Brazilian Portuguese-English
English-Brazilian Portuguese
Dictionary & Phrasebook

HIPPOCRENE DICTIONARY & PHRASEBOOKS

Albanian
Arabic(Eastern Arabic)
Arabic (Modern Standard)
Armenian (Eastern)
Armenian (Western)
Australian
Azerbaijani
Basque
Bosnian
Breton
British
Cajun French
Chechen
Croatian
Czech
Danish
Dari *Romanized*
Esperanto
Estonian
Finnish
French
Georgian
German
Greek
Hebrew *Romanized*
Hindi
Hungarian
Igbo
Ilocano
Irish
Italian
Japanese *Romanized*
Korean
Lao *Romanized*

Latvian
Lithuanian
Malagasy
Maltese
Mongolian
Nepali *Romanized*
Norwegian
Pashto *Romanized*
Pilipino (Tagalog)
Polish
Portuguese (Brazilian)
Punjabi
Québécois
Romanian
Romansch
Russian
Serbian
Shona
Sicilian
Slovak
Slovene
Somali
Spanish (Latin American)
Swahili
Swedish
Tajik
Tamil *Romanized*
Thai *Romanized*
Turkish
Ukrainan
Urdu *Romanized*
Uzbek
Vietnamese

Brazilian Portuguese-English
English-Brazilian Portuguese
Dictionary & Phrasebook

Osmar de Almeida-Santos

Hippocrene Books, Inc.
New York

For information, address:
  HIPPOCRENE BOOKS, INC.
  171 Madison Avenue
  New York, NY 10016
  www.hippocrenebooks.com

Library of Congress Cataloging-in-Publication Data

Almeida-Santos, Osmar de.
  Brazilian Portuguese-English/English-Brazilian Portu-
  guese dictionary & phrasebook / Osmar de Almeida-
  Santos
      p. cm.
  ISBN-10: 0-7818-1007-8
  ISBN-13: 978-0-7818-1007-4
      1. Portuguese language--Dictionaries--English.
  2. English language--Dictionaries--Portuguese.
  3. Portuguese language--Brazil--Provincialisms--
  Dictionaries. 4. Portuguese language--Conversation
  and phrase books--English. I. Title: Dictionary &
  phrasebook. II. Title: Dictionary and phrasebook.
  III. Title.

  PC5333.A598 2004
  469.3'21--dc22

                                        2004054351

Printed in the United States of America.

CONTENTS

ACKNOWLEDGMENTS

Many thanks to Elizabeth Monte Campaña who's tireless revisions and suggestions to the manuscript greatly contributed to the book's production.

BRAZIL — The Country

Geography and Climate

Brazil is the largest and most populous country in South America, and occupies an area slightly smaller than the continental United States. It has twenty-six federal states that are granted far less autonomy than in the US. The majority of cities are located on the coast, largely because of the mountains of Serra do Mar and Serra da Mantiqueira, as well as the impenetrable jungles of the Mata Atlântica, which made major settlements farther inland difficult. The plateaus were eventually conquered, however, and today there are quite a few larger cities located in the highlands. For instance, São Paulo, Brasília, Curitiba, Goiânia, Belo Horizonte, among others. The Brazilian landscape is never monotonous and contains mountains, jungles, valleys, rivers, waterfalls, and beaches.

Brazil has equatorial, tropical and subtropical climates. While there are no volcanoes, earthquakes or tornadoes, there are occasional floods and some droughts. In general the climate is pleasant throughout the year. The northern and northeastern regions of Brazil fluctuate between humid and dry, while drought is prevalent in the northeastern states. The southeast has a temperate climate, while the extreme south has cold winters with continual frost and, on rare occasions, snowfalls.

The People

Europeans, Africans, Asians, Arabs, and the indigenous peoples of Brazil, as well as many other nations, have contributed to a multiracial Brazilian society. Mixed race marriages are very common and it is said that that there are 49 shades of skin color, from white to black. The various facial features, eye colors, hair types, and range of heights may also surprise a first-time visitor to Brazil.

A lighter-skinned population is primarily found in the southern federal units, especially Paraná, Santa Catarina, and Rio Grande do Sul, where European settlers quickly migrated. The northeast is darker due to the mixing of indigenous populations, African slaves, and white Europeans.

The actual population of Brazil is around 170 million people. Of this figure, approximately 40 million are below the poverty line. As a rule, the southern industrialized states are wealthier than the northern ones. However, Brazil's tourism industry, with its beautiful beaches, warm climate, and tepid waters, has greatly benefited the northeastern regions. Excellent, first-class leisure services are available all year long, but they are especially popular during the cold winters of the Northern Hemisphere.

History and Economics

Portuguese explorers first arrived in Brazil around the beginning of the 16th century. The Portuguese Empire, however, took almost a hundred years before they began to heavily colonize the area.

The foundations of the Brazilian economy have transformed during almost every century of its

500-year history. For example, during the 16th century it survived on the export of a rare wood much sought after in Europe: *Pau Brazil*, or "Brazilwood." From the 17th century onwards, gold and sugarcane became the major exports. And, during the 19th century, coffee and cacao became the primary exports. Major industrialization of the country began around 1950 and today Brazil has a healthy, well-balanced economy divided relatively evenly among agriculture, manufacturing, and service industries. In volume, the Brazilian economy occupies the 8th to 9th position in the world. Brazil is one the largest exporters of food, with a large variety of fruits, vegetables, coffee, cacao, and meats.

At the onset of the 19th century Napoleon invaded Portugal. The Portuguese King João VI then decided to escape to Brazil, which became the capital of the Portuguese Empire. This gave Brazil a great push forward. Even after Napoleon's final defeat, the King was reluctant to go back to Europe. Only after rebellions in Lisbon did the Portuguese King return to Europe. Before his departure, however, he appointed his son Pedro to rule the budding nation. Dutifully, Pedro proclaimed independence in 1822, whereupon he became Pedro I of Brazil.

The "coffee boom" of the 19th century brought nearly one million European immigrants to Brazil. It also helped Brazil to become an independent republic similar to that of the United States. In 1889, wealthy coffee magnates backed a military coup and expelled the monarchy. Today, the Brazilian Royal family lives in Brazil after a century of exile in Europe.

The 20th Century and Beyond

During its 180 years as a Republic, Brazil has had only a handful of Presidents who completed their full terms. Two dictatorships lasted decades and coup d'états were frequent.

Intermittently Brazil has come onto the world stage. During World War I Brazil gave humanitarian aid to the Allies in the form of food, clothing, medicine, and medical personnel. Then, during World War II, the aid was extended to military action in the South Atlantic and in Italy. Brazil has the distinction of being the only Latin American country to participate militarily in Europe, where it contributed its Navy, Air Force and Army.

In 1962, Brazil founded a new capital, Brasília, located in the geographic center of the country. Its construction took less than three years. Today, Brasília is a large and beautiful city worth a visit. The construction of Brasília has also helped to stimulate economic activity in the interior of the country and in the highlands.

In 1989, Brazil had its first democratic election in three decades. Since that time it has become even more politically and economically stable, with far better administrators than it's had in the past. Moreover, the development of its industries, especially in the service sector and in the area of global trade, has helped Brazil become one of the most prominent leaders in both South America and the world.

BRAZILIAN PORTUGUESE —
The Language

Two hundred million people in Europe, South America, Africa and Asia speak the Portuguese language. It originated from the Latin, spoken by the Romans, who occupied Portugal during the 3rd century B.C. onwards. Today, Portuguese is the 6th most widely spoken language in the world.

Brazilian Portuguese is the larger branch of Portuguese with more than 170 million speakers.

Influences:

1. The Lusitanian tribes of Portugal accepted the Latin language almost in its entirety. They simplified it by cutting off the declinations and the neuter gender. They also contributed some native words to the language.
2. Hundreds of Arabic words were introduced to Portuguese during the centuries of Arabic occupation in Portugal. The Arabic language, however, did not change the structure or pronunciation of Portuguese.
3. More recently, loanwords from other modern European languages (French, English, as well as Slavic and Nordic languages) have influenced Portuguese.
4. After World War II, the main influence on Brazilian Portuguese has become American English—mainly in the fields of economics, trade, banking, entertainment, art, sports, science and technology.
5. In Brazil, hundreds of native tribes had their own specific languages. Nowadays, there are thousands of native words in Brazilian Portuguese.

These words are primarily restricted to names of places, plants, and fruits. Being localized nouns they had no equivalent in any other language; therefore, they became a part of modern Brazilian Portuguese.

European Portuguese

There are very few differences between European Portuguese and Brazilian Portuguese. However, Brazilian Portuguese is said to be softer and more melodious than other Portuguese-speaking peoples. Differences in written Portuguese are minimal. Similar to the relationship between American and British English some words are spelled with minor variations. For example, in Portugal, *director* and *facto* are spelled with a "c," whereas, in Brazil, the "c" was abolished because it is not pronounced in everyday speech. Therefore, a *director* is a *diretor*. The American-British equivalent, for example, is *colour* and *color*, which are easily understood and widely accepted by both sides. There are some different usages of words as well, such as *comboio* (Portugal) and *trem* (Brazil) for the word "*train*," and some colloquial expressions that are not mutually intelligible.

HOW TO USE THIS BOOK

Pronunciation Guide and Alphabet

A simple and essential introduction to Brazilian Portuguese pronunciation provides the first steps to learning the language. Since Portuguese is a phonetic language each sound corresponds to a written letter, and vice versa. Once the beginner learns some basic rules of spelling and pronunciation he/she will be able to *speak* a written word and to *write* a spoken one.

A Brief Modern Grammar

This section clearly explains elementary grammar in a modern way—the language as it is spoken in Brazil everyday. Only the most essential rules are given and in an abbreviated manner. All academic rigidity is avoided. Simple explanations about the various parts of speech are included; wherever possible, comparisons are made to the English language to aid comprehension. Lists of essential words, phrases, expressions and verb conjugations are displayed.

English-Portuguese/ Portuguese-English Dictionary

Studies suggest a person of average education has perfect comprehension of circa 10,000 different words; of these, only 3,000 are usually used during day-to-day activities. This book is designed for the traveler and contains approximately 4,000 essential words. These words were carefully chosen to cover the basic necessities of everyday life and travel. It has practical information as well as a selection of useful words and phrases. Both dictionaries are heavily charged with nouns and verbs. The traveler will learn quickly to guess the adjective corresponding to a noun, a verb, etc. The traveler can also use the dictionary to find words not listed in the phrasebook.

Phrasebook

This large section is divided into chapters according to everyday needs: *Transport, Currency, Accommodation, Shopping, Food,* etc.

Each section begins with a brief **explanation** about a particular topic. In Brazil, it is vital not only to know how to *say* things, but also to understand *how* things are done. Social behavior, cultural habits and other tips are thoroughly explained. There is also a list of **vocabulary words** where you will find the most common words for that subject. Finally, each chapter contains a section for **phrase construction** that offers fully conjugated verbs and other parts of speech (*I want. . . , I need. . . , How much. . . , etc*). These terms are used as bricks to help travelers build a fully functional sentence with the use of some basic words.

Quick Reference

This section contains the most elementary words needed—numbers, colors, days of the week, hours, etc.

We hope you find this book pleasant, informative, easy to learn from, and useful in your stay in Brazil.

Boa viagem!

PRONUNCIATION GUIDE

The vowels and consonants in Portuguese **always** have the same sounds in accordance with a few simple rules. To make it easier and to avoid mispronunciation, it is obligatory to use some graphic signs (accents), in certain words. These signs are called:

´   **acute accent**—it indicates that the **á** is open as in "cat."

~   **tilde**—it indicates that the **ã** and **õ** have a nasal tone as in "ant" and "bone," this sound is quite difficult for a beginner.

^   **circumflex**—it is used to indicate that the vowels (**â, ê, ô**) are "closed" as in "ant," "end" and "coma."

ç   **cedilla**—it is used *before* a, o, or u, otherwise the "c" would have the sound of a "k."

`   **grave accent**—(rarely used) for contraction of two vowels "a" together: a + a = à.

¨   **umlaut**—indicates that the **u** after a **q** or a **g** must be pronounced; e.g. **freqüente** (*frekuente* and not *frekent*).

The stress of a Portuguese word always falls on the **second to last syllable**. When this is not the case, one of the graphic accents above is used to indicate that the stress is elsewhere. A beginner should not worry about graphic accents, they are written only to help, not to confuse.

Brazilian Portuguese Pronunciation

VOWEL	EXAMPLE		ENGLISH SOUND
a, á, à	cada	[á]	as in *cat*
ã, an, â	amanhã	[ã]	as in *ant*
e, ê	letra	[ê]	as in *end*
é	é	[é]	as in *get*
i, í	íntimo	[i]	as in *it*
o, ô, õ	corredor	[ô]	as in *over*
ó	ótimo	[ó]	as in *top*
u, ú, ü	um, último	[u]	as in *to*

SEMIVOWEL

e	teatro	[j]	as in *yacht*
i	ciúme	[j]	as in *fume*
u	aquático	[w]	as in *aquatic*

DIPHTHONG

ãe	mãe	[aj]	as in *flying*
ai	vai	[aj]	as in *ride*
ao, au	aos, auxílio	[aw]	as in *shout*
ão	vão	[ãw]	as in *round*
ei	feira	[ej]	as in *they*

eu	deusa	[ew]	as in *feud*
oi	boi	[oj]	as in *point*
ou	cenoura	[o]	as in *local*
õe	limões	[õj]	as in g*oing*

CONSONANT	EXAMPLE		ENGLISH SOUND
c	casa	[k]	before *a, o, u*; hard as in *cat, cot, cut*
ce, ci	cedo, cinema	[c]	before *e* and *i*; soft as in *cell, cinema*
ç	aço	[c]	only before *a, o* and *u*; to indicate a soft *c* as in *so*
ch	chá	[sh]	sizzling as in *shock*
d	data	[d]	as in English, *date*
ga, go, gu	gola, gula	[gh]	before *a, o, u,* hard as in *gap, go, guru*
ge, gi	gente, giro	[ge]	before *e* and *i* soft as in *gentle, gin*
gue, gui	guerra, guiar	[gh]	before *e* and *i* hard as in *get, guide*

11

güe, güi	agüentar	[ghu]	before *e* and i, the *u* is pronounced as in *Guam*
h	homem	[h]	is always silent, except in combinations, such as ch, lh and nh
j	jogo	[j]	as in joy
l, lh	limpo, janela	[l]	as in English *late*, except when before *h* . . .
lh	milhão	[lee]	as in *million*
m	animal, massa	[m]	as in English, except . . .
m	cantam, sim	[ãw]	when a vowel comes before *m* it becomes nasal
n	nadar, penal	[n]	as in *no*, except when after a vowel it becomes nasal . . .
n	cansar	[ã]	as in *ant*
nh	tamanho	[n]	as in *onion*

qu	qual, quorum	[k]	before *a* and *o* the *u* is always pronounced as in *quarrel*, *quorum*
qu	que, quinto	[k]	before *e* and *i* the *u* is never pronounced as in *Quito*
qüe, qüi	freqüente	[kw]	as in *frequent*
r	rato	[rr]	before another consonant and at the beginning/ end of a word, hard as in *ring, rot*
r	florest	[r]	between vowels soft as in *forest*
rr	carro	[rr]	always hard as in *rock*
s	sol	[s]	before another consonant and at the beginning/ end of a word, soft as in *so*
s	mesa	[z]	between two vowels it sounds like a *z*, as in *case*

ss	nosso	[s]	soft as in *boss*
t	todo	[t]	as in English *total*
x	léxico	[*s, sh, z, eks, ekz*]	multiple pronunciation; there are no rules for this consonant. As a rule of thumb, you can pronounce it as you would a similar English word— *exam, expect, Xerox.*
z	zangar	[z]	as in English *zoo*

b, d, f, k, p, t, v, w, y are pronounced as they are in English.

ACCENTUATION CHANGES

Brazilian *gü* and *qü* become *gu* and *qu,* e.g. agüentar, cinqüenta, i.e. the *u* is always pronounced when it has an umlaut ü.

Brazilian *c* and *ç* double to *cc* and *cç,* e.g., seccionar, secção.

The Rules of Stress in Portuguese are as follows:

(a) when a word ends in *a, e, o, m* (except *im, um* and their plural forms) or *s*, the second to last syllable is stressed; cama*ra*da, cama*ra*das, *par*te, *par*tem.

(b) when a word ends in *i, u, im, um, n* or a consonant other than *m* or *s*, the stress falls on the last syllable: ven*di*, alg*um*, alg*uns*, fal*ar*.

(c) when the rules set out in (a) and (b) are not applicable, an acute or circumflex accent appears over the stressed vowel: *ó*tica, *â*nimo, ingl*ê*s.

ALPHABET

A	ah	N	en
B	bay	O	oh
C	say	P	pay
D	day	Q	kay
E	er	R	ayr
F	ef	S	ays
G	jay	T	tay
H	agah	U	ooh
I	ee	V	vay
J	jota	X	schees
L	el	Z	zay
M	em		

* * *

K (kah)
W (dah-blee-u)
Y (ee-psilon)

The letters **K, W, Y** do not exist in Portuguese. They are, however, used in the following:

1. Abbreviations of measurements—e.g. Kg, Km, KB, W (watts)
2. Proper names—e.g. Mary, Ary, Ruy, Darcy, Williams, Walter, Washington
3. Foreign words widely accepted—e.g. layout, copy desk, check in, back up

A BRIEF GRAMMAR

Portuguese grammar is similar to English in that it contains the same parts of speech: articles, adjectives, nouns, adverbs, verbs, etc. There are, however, **three very important differences** that one must *always* keep in mind.

1. The articles, adjectives, pronouns, and the majority of nouns always have four forms—**masculine, feminine, singular and plural.** In English, normally, only nouns have a plural form.
2. In Portuguese, the adjectives come **after** the noun, whereas in English the adjectives come **before** the noun. Yet there are exceptions to this rule, for poetic and literary effects, e.g. "**um grande homem**" (*a great man*) is different from "**um homem grande**" (*a man who is tall*); "**linda mulher**" (*beautiful woman*) is more poetic / emphatic than "**mulher linda**" (see also *articles, adjectives and pronouns*).
3. Although modern Portuguese is getting closer to the English way of expressing the mode and tense of a verb (subjunctive, conditional, future and past tenses), they are expressed in a different manner.

Definite Article — the

All nouns in Portuguese are either masculine or feminine. Their articles are indications of gender (masculine or feminine) and number (singular or plural).

The definite articles are: **o** *m*, **os** *m pl*
a *f*, **as** *f pl*

o meni<u>o</u>	— *the boy*
a menin<u>a</u>	— *the girl*
os menin<u>os</u>	— *the boys*
as menin<u>as</u>	— *the girls*

Every object is a "he" or "she," there are no neutral genders in Portuguese.

o carro	— *the car* (he)
os carros	— *the cars* (they)
a máquina	— *the machine* (she)
as máquinas	— *the machines* (they)

Note:
1. The above rule of four forms applies to every **noun**, **adjective**, and **article**.
2. In a **mix-gender group** of persons, or objects, it is enough to have **one male** person/object for the whole group to be treated as **male plural**.

Indefinite Article — a, some

Um menino	— *a boy*
Uma menina	— *a girl*
Uns meninos	— *some boys*
Umas meninas	— *some girls*

Demonstrative Article — this, that, these, those

esse *m*, **essa** *f* = *this;* **esses** *m pl* = *these*
aquele *m*, **aquela** *f* = *that;* **aqueles** *m f pl* = *those*

One can guess the gender and number of a word by its ending (~**o**, ~ **a**, ~ **os**, ~ **as**) in 90% of the cases. In general, nouns and adjectives ending in ~**o** are masculine; nouns and adjectives ending in ~**a** are feminine. Likewise, the _s_ at the end of most words, most certainly indicates a plural.

Nouns (n.) — Substantivos

Nouns and verbs are the backbone of basic speech. Always, **someone (or something) wants (or is doing) something.** The more nouns of a foreign language you know, the better your basic communication skills in that language will be. The same applies to basic verbs.

Therefore, we have given a great deal of attention in this dictionary to the choice of the most common "things," as well as the things that we "do." Amongst the 4,000 words of each language you'll find in this dictionary, the overwhelming majority are nouns and verbs.

Portuguese nouns have **diminutives**, i.e., forms that indicate that something is small; they are also used as terms of endearment. The diminutive nouns always end in **~inho** (*m*) and **~inha** (*f*). No matter how big or tall a person may be, someone in love may call this person *meu Anjinho* = "my little Angel." English-speakers try to use "*y*" to take up this function; for example, *Dad* becomes *Daddy*.

Adjectives (adj.) — Adjetivos

Portuguese adjectives come *after the noun*, whereas in English, the adjective usually comes first. Portuguese adjectives follow the same rules as already described for articles and nouns regarding number and gender.

As in English, some basic adjectives *(good, bad)* have irregular **superlatives** *(better, worse)*. The bilingual Dictionary helps to clarify those irregularities.

English adjectives do not have diminutives. To compensate for this, English-speaking people try to use the sufix ~**ish**. For example, "sweetish, smallish." In Portuguese there are diminutives for adjectives, and, like nouns, they usually end in ~*inho, ~inha*. In the example above, **sweet** *adj* = doce, the diminutive is *docinho adj* = sweetish.

Pronouns (pron.) — Pronomes

These are words we use instead of a noun. There are two kinds—direct and indirect. The direct is the subject who speaks (I, you, he, she, we, they). The indirect is the complement of something else (me, us, him, her, them). In this book we have excluded the old-fashioned ones' corresponding to the English "thou, thee," which are rarely used in either Portuguese or in English.

			Indirect/Direct Object of the Action
Subject			
I	= **eu**	me	= **para mim, me**
you	= **você**	you	= **para você, te**
he	= **ele**	him	= **para ele, lhe**
she	= **ela**	her	= **para ela, lhe**
we	= **nós**	us	= **para nós, nos**
you *pl*	= **vocês**	you	= **para vocês, lhes**
they	= **eles**	them	= **para eles, lhes**

Possessive

My = **meu** *m*, **minha** *f* (add an *s* to either, if more than one object is possessed)

Your = **teu** *m*, **tua** *f* (add an *s* to either, if more than one object is possessed)

His = **dele**

Her = **dela**

Our = **nosso** *m*, **nossa** *f* (add an *s* to either, if more
than one object is possessed)
Your *pl* = **de vocês**
Their = **deles** *m*, **delas** *f*

Impersonal Noun and Pronoun

In Portuguese, impersonal nouns and pronouns
are widely used.

Impersonal noun:
a gente = the people, we

Impersonal pronoun:
se = people, we, us, one

The terms *a gente* and *se* are interchangeable, they
are equivalents and you will hear them a thousand
times a day. It is easy and worthwhile to remember
them.

Note:
Although the significance of *a gente* and *se* is something like *"we, one of us, someone of us, anybody
from our group, we the people . . ."* it has a collective
meaning as well, something like *"one of our group,
us"* and the verb that follows it is *always* the 3rd
person singular. The most approximate understanding of these two terms is that they are similar
to the English *one* in the phrases: *"one works, but
one gets nowhere . . ."* or *"one fights for Liberty, but,
in the end, tyranny prevails.*

Examples:
a gente é = one is
a gente foi = we went
se faz tudo = our group does everything.

Negation

Portuguese negation is simple: just add *não* before the verb or just say *não*. Make sure that the word *não* is the strongest, i.e. most stressed word of your statement.

EXAMPLES:
Eu não quero = I do **not** want
Não, obrigado = **no**, thank you.

Asking Questions

This is done by the **intonation** of the statement. To ask a question, say the phrase *as if* it were a positive statement, putting an emphasis (stress) on the last word and raising the tone of your voice slightly. Once you've heard a couple of questions, you get the knack of it. Watch the person closely because his/her facial expression may also indicate whether the person is saying something or asking a question.

SAMPLES:
— Você quer uma **cerveja**? [*Do you want a **beer**?*]
— **Não.** Você tem **vinho**? [*No. Do you have **wine**?*]

You don't need to shout. Just make a pause before *cerveja*, *não* and *vinho*, and say these three words clearly.

To help you, below is a list of some interrogative words. In most cases, if a phrase starts with any of these words (or if it is the *only* word), you can be confident that the phrase is most likely a question.

onde? = where?
porque? = why?
qual? = which one?
quando? = when?

quanto? = how much?
que? = which? what?
quem? = who?

Adverbs (adv.) — Advérbios

As in English, adverbs do not designate gender or the plural.

In **English**, one can "make" an adverb by adding "**ly**" or "**lly**" to another word.

EXAMPLES:
great (adjective) becomes **greatly**
legal (adjective) becomes **legally**

In **Portuguese**, the "*ly*"is replaced by the ending "*-mente.*"

EXAMPLES:
grande (adjective) becomes **grandemente**
legal (adjective) becomes **legalmente**
[In the case of a word having feminine and masculine—**simétrico** *m*, **simétrica** *f*—it is the *feminine* form that receives the addition of "-mente." Thus the adverb is **simetricamente**].

Prepositions (prep.) — Preposições

Prepositions are words that indicate the relation of a noun and a verb, an adjective, or another noun. The most common in Portuguese are:

a	to, towards, for
antes de	before
ao lado de	next to, beside
ao redor de	around
após	after
até	until, till
atrás de	behind

através de	through, across
cerca de	circa, near, close, approximate
com	with
contra	against
de	of, from
depois de	after
durante	during
em	in, on
em volta de	around
entre	between, amongst
fora de	outside
longe de	far from
para	for, towards
perto de	near, close to, next to
por	by
sem	without
sobre	on, about
sub	under

Interjection (interj.) — Interjeições

Interjections are spontaneous, short words and sounds; they are exclamations that express joy, surprise, anger, greeting, etc. Some are rude and some are slang.

Ah! . . . = Ha! . . . (surprise or sudden understanding)
Ai! (*aee*) = Agh! (pain)
Oba! (*oubah!*) = Great! (joy)
Oh! . . . = Oh! . . . (pity, sorrow)
Oi! (*oee*) = Hi! (greeting*)*
Oxente (*oschente*) = Wow! (surprise)
Pô! (*pou*) = Wow! (surprise, short for *poxa* or *porra*)
Pôxa! (*pousha*) = Wow! (surprise, considered rude)
Putz! (*pootz*) = Shit! (short for *puta merda*, rude expression of surprise/anger)
Puxa! (*poosha*) = Wow! (surprise, considered rude)
Ui! (*ooee*) = Ouch! (pain)
Upa! (*oopah*) = Whoops!
Ups! (*oops*) = Whoops!
Xiii! . . . (*shee!*) = Uh, oh! (a great disgust/regret)

Conjunction (conj.) — Conjunções

A conjunction is a word that connects two phrases. The most common in Portuguese are:

assim = so
com = with
como = as, like
contudo = however
e = and
mas = but
não obstante = nevertheless
nem = neither, nor
ou = or
pois = because, thus, then
porém = but
que = that, which
se = whether

Verbs (v.) — Verbos

PORTUGUESE VERBS

- All Portuguese verbs end in ~*r.* This is the infinitive form corresponding to the English **to**. For brevity, in parts of this book, the English *to* was omitted; it is indicated, however, in parts of speech as *v.*
- Thus, all Portuguese verbs have an ending of ~*ar, ~er, ~ir* or ~*or,* in their infinitive (general) form. It is in this manner that they are listed in this Dictionary. By the various verb endings—**ar, er, ir, or**—one can say that such and such a verb belongs to the 1st, 2nd, 3rd or 4th *conjugation.*
- A conjugation is a model in which a verb varies according to its mode, person, and time. Portuguese (as well as English) has many modes, persons and times. In English these variations are much more simple because it has the verbs *can, may, be, have, will, shall, go* to modify the verb. Classical Portuguese would have a different variation for *each* mode, person and time. However,

modern Brazilian Portuguese is also beginning to use auxiliary verbs to indicate which mode, person and time we are talking about.

<u>PARTICIPLES</u>

Present and Past Participles are used to form compound verbs (auxiliary + participle). In English, these participles are recognized by:

1) ~**ing** = present participle, e.g., being, doing, making
2) a variable past participle usually ending in ~**ed** or ~**en**, e.g., talked, taken, and some other irregular past participles.

In Portuguese, the participles are much more predictable. They follow the four verb conjugations; this applies to irregular verbs as well. The participles are very much used, so it is worthy to learn these participles.

The **Present Participle** for all verbs are:

- verbs ending in ~**ar** pp. ~*ando*; e.g. *amar*, pp = *amando*
- verbs ending in ~**er** pp ~*endo*; e.g.*vender*, pp = *vendendo*
- verbs ending in ~**ir** pp ~*indo*; e.g. *partir*, pp = *partindo*
- verbs ending in ~**or** pp ~*ondo*; e.g. *por*, pp = *pondo*

The **Past Participle** in Portuguese are:

- verbs ending in ~**ar** = ~**ado**; e.g. *amar*, ptp = *amado*
- verbs ending in ~**er** = ~**ido**; e.g. *vender*, ptp = *vendido*
- verbs ending in ~**ir** = ~**ido**; e.g. *partir*, ptp = *partido*

• the verb **por** and its composites (**supor, com por, propor**) has the past participle as *posto* and composites as *~posto* (i.e. *suposto, composto, proposto*, etc.)

<u>IRREGULAR VERBS</u>

SER and ESTAR

There are **two** verbs for "**to be**" in Portuguese.

*To **always** be* = **ser**
*To **temporarily** be* = **estar**

For example, "I am a man" uses the verb ser, "Eu **sou** um homem;" whereace "I am here" (location) uses the verb estar, "Eu **estou** aqui."

SER (*to "always" be*)

<u>Present</u> (*see pronouns for I, you etc.*)[1]
Eu **sou** — I am (permanently, most of the time)
Você, ele, ela, a gente **é** — you/he/she/it/one is
Nós **somos** — we are
Vocês, eles, elas **são** — they/you all are

<u>Past</u>
fui — I was
foi — you were
foi — he/she/it was
fomos — we were
foram — they/you all were

<u>Future</u>
vou ser — I will be
vai ser — you/he/she/it will be
vamos ser — we will be
vão ser — they/you all will be

---

1. In Portuguese, one can dispense the pronouns because the *form* of the verb already indicates **who** is talking.

ESTAR (*to "temporarily" be*)

Present
estou — I am
está — you/he/she/it is
estamos — we are
estão — they/you all are

Past
estive — I was
esteve — you/he/she/it were
estivemos — we were
estiveram — they/you all were

Future
vou estar — I will be
vai estar — you/he/she/it will be
vamos estar — we will be
vão estar — they/you all will be

IR (*to go*)

Present
vou — I go (or *I am going*)
vai — you/he/she/it goes (or *is going*)
vamos — we go (or *are going*)
vão — they/you all go (or *are going*)

Past (you will notice that these forms are identical to the Past form of *ser* (to be))
fui — I went
foi — you/he/she/it went
fomos — we went
foram — they/you all went

Future (identical to the present, because it forms the future of all verbs, see "Note")
vou — I will go
vai — you/he/she/it will go

vamos — we will go
vão — they/you all will go

Note:
The present tense of **the verb "ir"** + an **Infinitive** of any verb = the **future** tense. It is the equivalent of saying "I am going to. . . ." in English.

Ter (*to have*)[2]

<u>Present</u>[3]
tenho — I have
tem — you/he/she/it has
temos — we have
tém — they/you all have

<u>Past</u>
tive — I had
teve — you/he/she/it had
tivemos — we had
tiveram — they/you all had

<u>Future</u>
vou ter — I will have
vai ter — you/he/she/it will have
vamos ter — we will have
vão ter — they/you all will have

---

2. There is also the verb *haver* in Portuguese. However, its usage is disappearing, and it is used mostly in impersonal expressions— "*há, houve*"—the equivalent of "there is, there are, there was".

3. The verb **ter** is used as an auxiliary verb, exactly in the same way the verb *to have* is used in English to make the compound past. Example: *I have bought* = **eu tenho comprado**, i.e. **present** of to have (**ter**) + **past participle.** The same formula is used for more forms, e.g. past of "to have" (I had) + past participle (bought) and so on. This way of "making" tenses is identical to the Portuguese way.

Regular Verbs

Regular Portuguese verbs can be divided into four conjugations based on their infinitive word endings: **~ar, ~er, ~ir** and **~or.** Below are the models of such conjugations. When you see any verb (indicated by *v.* in this book) it is likely that it is a **regular** verb; therefore you will know how to say the various forms for persons and tenses.

~AR Verb Endings

EXAMPLE: **Amar** (to love)

Present
amo — I love
ama — you/he/she/it loves
amamos — we love
amam — they/you all love

Past
amei — I loved
amou — you/he/she/it loved
amamos — we loved
amaram — they/you all loved

Future
vou amar — I will love
vai amar — you/he/she/it will love
vamos amar — we will love
vão amar — they/you all will love

~ER Verb Endings

EXAMPLE: **Vender** (to sell)

Present
vendo — I sell
vende — you/he/she/it sells

vendemos — we sell
vendem — they/you all sell

Past
vendi — I sold
vendeu — you/he/she/it sold
vendemos — we sold
venderam — they/you all sold

Future
vou vender — I will sell
vai vender — you/he/she/it will sell
vamos vender — we will sell
vão vender — they/you all will sell

~IR Verb Endings

EXAMPLE: **Partir** (to depart)

Present
parto — I depart
parte — you/he/she/it departs
partimos — we depart
partem — they/you all depart

Past
parti — I departed
partiu — you/he/she/it departed
partimos — we departed
partiram — they/you all departed

Future
vou partir — I will depart
vai partir — you/he/she/it will depart
vamos partir — we will depart
vão partir — they/you all will depart

~POR[4] Verb Endings

EXAMPLE: **Pôr** (to put)

Present
ponho — I put
põe — you/he/she/it puts
pomos — we put
põem — they put

Past
pus — I put
pôs — you/he/she/it put
pusemos — we put
puseram — they put

Future
vou pôr — I will put
vai pôr — you/he/she/it will put
vamos pôr — we will put
vão pôr — they will put

---

4. The verb *pôr* is the only one of this model. All the other verbs using a prefix + **por** (*supor* = suppose, *compor* = compose, *propor* = propose, etc) follow the same model.

ABBREVIATIONS

abbrev.	abbreviation
adj.	adjective
adv.	adverb
art.	article
coll.	colloquial
conj.	conjunction
dimin.	diminutive
excl.	exclamatory
f.	feminine, female
imp.	imperative
interj.	interjection
interrog.	interrogative
m.	masculine, male
n.	noun
num.	numeral
pl.	plural
pref.	prefix
prep.	preposition
pron.	pronoun
pp.	past participle
reflex.	reflexive
v.	verb

PORTUGUESE – ENGLISH DICTIONARY

A

a *prep.* to
abacate *n.m* avocado
abafar *v.* to muffle
abaixar *v.* to lower
abaixo *adv.* down
abajur *n.m* lamp
abelha *n.f* bee
abençoar *v.* to bless
aberto(a) *adj.m(f)* open
abertura *n.f* gap
abobrinha *n.f* zucchini
abordagem *n.f* approach
abordar *v.* to approach
aborrecer *v.* to annoy, nag
aborrecido(a) *adj.m(f)* dull
abortar *v.* to abort,
    miscarry
aborto *n.m* abortion
aborto espontâneo *n.m*
    miscarriage
abraçar *v.* to cuddle, hug
abraço *n.m* hug
abreviar *v.* to abbreviate
abreviatura *n.f*
    abbreviation
abrigar *v.* to shelter
abrigo *n.m* shelter
abril *n.m* April
abrir *v.* to open
absorver *v.* to absorb
abundância *n.f* plenty
abusar *v.* to abuse
abuso *n.m* abuse

acabar *v.* to finish, end
acalmar *v.* to pacify
acampar *v.* to camp
acanhado(a) *adj.m(f)* shy,
    timid
ação *n.f* action
ação da bolsa *n.f* share
acariciar *v.* to cuddle
acasalar *v.* to mate
aceitar *v.* to accept
acelerador *n.m* accelerator
acelerar *v.* to accelerate
acenar com a mão *v.* to
    wave
aceno de cabeça *n.m* nod
acessar *v.* to access
acesso *n.m* access, seizure
acessório *n.m* accessory
achados *n.m.pl* finding
achar *v.* to find
acidente *n.m* accident
acima *prep.* above
acima de *adv.* up
ACM *n.m* YMCA
aço inoxidável *n.m*
    stainless steel
acolchoado *n.m* comforter
acolher *v.* to welcome
acomodação *n.f*
    accommodations
acomodar *v.* to
    accommodate, adapt
acompanhar *v.* to follow
acontecer *v.* to happen
acordar *v.* to wake

acordo *n.m* agreement
acostumar *v.* to accustom
açougueiro(a) *n.m(f)* butcher
acreditar *v.* to believe
açúcar *n.m* sugar
acusar *v.* to accuse, indict
adaptar *v.* to adapt
adega *n.f* cellar
adequado(a) *adj.m(f)* fit
adição *n.f* addition
adicional *adj.* additional
adicionar *v.* to add
adjetivo *n.m* adjective
administração *n.f* administration
admirar *v.* to admire
adolescência *n.f* adolescence
adolescente *n.* teenager
adormecer[1] *v.* to fall asleep
adormecer[2] *v.* to go numb
adormecido(a) *adj.m(f)* asleep
adotar *v.* to adopt
adultério *n.m* adultery
adulto(a) *n.m(f)* adult, grown-up
advogado(a) *n.m(f)* attorney, lawyer
aeroporto *n.m* airport
afastado(a) *adj.m(f)* remote, away
afetar *v.* to affect
afiado(a) *adj.m(f)* sharp
afilhada *n.f* goddaughter
afilhado *n.m* godson
afluência *n.f* affluence
afogar *v.* to drown
África *n.f* Africa
africano(a) *n.m; adj.m(f)* African
afrouxar *v.* to sag
afundar *v.* to sink

agarrar *v.* to grab, seize
agência *n.f* agency
agência de correio *n.f* post office
agente *n.* agent
agir *v.* to act
agitar *v.* to shake
agora *adv.* now
agosto *n.m* August
agradável *adj.* nice
agradecer *v.* to thank
agradecido(a) *adj.m(f)* thankful
agredir *v.* to attack
agressão *n.f* aggression
agressivo(a) *adj.m(f)* aggressive
agrupar *v.* to group
água *n.f* water
água da torneira *n.f* tap water
água-viva *n.f* jellyfish
agulha *n.f* needle
AIDS *n.f* AIDS
ainda *adv.* yet
ajuda *n.f* help
ajudar *v.* to help
ajustar *v.* to fit, adjust
ajuste *n.m* adjust
ala *n.f* ward, wing
alameda *n.f* boulevard
alaranjado(a) *adj.m(f)* orange color
alarmar *v.* to alarm
alarme *n.m* alarm
albergue *n.m* hostel
alça *n.f* handle
alcançar *v.* to reach
alcance *n.m* reach, grasp
álcool *n.m* alcohol
aldeia *n.f* village
aleatório(a) *adj.m(f)* random

alegrar *v.* to cheer up
alegre *adj.* cheerful, jolly
alegria *n.f* joy
aleijar *v.* to maim
além de *prep.* beyond
além do mais *adv.* moreover
alemã(~o) *n.; adj. f(m)* German
Alemanha *n.f* Germany
alergia *n.f* allergy
alérgico(a) *adj.m(f)* allergic
alfabeto *n.m* alphabet
alface *n.f* lettuce
alfaiate *n.m* tailor
alfândega *n.f* customs
alfinete *n.m* pin
alga marinha *n.f* seaweed
algo *pron.* something
algodão *n.m* cotton
alguém *pron.* somebody
algum(~a) *pron.m(f); adj.m(f)* any
alguns, algumas *pron.m(f)pl; adj.m(f)pl* some
alho *n.m* garlic
alho-poró *n.m* leek
ali *adv.* there
aliança *n.f* wedding ring
alisar *v.* to smooth
aliviar *v.* to relieve
alívio *n.m* relief
almoçar *v.* to lunch
almoço *n.m* lunch
almofada *n.f* cushion
altitude *n.f* altitude
alto(a) *adj.m(f)* tall, high
alto-falante *n.m* loudspeaker
altos e baixos *n.m* ups-and-downs
altura *n.f* height

alugar *v.* to rent, let, lease; hire
aluguel *n.f* rent, lease; hire
alvo *n.m* target
alvorecer *n.m* dawn
amadurecer *v.* to ripen, mature
amalucado(a) *n.m(f)* haywire; *adj.* crazy, whacky
amanhã *n.m; adv.* tomorrow
amante *n.* lover
amar *v.* to love
amarelo(a) *adj.m(f)* yellow
amargo(a) *adj.m(f)* bitter
amarrar *v.* to tie someone, something
amassar *v.* to knead
ambição *n.f* ambition
ambiente *n.m* environment
ambígüo(a) *adj.m(f)* ambiguous
ambos(as) *adj.m(f)pl* both
ambulância *n.f* ambulance
ameaça *n.f* threat, menace
ameaçar *v.* to jeopardize, threaten
ameixa *n.m* plum
América *n.f* America
americano(a) *n.m; adj.m(f)* American
amigável *adj.* friendly
amigo(a) *n.m(f)* friend
amizade *n.f* friendship
amolecer *v.* to soften
amolecido(a) *adj.m(f)* mellow
amor *n.m* love
amostra *n.f* sample
anã(~o) *n.f (m)* dwarf, midget
âncora *n.f* anchor
andar *v.* to walk

anel *n.m* ring
anemia *n.f* anemia
anestesia *n.f* anesthesia
anexar *v.* to attach, annex
anexo *n.m* enclosure
anfitriã *n.f* hostess
anfitrião *n.m* host
ângulo *n.m* angle
animal *n.m* animal
animal de estimação *n.m*
     pet
aniversário *n.m* birthday,
     anniversary
anjo *n.m* angel
ano *n.m* year
ano bissexto *n.m* leap year
Ano Novo *n.m* New Year
anoitecer *n.m* dusk
anotar *v.* to annotate, to
     take note
ansiedade *n.f* anxiety
ante- *pref.* fore
antebraço *n.m* forearm
antena *n.f* antenna
antepassado(a) *n.m(f)*
     ancestor
anterior *adj.* former, prior
antes *prep; adv.* before
antigo(a) *adj.m(f)* ancient
antigüidade *n.f* antiquity
antiquado(a) *adj.m(f)* old-
     fashioned, outdated
anual *adj.* annual
anular *v.* to nullify, disallow
anunciar *v.* to advertise
anúncio *n.m*
     announcement
ao lado de *prep.* beside
ao redor de *prep.* around
apagar *v.* to erase, fade
aparar *v.* to trim
aparência *n.f* appearance
apartamento *n.m*
     apartment

apelido *n.m* nickname
apenas *adv.* only
apendicite *n.f* appendicitis
aperfeiçoar *v.* to upgrade
aperitivo *n.m* appetizer
apertado(a) *adj.m(f)* tight
apertar *v.* to squeeze
aperto *n.m* squeeze
aperto de mão *n.m*
     handshake
apesar de *prep.* despite
apetite *n.m* appetite
apetrechos *n.m.pl* tackle
aplaudir *v.* to applaud
aplauso *n.m* applause
aplicação *n.f* application
aplicar *v.* to apply
apogeu *n.m* heyday
apoiar *v.* to support,
     back up
apontar *v.* to point, show,
     indicate
apoquentação *n.f* nagging
apoquentar *v.* to nag
aposentar *v.* to retire
aposta *n.f* bet
apostar *v.* to gamble, bet
apreensão *n.f* arrest
aprender *v.* to learn
aprendiz *n.* apprentice
aprendizagem *n.f*
     apprenticeship
apropriado(a) *adj.m(f)*
     appropriate
aprovado(a) *adj.m(f)*
     approved
aprovar *v.* to approve
aproximação *n.f* approach
aproximar *v.* to approach
aquecedor *n.m* heater
aquela(e) *pron.f(m)* that
aqui *adv.* here
ar *n.m* air

ar condicionado *n.m* air-conditioning
árabe *n.m; adj.* Arab, Arabian
arame *n.m* wire
aranha *n.f* spider
árbitro *n.m* referee
arco *n.m* arch, hoop
arco-íris *n.m* rainbow
área *n.f* area
areia *n.f* sand
arejar *v.* to air
arenque defumado *n.m* kipper
argumento *n.m* argument
arma *n.f* weapon
armadilha *n.f* trap
armar *v.* to arm
armário *n.m* cupboard
armazenamento *n.m* storage
aroma *n.m* scent
arquitetura *n.f* architecture
arquivar *v.* to file, shelve
arquivo *n.m* archive, file
arranhão *n.m* scratch
arranhar *v.* to scratch
arrebentar *v.* to burst
arredores *n.m.pl* surroundings
arreio *n.m* harness
arriscado(a) *adj.m(f)* dodgy
arriscar *v.* to risk, jeopardize
arrogante *adj.* overbearing
arroz *n.m* rice
arrumar *v.* to settle, fix
arrumar malas *v.* to pack
arte *n.f* art
artesã(~o) *n.m(f)* craftsman
artificial *adj.* artificial
artigo *n.m* article
artigos de valor *n.m.pl* valuables

artista *n.* artist
árvore *n.f* tree
às vezes *adv.* sometimes
asa *n.f* wing
ascender *v.* to rise
Ásia *n.f* Asia
asiático(a) *n.m; adj.m(f)* Asian
asilar *v.* to shelter
asilo *n.m* refuge, asylum
áspero(a) *adj.m(f)* rough
aspirador de pó *n.m* vacuum cleaner
aspirina *n.f* aspirin
assaltante *n.* mugger
assar *v.* to bake
assassinar *v.* to murder
assassinato *n.m* murder
assassino(a) *n.m(f)* killer, murderer
assegurar *v.* to assure, insure
assento *n.m* seat
assinar *v.* to sign
assinatura *n.f* signature
assistente *n.* assistant
associação *n.f* association
assunto *n.m* matter, subject
assustado(a) *adj.m(f)* scared
assustar *v.* to scare
atacar *v.* to tackle
atadura *n.f* bandage
ataque *n.m* seizure
até *prep.* until
atenção *n.f* attention
atencioso(a) *adj.m(f)* attentive
aterrissar *v.* to land
atingir *v.* to reach
atirar *v.* to shoot
atitude *n.f* attitude
atividade *n.f* activity

ativo(a) *adj.m(f)* active
ativo fixo *n.m* fixed assets
atleta *n.* athlete
ato *n.m* act
ator *n.m* actor
atraente *adj.* attractive
atrair *v.* to attract
atrás *adv.* behind, back
atrás de *prep.* behind
atrasado(a) *adj.m(f)*
    overdue, late
atrasar *v.* to delay
atraso *n.m* delay
através de *prep.* across,
    through
atribuir *v.* to assign
atriz *n.f* actress
atualizar *v.* to update
atum *n.m* tuna
audição *n.f* hearing
aumentar *v.* to enlarge
aumento *n.m* increase,
    raise
ausência *n.f* absence
autêntico(a) *adj.m(f)*
    authentic
auto-, se *pron.reflex.* self
auto-estrada *n.f* highway
automático(a) *adj.m(f)*
    automatic
autor(~a) *n.m(f)* author
autoridade *n.f* authority
autorização *n.f*
    authorization
autorizar *v.* to authorize
auto-serviço *n.m* self-
    service
avaliar *v.* to evaluate
avançar *v.* to advance
avanço *n.m* advance
avaria *n.f* damage
aveia *n.f* oats
avenida *n.f* avenue
aventura *n.f* adventure

aversão *n.f* disgust
ave *n.f* bird
aves comestíveis *n.f.pl*
    poultry
avião *n.m* airplane
avisar *v.* to warn, inform
aviso *n.m* notice, signal
avó *n.f* grandmother
avô *n.m* grandfather
avós *n.m.pl* grandparents
axila *n.f* armpit
azarado(a) *adj.m(f)* hapless
azedo(a) *adj.m(f)* sour
azeitona *n.f* olive
azul *adj.* blue

B
babá *n.f* baby-sitter
babador *n.m* bib
babar *v.* to drool
bacia *n.f* basin, bowl
bactéria *n.f* bacteria
baderna *n.f* commotion,
    melee
bagageiro *n.m* rack
bagagem *n.f* baggage,
    luggage
baía *n.f* bay
bainha *n.f* hem
bairro *n.m* ward
baixar *v.* to lower
baixo(a) *adj.m(f)* low
bala *n.f* bullet
balançar *v.* to swing
balanço *n.m* swing
balcão *n.m* balcony,
    counter
balde *n.m* bucket
balé *n.m* ballet
balsa *n.f* ferry
banca de jornal *n.f*
    newsstand
banco *n.m* bank, bench

banda *n.f* band
bandeira *n.f* flag
bandeja *n.f* tray
bando *n.m* gang
banha *n.f* lard
banhar *v.* to bathe
banheira *n.f* bathtub, tub
banheiro *n.m* bathroom
banheiro público *n.m*
    restroom
banho *n.m* bath
banir *v.* to disallow
banqueiro(a) *n.m(f)* banker
banquete *n.m* banquet
banquinho *n.m* stool
bar *n.m* bar, pub
baratear *v.* to cut the price
barato(a) *adj.m(f)* bargain,
    cheap
barba *n.f* beard
barbante *n.m* string
barbeador *n.m* shaver
barbear *v.* to shave
barbeiro *n.m* barber
barco *n.m* boat
barra *n.f* bar
barriga *n.f* belly
barrilzinho *n.m* keg
barulhento(a) *adj.m(f)*
    loud, noisy
barulho *n.m* noise, fight
base *n.f* basis
bastante *adv.* pretty, quite,
    enough
bate-papo *n.m* chatter
bater *v.* to beat, hit, knock
bater-papo *v.* to chat
batida *n.f* cocktail, beat,
    knock
batismo *n.m* baptism
batizar *v.* to baptize
batom *n.m* lipstick
baunilha *n.f* vanilla
bêbado(a) *adj.m(f)* drunk

bebê *n.m* baby, infant
beber *v.* to drink
bebida *n.f* beverage, drink
bebida destilada *n.f* liquor
beijar *v.* to kiss
beijo *n.m* kiss
beira *n.f* verge
beleza *n.f* beauty
belga(o) *adj.f(m)* Belgian
Bélgica *n.f* Belgium
beliscão *n.m* pinch
beliscar *v.* to pinch
bem *adv.* well, very, quite
bem-vindo(a) *adj.m(f)*
    welcome
beneficiar *v.* to benefit
benefício *n.m* benefit
berço *n.m* cot, cradle
berrar *v.* to yell
berro *n.m* yell
bexiga *n.f* bladder
Bíblia *n.f* Bible
biblioteca *n.f* library
bibliotecário(a) *n.m(f)*
    librarian
bicar *v.* to peck
bicicleta *n.f* bicycle
bico *n.m* nipple
bife *n.m* steak
bilhão *n.m* billion
bilhete *n.m* ticket
bilíngüe *adj.* bilingual
bisavó *n.f* great-
    grandmother
bisavô *n.m* great-
    grandfather
bloco *n.m* block
bloco de papel *n.m* pad
blusa *n.f* blouse
boa *adj.f* good
boas vindas *n.f* welcome
boato *n.m* gossip
bobagem *n.f* folly
boba(o) *n.f (m)* fool, silly

boca *n.f* mouth
bocejar *v.* to yawn
bocejo *n.m* yawn
bochecha *n.f* cheek
bodas *n.f.pl* wedding
bóia *n.f* buoy
boina *n.f* beret
bola *n.f* ball
bolha *n.f* blister, bubble
bolo *n.m* cake
bolsa *n.f* purse
bolsa de estudos *n.f*
　scholarship
bolso *n.m* pocket
bom *adj.m* good
bom gosto *adj.m* good
　taste, elegant
bomba *n.f* bomb, pump
bombardear *v.* to bomb,
　pump
bombear *v.* to pump
bombeiro *n.m* fireman
bondade *n.f* kindness
boné *n.m* cap
boneca *n.f* doll
bonita(o) *adj. f(m)*
　beautiful, nice, pretty
bonitinha(o) *adj. f(m)* cute
borbulhar *v.* to fizz
borda *n.f* edge
bota *n.f* boot
botão *n.m* button
boxe *n.m* boxing
braço *n.m* arm
branco(a) *adj.m(f)* white
brechó *n.m* flea market
breve *adj.* brief
briga *n.f* fight
brigar *v.* to fight
brilhante *adj.* bright
brilhar *v.* to glare, shine
brilho *n.m* glare, shine
brincadeira *n.f* jest, hoax
brincar *v.* to toy

brinco *n.m* earring
brinquedo *n.m* toy
brisa *n.f* breeze
bronzeado(a) *n.m; adj.m(f)*
　tan
bronzear *v.* to tan
bruto(a) *adj.m(f)* brutish,
　gross
bulbo *n.m* bulb
bule de chá *n.m* teapot
buraco *n.m* hole
buraco de fechadura *n.m*
　keyhole
burocracia *n.f* red tape,
　bureaucracy
burro *n.m* donkey
busca *n.f* quest, search
buscar *v.* to fetch, search
bússola *n.f* compass

C

cabana *n.f* hut
cabeça *n.f* head
cabeça para baixo *adv.*
　upside-down
cabelereiro(a) *n.m(f)*
　hairdresser
cabelo *n.m* hair
cabide *n.f* hanger
cabo *n.m* cable
cabo de ligação *n.m*
　jumper cables
cabra *n.f* goat
cabrito(a) *n.m(f)* baby
　goat, kid
caça *n.f* hunt
caçador(~a) *n.m(f)* hunter
caçar *v.* to hunt
cachecol *n.m* scarf
cachimbo *n.m* pipe
cachorro *n.m* dog
cada *adj.* every, each
cadáver *n.m* corpse

cadeado *n.m* locker
cadeia *n.f* jail
cadeira *n.f* chair
caderno *n.m* notebook
café *n.m* coffee, coffee bar
café da manhã *n.m* breakfast
caixa *n.f* box, cashier, case
caixa de papelão *n.f* carton
caixa postal *n.f* mailbox
caixão *n.m* big box, coffin
calçada de rua *n.f* sidewalk
calcanhar *n.m* heel
calças *n.f.pl* pants
calcinhas *n.f.pl* panties, knickers, briefs
calculadora *n.f* calculator
calcular *v.* to calculate, reckon
caldeira *n.f* boiler
calendário *n.m* calendar
calha *n.f* gutter
calma(o) *n.f; adj.f(m)* calm, quiet
calor *n.m* heat
cama *n.f* bed
camada *n.f* layer
camarão *n.m* prawn, shrimp
camelô *n.m* peddler
câmera *n.f* camera
caminhada *n.f* walk
caminhão *n.m* truck
caminhar *v.* to hike
caminho *n.m* path, route
caminhonete *n.f* van
camisa *n.f* shirt
camisinha *n.f* condom
campo *n.m* field
Canadá *n.m* Canada
canadense *n; adj.* Canadian
canção *n.m* song
cancelamento *n.m* cancellation

cancelar *v.* to cancel
câncer *n.m* cancer
caneca *n.f* mug
caneta *n.f* pen
canivete *n.m* pocketknife
cano *n.m* pipe
canoa *n.f* canoe
cansado(a) *adj.m(f)* tired
cansar *v.* to tire
cantar *v.* to sing
cantarolar *v.* to hum
canto *n.m* corner
cantor(~a) *n.m(f)* singer
capa *n.f* hood, cover
capa de chuva *n.f* raincoat
capacete *n.m* helmet
capaz *adj.* able, capable
capital *n.m* capital
capitão *n.m* captain
capítulo *n.m* chapter
caráter *n.m* character
cardápio *n.m* menu
careca *adj.* bald
carga *n.f* load, charge
carne *n.f* meat
carne de caça *n.f* venison
carne de porco *n.f* pork
caro(a) *adj.m(f)* dear, expensive
carona *n.f* hike
carregador(~a) *n.m(f)* porter
carregar *v.* to carry, load
carro *n.m* car
carta *n.f* letter
cartão *n.m* card
cartão de crédito *n.m* credit card
cartão de embarque *n.m* boarding pass
cartão de visita *n.m* business card
cartão postal *n.m* postcard
carteira *n.f* wallet

carteira de identidade *n.f*
identity card
carteira de motorista *n.f*
driver's license
carvalho *n.m* oak
casa *n.f* house
casal *n.m* couple
casamento *n.m* marriage,
wedding
casar *v.* to marry, wed
caso *n.m* case
cassino *n.m* casino
castelo *n.m* castle
catálogo *n.m* catalog
catedral *n.f* cathedral
Catolicismo *n.m*
Catholicism
católico(a) *n.m; adj.m(f)*
catholic
causa *n.f* motive, sake,
cause
causar *v.* to cause
cauteloso(a) *adj.m(f)*
cautious
cavalo *n.m* horse
caverna *n.f* cave
caxumba *n.f* mumps
CD *n.m* CD
CD player *n.m* CD player
CD-rom *n.m* CD-ROM
cebola *n.f* onion
cedo *adv.* early
cegar *v.* to blind
cego(a) *adj.m(f)* blind
cegueira *n.f* blindness
ceia *n.f* supper
cela *n.f* cell
celebrar *v.* to celebrate
celeiro *n.m* barn
célula *n.f* cell
cem *num.* hundred
cemitério *n.m* cemetery,
graveyard
cenário *n.m* scenery

centímetro *n.m* centimeter
central *adj.* central
centrar *v.* to center
centro *n.m* center
CEP *n.m* ZIP, postal code
cera *n.f* wax
cerâmica *n.f* pottery
cerca *n.f* fence
cereal *n.m* cereal
cerimônia *n.f* ceremony
certo(a) *adj.m(f)* sure
cerveja *n.f* beer
cerveja clara *n.f* lager
cesta *n.f* basket
céu *n.m* heaven, sky
chá *n.m* tea
chácara *n.f* country house,
small farm
chaleira *n.f* kettle
chama *n.f* flame, flare
chamada *n.f* call
chamada a cobrar *n.f*
collect call
chamar *v.* to call
chance *n.f* chance
chantagear *v.* to blackmail
chantagista *n.* racketeer,
blackmailer
chão *n.m* floor
chapéu *n.m* hat
charuto *n.m* cigar
chave *n.f* key
chave de fenda *n.f*
screwdriver
chaveiro *n.m* locksmith
chefe *n.m* boss, chief
chegada *n.f* arrival
chegar *v.* to arrive
cheio(a) *adj.m(f)* full
cheirar *v.* to smell
cheiro *n.m* smell
cheque *n.m* check
cheque de viagem *n.m*
traveler's check

chicote *n.m* lash
chicotear *v.* to lash
chifre *n.m* horn
chinelo *n.m* slipper
chocar *v.* to shock
choque *n.m* shock
chorar *v.* to weep, cry
choro *n.m* cry
choroso(a) *adj.m(f)* tearful
chover *v.* to rain
chumbo *n.m* lead
chupar *v.* to suck
chutar *v.* to kick
chute *n.m* kick
chuva *n.f* shower, rain
chuveiro *n.m* shower, rain
chuvoso(a) *adj.m(f)* rainy
cicatriz *n.f* scar
cidadã(~o) *n.f(m)* citizen
cidade *n.f* city, town
ciência *n.f* science
ciente *adj.* aware
científico(a) *adj.m(f)*
    scientific
cigarro *n.m* cigarette
cílio *n.m* eyelash
cinco *num.* five
cinema *n.m* movie theater
cinto *n.m* belt
cinto de segurança *n.m*
    seat belt
cintura *n.f* waist
cinza *n.f* ash; *adj.* gray
cinzeiro *n.m* ashtray
cinzento(a) *adj.m(f)* gray
circo *n.m* circus
círculo *n.m* circle
circunstância *n.f*
    circumstance
cirurgia *n.f* surgery
cirurgiã(~o) *n.f (m)*
    surgeon
cirurgia plástica da face *n.f*
    face-lift

citação *n.f* quote
citar *v.* to quote
ciúme *n.m* jealousy
ciumento(a) *adj.m(f)*
    jealous
civilização *n.f* civilization
claro(a) *adj.m(f)* clear,
    bright, evident
clássico(a) *adj.m(f)* classic
cliente *n.* client, customer
clima *n.m* climate
clínica *n.f* clinic
clube de dança *n.m* dance
    club
coberta *n.f* quilt
cobertor *n.m* blanket
cobiça *n.f* greed
cobiçar *v.* to covet
cobra *n.f* snake
cobrar *v.* to charge
coceira *n.f* itch
código *n.m* code
código postal, CEP *n.m*
    postal code, ZIP
coelho *n.m* rabbit
cofre *n.m* safe
cogumelo *n.m* mushroom
coisa *n.f* thing
cola *n.f* glue
colar¹ *n.m* necklace
colar² *v.* to glue
colcha *n.f* quilt
colchão *n.m* mattress
colchete *n.m* safety pin
coleção *n.f* collection
colega *n.* peer, colleague
colégio *n.m* college
colete salva-vida *n.m* life
    jacket
colheita *n.f* harvest
colher *n.f* spoon
colher de chá *n.f* teaspoon
colher de sopa *n.f*
    tablespoon

colidir *v.* to collide
colina *n.f* hill
colisão *n.f* collision
colméia *n.f* hive
colo *n.m* lap
colocar *v.* to place, put
colônia *n.f* settlement
colonizar *v.* to colonize
colonizador(~a) *n.m(f)*
  settler
coluna *n.f* column
com *prep.* with
com respeito a *prep.*
  regarding
com sede *adj.* thirsty
combinação *n.f*
  combination
combinado(a) *adj.m(f)*
  matching
combinar *v.* to combine,
  agree, arrange
combustível *n.m* fuel
começar *v.* to begin, start
começo *n.m* beginning,
  onset, start
comentar *v.* to comment
comentário *n.m* comment
comer *v.* to eat
comercializar *v.* to market,
  commercialize
comerciar *v.* to trade
comércio *n.m* trade
comestível *adj.* edible
comida *n.f* food,
  refreshment
comissão *n.f* commission
comissário(a) de bordo
  n.m(f) flight attendant
comitê *n.m* committee
como *conj.* as; *prep.* like;
  adv. how
companheiro(a) *n.m(f)*
  fellow, pal, companion,
  mate

companhia *n.f* company
comparação *n.f*
  comparison
comparar *v.* to compare
compartilhar *v.* to share
compartimento *n.m*
  compartment, room
compensar *v.* to
  compensate
competência *n.f*
  competence
competição *n.f*
  competition
completar *v.* to utter
completo(a) *adj.m(f)*
  complete
complicação *n.f* hassle
complicado(a) *adj.m(f)*
  complicated
complicar *v.* to complicate,
  hassle
compor *v.* to compose
comportamento *n.m*
  behavior
comportar *v.* to behave
composição *n.f*
  composition
compra *n.f* purchase
comprar *v.* to buy,
  purchase
compreender *v.* to
  understand
comprimento *n.m* length
comprimido *n.m* tablet,
  pill
compromisso *n.m*
  engagement
computador *n.m*
  computer
comum *adj.* common,
  ordinary
comunicação *n.f*
  communication

comunicar *v.* to comunicate

concentrar *v.* to concentrate

concerto *n.m* concert

concha *n.f* shell

conclusão *n.f* completion, conclusion

concordar *v.* to agree

concreto(a) *adj.m(f)* concrete

condenar *v.* to condemn

condição *n.f* condition

condolências *n.f.pl* condolences

condutor(~a) *n.m(f)* conductor

conectar *v.* to connect

conexão *n.f* connection

conferir *v.* to check

confessar *v.* to confess

confiança *n.f* confidence, trust

confiar *v* to trust, rely

confiável *adj.* reliable

confirmar *v.* to confirm

confiscar *v.* to impound

confissão *n.f* confession

conflito *n.m* conflict

confortável *adj.* comfortable

confundir *v.* to confuse

confusão *n.f* mess

congelado(a) *adj.m(f)* frozen

congelador *n.m* freezer

congelar *v.* to freeze

conhecer *v.* to know

conhecido(a) *adj.m(f)* known, acquaintance

conhecimento *n.m* knowledge

conjunto(a) *n.m* group; *adj.m(f)* joint

conjunto de objetos *n.m* kit

consciente *adj.* conscious

conseguir *v.* to achieve

conselho *n.m* advice

conseqüência *n.f* consequence

consertar *v.* to fix, repair

conserto *n.m* repair

conservar *v.* to conserve

consideração *n.f* regard

considerar *v.* to consider, regard

consoante *n.f* consonant

constranger *v.* to embarrass

construir *v.* to build

cônsul(~esa) *n.m(f)* consul

consulado *n.m* consulate

consultar *v.* to refer

conta *n.f* account, bill

contador(~a) *n.m(f)* accountant

contagem *n.f* score, count

contagioso(a) *adj.m(f)* contagious

contaminar *v.* to contaminate

contar *v.* to count, tell

contatar *v.* to contact

contato *n.m* contact

contente *adj.* happy, glad, content

conter *v.* to contain

conteúdo *n.m* content

continente *n.m* continent

continuar *v.* to continue

conto *n.m* tale

contra *prep.* against

contrabandear *v.* to smuggle

contraceptivo(a) *adj.m(f)* contraceptive

contrário(a) *n.m; adj.m(f)* contrary, opposite

contratar *v.* to contract

contrato *n.m* contract
controlar *v.* to control
controle *n.m* control
contudo *conj.* however
convencer *v.* to convince
convento *n.m* convent
conversa *n.f* talk
conversação *n.f*
conversation
conversar *v.* to talk
conversível *adj.* convertible
converter *v.* to convert
convertido(a) *n.m(f)*
convert
convidado(a) *n.m(f)* guest
convidar *v.* to invite
convite *n.m* invitation
cópia *n.f* copy
copiar *v.* to copy
cor *n.f* color
cor-de-rosa *adj.* pink
coração *n.m* heart
corar *v.* to blush, change
color
corcunda *n.f; adj.*
hunchback
corda *n.f* rope
cordão de sapato *n.m*
shoelace
cordeiro *n.m* lamb
corpo *n.m* body
correção *n.f* correction
correio *n.m* post, mail
correio aéreo *n.m* air mail
corrente *n.f* chain, current
correr *v.* to race
correspondência *n.f*
correspondence
correto(a) *adj.m(f)* correct
corrida *n.f* race
corrigir *v.* to correct
cortar *v.* to disconnect,
chop, cut
corte *n.m* court; cut

corte de cabelo *n.m*
haircut
cortês *adj.* polite
cortina *n.f* curtain, blind
costas *n.f.pl* back
costela *n.f* rib
costume *n.m* custom, habit
costura *n.f* seam
costurar *v.* to sew
cotovelo *n.m* elbow
couro *n.m* leather
coxa *n.f* thigh
coxo(a) *adj.m(f)* lame
cozinha *n.f* kitchen
cozinhar *v.* to cook
cozinheiro(a) *n.m(f)* cook
crânio *n.m* skull
creme *n.m* cream
creme de proteção solar
n.m sunblock
crença *n.f* belief
crescer *v.* to grow, thrive
crescimento *n.m* growth
crespa(o) *adj.f(m)* curl
criança *n.f* child, kid
criação *n.f* creation
criar *v.* to create
crime *n.m* crime
criminoso(a) *adj.m(f)*
outlaw, criminal
cristã(~o) *n.f(m); adj.f(m)*
Christian
Cristianismo *n.m*
Christianity
crítica *n.f* criticism
criticar *v.* to criticize
crosta *n.f* crust
cru(~a) *adj.m(f)* raw
crustáceo *n.m* shellfish
cruz *n.f* cross
cruzamento *n.m* crossing
cruzamento de estrada
n.m junction
cruzar *v.* to cruise

cruzeiro *n.m* cruise
cubo de gelo *n.m* ice cube
cuecas *n.f.pl* underwear
cuidado *n.m* caution, care
cuidadoso(a) *adj.m(f)* careful
cuidar *v.* to care
cuidar de bebê *v.* to baby-sit
culpa *n.f* guilt
culpado(a) *n.m(f)* culprit; *adj.m(f)* guilty
culpar *v.* to blame
cultivar *v.* to cultivate, grow
culto(a) *n.m* worship, cult; *adj.m(f)* cultured
cultura *n.f* culture
cumprimentar *v.* to greet
cumprir *v.* to comply
cunhada *n.f* sister-in-law
cunhado *n.m* brother-in-law
cura *n.f* cure
curar *v.* to heal, cure
curioso(a) *adj.m(f)* curious
curso *n.m* course
curva *n.f* bow
curvar *v.* to bend
cuspir *v.* to spit
custar *v.* to cost
custo *n.m* cost

D

dado *n.m* die
dama *n.f* lady
dança *n.f* dance
dançar *v.* to dance
danificar *v.* to damage
dano *n.m* damage, harm
daqui prá frente *adv.* henceforth
dar *v.* to give
data *n.f* date
datar *v.* to set the date

de *prep.* of; from; off
de fora *adv.* from outside
de lado *adv.* aside
débito *n.m* debt
década *n.f* decade
decadência *n.f* decay
decano *n.m* dean
decência *n.f* decency
decepção *n.f* disappointment
decepcionar *v.* to disappoint
decimal *adj.* decimal
décimo(a) *num.m(f)* tenth
decisão *n.f* decision, judgment
declarar *v.* to declare
declinar *v.* to decline
declínio *n.m* decline
decodificar *v.* to decode
decoração *n.f* decoration
decorar *v.* to decorate
dedicação *n.f* dedication
dedicar *v.* to dedicate
dedo da mão *n.m* finger
dedo do pé *n.m* toe
dedo indicador *n.m* forefinger
defeito *n.m* defect
defender *v.* to defend, protect
defesa *n.f* defense
definição *n.f* definition
definir *v.* to define
degrau *n.m* step
deitado(a) *adj.m(f)* lying down
deitar *v.* to lay down
deixar *v.* to let, quit
dela(e) *adj.f(m)* her, his, its
delegacia de polícia *n.f* police station
deles(as) *adj.m(f)pl* their

delicioso(a) *adj.m(f)* delicious

demais *adv.* too much

demanda *n.f* demand

demandar *v.* to demand

demitir *v.* to dismiss

democracia *n.f* democracy

demonstração *n.f* demonstration

demorar *v.* to linger

dente *n.m* tooth

denteado(a) *adj.m(f)* jagged

dentista *n.* dentist

dentro *adv.* within, inside

depauperado(a) *adj.m(f)* depleted

depender *v.* to depend

deplorar *v.* to deplore

depois *adv; prep; conj.* after

deportar *v.* to deport

depositar *v.* to deposit

depósito *n.m* deposit

depósito de lixo *n.m* dump

depressa *adv.* fast

depressão *n.f* depression

derramar *v.* to spill, pour

derrame *n.m* stroke (apoplexy)

derreter *v.* to melt

derrota *n.f* defeat

derrubar *v.* to topple

desacordo *n.m* disagreement

desagradável *adj.* unpleasant

desagrado *n.m* dislike

desajustado(a) *adj.m(f)* maladjusted

desalojar *v.* to dislodge

desaparecer *v.* to disappear

desarmar *v.* to disarm, defuse

desastre *n.m* disaster

desautorizado(a) *adj.m(f)* unauthorized

desautorizar *v.* to disallow, discredit

desbotar *v.* to fade

descafeinado(a) *adj.m(f)* decaffeinated

descalço(a) *adj.m(f)* barefoot

descansar *v.* to rest, relax

descanso *n.m* rest

descarregar *v.* to unload

descartar *v.* to dismiss

descartável *adj.* disposable

descentralização *n.f* decentralization

descer *v.* to descend

descida *n.f* descent

descobrir *v.* to discover

desconhecer *v.* to not know, not accept, ignore

desconhecido(a) *adj.m(f)* stranger

descontar *v.* to deduct, discount

descontentar *v.* to displease

descontente *adj.* unhappy

desconto *n.m* discount

descontrair *v.* to rest, relax

descorante *n.m* bleach

descorar *v.* to bleach

descrever *v.* to describe

descrição *n.f* description

descuidado(a) *adj.m(f)* reckless

descuidar *v.* to neglect

descuido *n.m* oversight, neglect

desculpa *n.f* excuse

desculpar *v.* to excuse

desculpe! *interj; adj.* sorry!

desde *prep; conj.* since

desdobrar *v.* to unfold
desejar *v.* to desire, wish
desejo *n.m* desire, wish
desejoso(a) *adj.m(f)* keen,
  wishing to
desembarcar *v.* to
  disembark
desempacotar *v.* to unpack
desempenhar *v.* to
  perform, fulfill
desempenho *n.m*
  peformance
desempregado(a) *n.m(f)*
  unemployed
desenhar *v.* to draw, design
desenho *n.m* drawing
desenvolver *v.* to develop
desertar *v.* to desert
deserto *n.m* desert
desesperado(a) *adj.m(f)*
  hopeless
desesperar *v.* to infuriate,
  despair
desfavorável *adj.* untoward
desfazer *v.* to undo
desidratação *n.f*
  dehydration
desidratar *v.* to dehydrate
desigual *adj.* uneven
desleixado(a) *adj.m(f)*
  unkempt, careless
desligado(a) *adj.m(f)* off
desligar *v.* to switch off,
  unplug
desmaiar *v.* to faint
desmaio *n.m* faint
desnecessário(a) *adj.m(f)*
  unnecessary
desobedecer *v.* to disobey
desocupado(a) *adj.m(f)*
  vacant
desocupar *v.* to vacate, free
desodorante *n.m*
  deodorant

desordeiro(a) *n.m(f)* lout
desordem *n.f* disarray
despedir *v.* to dismiss
despejar *v.* to pour
desperdiçar *v.* to waste
desperdício *n.m* waste
despesa *n.f* expense
despir *v.* to undress, strip
desprezar *v.* to despise
desprezo *n.m* contempt
destinação *n.f* destination
destino *n.m* fate, destiny
destruição *n.f* destruction
destruir *v.* to destroy, raze,
  shatter
desvantagem *n.f*
  disadvantage
desviar *v.* to divert, deflect
desvio *n.m* detour
detalhado(a) *adj.m(f)*
  detailed
detalhar *v.* to detail
detalhe *n.m* detail
detectar *v.* to detect,
  discover
detetive *n.* detective
Deus *n.m* God
dever[1] *n.m* duty
dever[2] *v.* owe, must
dever fazer *v.* to ought
devidamente *adv.* duly
devido(a) *adj.m(f)* due
dez *num.* ten
dezembro *n.m* December
dia *n.m* day
dia de semana *n.m*
  weekday
diabete *n.f* diabetes
diabo(a) *n.m; adj.m(f)*
  devil
diagnóstico *n.m* diagnosis
diagonal *n.f* diagonal
dialeto *n.m* dialect
diálogo *n.m* dialogue

diamante *n.m* diamond
diário(a) *n.m* diary, newspaper; *adj.m(f)* daily
dica *n.f* hint, tip
dicionário *n.m* dictionary
didático(a) *adj.m(f)* didactic
dieta *n.f* diet
diferença *n.f* difference
diferente *adj.* different, unlike
difícil *adj.* difficult
dificuldade *n.f* difficulty
dificultar *v.* to complicate, make difficult
digestão *n.f* digestion
digital *adj.* digital
dimensão *n.f* dimension
diminuição *n.f* decrease
diminuir *v.* to decrease
dinheiro *n.m* money, cash
diplomacia *n.f* diplomacy
direito(a) *n.m* justice; *adj.m(f)* right, direct, just
diretor(~a) *n.m(f)* director
discar *v.* to dial
disciplina *n.f* discipline
disco *n.m* disk
discordar *v.* to disagree
discreção *n.f* discretion
discreto(a) *adj.m(f)* discreet
discursar *v.* to speak, make a speech
discurso *n.m* speech
discussão *n.f* discussion; argument, quarrel
discutir *v.* to discuss
disponível *adj.* available
dispositivo *n.m* appliance
distância *n.f* distance
distanciar *v.* to distance, move away
distante *adj.* distant, far-away
distinguir *v.* to differentiate, distinguish
distinto(a) *adj.m(f)* distinct, different
distrair *v.* to distract
distribuição *n.f* distribution
distribuir *v.* to distribute
distrito *n.m* district, precinct
diversos(as) *adj.m(f)pl* several
divertimento *n.m* fun
dividir *v.* to divide, split
divorciar *v.* to divorce
divórcio *n.m* divorce
dizer *v.* to say
dizimar *v.* to decimate
do que *conj.* than
doação *n.f* donation, gift
doar *v.* to donate, give
dobra *n.f* fold
dobrar *v.* to fold
doce *n.m; adj.* sweet
doença *n.f* disease, illness
doença venérea *n.f* venereal disease
doente *adj.* sick, ill
doer *v.* to hurt, ache
dois, duas *num.m,f* two
dólar *n.m* dollar
dolorido(a) *adj.m(f)* sore
doloroso(a) *adj.m(f)* painful
dominar *v.* to dominate, prevail
domingo *n.m* Sunday
domínio *n.m* domain
dor *n.f* ache, pain
dor de cabeça *n.f* headache

dor de dente *n.f* toothache
dormir *v.* to sleep
dormitório *n.m* dormitory
dose *n.f* dose
dose excessiva *n.f* overdose
dotar *v.* to endow
doutor(~a) *n.m(f)* doctor
drama *n.m* drama
droga *n.f* drug
duas vezes *adv.* twice
durante *prep.* during
duro(a) *adj.m(f)* hard,
    tough, harsh
dúvida *n.f* query, doubt
duvidar *v.* to doubt
dúzia *n.f* dozen

E

e *conj.* and
eclipsar *v.* to overshadow
economia *n.f* economy
economizar *v.* to
    economize, save
edição *n.f* edition, issue
edificante *adj.* exemplary
edificar *v.* to build, edify
edifício *n.m* building
editar *v.* to publish, edit
educação *n.f* education
educado(a) *adj.m(f)* polite,
    educated
educar *v.* to educate, bring
    up, train
eficaz *adj.* effective
égua *n.f* mare, female
    horse
ela *pron.f* she, it
elástico(a) *n.m* rubber
    band; *adj.m(f)* elastic
ele *pron.m* he, it
elegante *adj.* elegant, smart
esperto(a) *adj.m(f)* smart
eleição *n.f* election

eleger *v.* to elect, choose
eles *pron.pl* they
eletricidade *n.f* electricity
eletricista *n.m* electrician
elétrico(a) *adj.m(f)* electric
elevador *n.m* elevator; lift
elevar *v.* to lift, raise
elogiar *v.* to compliment,
    praise
elogio *n.m* compliment,
    praise
em *prep.* in, on, at, into
em frente *adv.* in front of
em lugar fechado *adv.*
    indoors
em nenhuma parte *adv.*
    nowhere
em torno *adv.* around
em vez de *adv.* instead of
e-mail *n.m* E-mail
emagrecer *v.* to slim
emagrecimento *n.m*
    slimming
embaixada *n.f* embassy
embaixador(~a) *n.m(f)*
    ambassador
embalado(a) *adj.m(f)* fast,
    eager
embalagem *n.f* packing
embalar *v.* to pack
embora *conj.* though
embrulhar *v.* to wrap,
    cheat, deceive
emergência *n.f* emergency
emigrar *v.* to emigrate
emoção *n.f* emotion, thrill
emocionar *v.* to move,
    upset, excite, thrill
empada *n.f* pastry
empatar *v.* to tie, draw;
    waste time
empate *n.m* draw,
    stalemate, deadlock, tie
empilhar *v.* to pile

empobrecer *v.* to impoverish

empreender *v.* to undertake

empreendimento *n.m* venture

empregado(a) *n.m(f)* employee

empregador(~a) *n.m(f)* employer

empregar *v.* to employ

emprego *n.m* job, employment

emprestar *v.* to lend (give a loan), borrow (take a loan)

empréstimo *n.m* loan

empurrar *v.* to push

encaminhado(a) *adj.m(f)* forward

encaminhar *v.* to forward

encanador *n.m* plumber

encantado(a) *adj.m(f)* overjoyed

encerar *v.* to wax

encher *v.* to fill; nag, annoy

enciclopédia *n.f* encyclopedia

encolher *v.* to shrink

encomenda *n.f* order

encomendar *v.* to order

encontrar *v.* to meet, encounter

encontro *n.m* encounter, meeting

encontro amoroso *n.m* date

encurtar *v.* to shorten

endereço *n.m* address

endossar *v.* to endorse

endurecer *v.* to harden

energético(a) *adj.m(f)* energetic

energia *n.f* energy, drive

enfermeiro(a) *n.m(f)* nurse

enferrujar *v.* to rust, corrode

enfurecer-se *v.* to rave

enfurecido(a) *adj.m(f)* angry

enganar *v.* to deceive, mislead

engano *n.m* misunderstanding, deceit, overlook

engasgar *v.* to choke

engenheiro(a) *n.m(f)* engineer

engraçado(a) *adj.m(f)* funny

enjoado(a) *adj.m(f)* queasy

enjoar *v.* to nauseate, bore, make sick

enjôo de mar *n.m* seasickness

enorme *adj.* enormous, huge, massive

enquanto *conj.* while

enrolar *v.* to curl

ensinar *v.* to teach

ensolarado(a) *adj.m(f)* sunny

ensopar *v.* to soak

então *adv.* then

enteada *n.f* stepdaughter

enteado *n.m* stepson

entender *v.* to grasp

enterrar *v.* to bury

entrada *n.f* entrance, input

entrar *v.* to enter, come in

entre *prep.* among(st), between

entrega *n.f* delivery

entregar *v.* to deliver

entrementes *adv.* meantime

entreter *v.* to entertain

entrevista *n.f* interview

entrevistar *v.* to interview

entusiasmado(a) *adj.m(f)* keen, eager

entusiasmar *v.* to excite

entusiasmo *n.m* enthusiasm, zest

envelhecer *v.* to age

envelope *n.m* envelope

envenenar *v.* to poison

enviado(a) *n.m* envoy; *adj.m(f)* sent

enviar *v.* to send

enxaguar *v.* to rinse

enxaqueca *n.f* migraine, headache

enxertar *v.* to graft

enxerto *n.m* graft

epidemia *n.f* epidemic

equilibrar *v.* to balance

equipamento *n.m* equipment, gear

equipar *v.* to equip

equipe *n.f* team

equivalente *n.m* equivalent; *adj.* equal

era *n.f* era

errado(a) *adj.m(f)* wrong

errar *v.* to err, make mistake

erro *n.m* error, mistake

erva *n.f* herb; marijuana

esbanjar *v.* to squander, waste

esbofetear *v.* to slap

escada *n.f* ladder, stairs

escada rolante *n.f* escalator

escama *n.f* scale

escoadouro *n.m* outlet

escola *n.f* school

escola secundária *n.f* high school

escolha *n.f* choice

escolher *v.* to choose, pick

escolta *n.f* escort

escoltar *v.* to escort

esconder *v.* to hide

escorregador *n.m* slide

escorregar *v.* to slide

escova *n.f* brush

escova de dente *n.f* toothbrush

escovar *v.* to brush

escrever *v.* to write

escritor(~a) *n.m(f)* writer

escritório *n.m* office

escritura *n.f* deed (to a house)

escultor(~a) *n.m(f)* sculptor

escultura *n.f* sculpture

escurecer *v.* to darken

escuridão *n.f* darkness

escuro(a) *adj.m(f)* dark

escutar *v.* to listen

esferográfica *n.f* ballpoint pen

esforçar *v.* to try hard

esforço *n.m* effort

esfregar *v.* to rub

esgotado(a) *adj.m(f)* exhausted

esgotar *v.* to drain, empty, exhaust

esmalte para unhas *n.m* nail polish

esmigalhar *v.* to crumble

esmola *n.f* handout

espaçar *v.* to space out

espaço *n.m* space

espaço em branco *n.m* blank

Espanha *n.f* Spain

espanhol(~a) *n.m*; *adj.m(f)* Spanish, Spaniard

espantar *v.* to amaze, scare

especial *adj.* special

especialidade *n.f* specialty

especialmente *adv.* especially

espectador(~a) *n.m(f)*
spectator

espelho *n.m* mirror

espera *n.f* wait

esperar *v.* to hope, expect, wait

esperança *n.f* hope

espessura *n.f* thickness

espeto *n.m* poker, spit, prick

espinha dorsal *n.f* backbone, spine

espírito *n.m* spirit, mind, soul, ghost

espirrar *v.* to sneeze

espirro *n.m* sneeze

esponja *n.f* sponge

espontâneo(a) *adj.m(f)* spontaneous

esporte *n.m* sport

esposa *n.f* wife

esposar *v.* to marry

esquecer *v.* to forget

esquecimento *n.m* forgetfulness, oblivion

esquentar *v.* to heat

esquerdo(a) *adj.m(f)* left

esqui *n.m* ski

esqui aquático *n.m* water-skiing

esquiar *v.* to ski

esquisito(a) *adj.m(f)* strange, odd

essencial *adj.* essential

essencialmente *adv.* essentially

estabelecer *v.* to establish

estabelecimento *n.m* establishment

estação *n.f* station, season

estação de férias *n.f* resort

estacionar *v.* to park a car

estacionamento *n.m* parking lot

estadia *n.f* stay

estádio *n.m* stadium

estado *n.m* state

estado de espírito *n.m* mood, state of mind

Estados Unidos *n.m* United States

estagiar *v.* to do a traineeship, to receive training

estagiário(a) *n.m(f)* trainee, apprentice

estágio *n.m* stage, period of training

estância *n.f* spa

estante de livros *n.f* bookcase

estar *v.* to be

estátua *n.f* statue

este, esta; isto *pron.* this

estes, estas *pron. pl* these

estima *n.f* affection, respect, esteem

estimar *v.* to estimate, appreciate

estimativa *n.f* estimate

estômago *n.m* stomach

estória *n.f* story, tale

estrada *n.f* road

estrada de ferro *n.f* railroad

estragado(a) *adj.m(f)* stale, rotten, broken

estragar *v.* to spoil, upset

estrago *n.m* upset

estrangeiro(a) *adj.m(f)* foreign; *n.m(f)* foreigner, alien

estranhar *v.* to be surprised, find strange

estranho(a) *adj.m(f)* strange, odd, weird, unfamiliar

estreitar *v.* to narrow

estreito(a) *adj.m(f)* narrow
estrela *n.f* star
estrelar *v.* to star
estresse *n.m* stress
estrondo *n.m* loud noise
estudante *n.* student
estudar *v.* to study
estudo *n.m* study
esvaziar *v.* to deflate, empty
eterno(a) *adj.m(f)* eternal
etiqueta *n.f* tag, label, etiquette
eu *pron.* I
euro *n.m* euro
Europa *n.f* Europe
europeu, européia *adj.m(f)* European
evacuar *v.* to evacuate
evadir *v.* to evade
evento *n.m* event
evidência *n.f* evidence
evidenciar *v.* to show, prove
evitar *v.* to avoid
exagerar *v.* to exaggerate, overdo, overstate
exagero *n.m* exaggeration, overkill
exame *n.m* examination
examinar *v.* to examine, peruse
exato(a) *adj.m(f)* exact, precise, accurate
exaurir *v.* to exhaust, drain, tire
exaustor *n.m* exhaust, extractor
exceção *n.f* exception
exceder *v.* to exceed
excelente *adj.* excellent
excesso *n.m* excess
excesso de trabalho *n.m* overwork
exceto *prep.* except
excetuar *v.* to except

excitação *n.f* excitement
excitar *v.* to excite
excluir *v.* to exclude
excursão *n.f* excursion, tour
execução *n.f* execution
executar *v.* to execute, perform
exemplificar *v.* to exemplify
exemplo *n.m* example
exercício *n.m* exercise
exercitar *v.* to exercise
exército *n.m* army
exibição *n.f* exhibition
exibir *v.* to exhibit
exigência *n.f* requirement
exigir *v.* to demand
exigente *adj.* demanding, fussy
exilado(a) *n.m(f)* exile
exilar *v.* to exile
exílio *n.m* exile
existência *n.f* existence
existir *v.* to exist
expectativa *n.f* expectation
experiência *n.f* experience, know-how
experimentar *v.* to try out, taste, test
expirar *v.* to expire
explicação *n.f* explanation
explicar *v.* to explain
explodir *v.* to explode, blow up
explosão *n.f* explosion, outburst
expor *v.* to expose, display
exportação *n.f* export
exportar *v.* to export
exposição *n.f* display, explanation
expressar *v.* to express
expresso(a) *adj.m(f)* express
expulsão *n.f* expulsion

expulsar *v.* to expel

extensão *n.f* extension, range, distance

exterior *n.m; adj.* outside

externo(a) *adj.m(f)* external, outer

extintor *n.m* fire extinguisher

extrair *v.* to extract

extraordinário(a) *adj.m(f)* extraordinary

extrato *n.m* extract

extraviar *v.* to mislay

extremo(a) *adj.m(f)* extreme

extrovertido(a) *adj.m(f)* outgoing, talkative

exuberância *n.f* exuberance

F

fã *n.* fan

fábrica *n.f* factory

fabricar *v.* to make, produce, manufacture

faca *n.f* knife

face *n.f* face

fachada *n.f* façade

fácil *adj.* easy

facilitar *v.* to facilitate, make easy

facilmente *adv.* easily

faísca *n.f* spark

faixa *n.f* band, strip

faixa de cruzamento *n.f* pedestrian crossing

falar *v.* to speak

falcão *n.m* hawk

falecer *v.* to die

falecimento *n.m* decease

falha *n.f* failure

falhar *v.* to fail

falsificação *n.f* fake

falsificar *v.* to forge, falsify

falso(a) *adj.m(f)* false, phony, mock

falta *n.f* lack, fault, want

falta de ar *n.f* short of breath

faltar *v.* to lack, be absent

família *n.f* family

faminto(a) *adj.m(f)* hungry

famoso(a) *adj.m(f)* famous

fantasma *n.m* ghost, phantom

farinha *n.f* flour

farmácia *n.f* pharmacy

farol *n.m* light; lighthouse

farol alto *n.m* headlight

farsa *n.f* farce

fase *n.f* phase

fatia *n.f* slice

fatiar *v.* to slice

fato *n.m* fact

fatura *n.f* invoice

faturar *v.* to invoice, make money

favor *n.m* favor

favorecer *v.* to favor, benefit

favorito(a) *n.m(f); adm(f)* favorite

fazenda *n.f* farm

fazendeiro(a) *n.m(f)* farmer

fazer *v.* to do, make

fé *n.f* faith

febre *n.f* fever

febre do feno *n.f* hay fever

fechado (a) *adj.m(f)* closed

fechadura *n.f* lock

fechar *v.* to shut, lock

feder *v.* to stink

fedor *n.m* stink

feijão *n.m* beans

feijoada *n.f* bean and meat stew

feio(a) *adj.m(f)* ugly

feira *n.f* fair, open market

feitiço *n.m* spell, charm, curse

feito(a) *adj.m(f)* made

felicidade *n.f* happiness

felicitações *n.f.pl* congratulations

felicitar *v.* to congratulate

feliz *adj.* happy

Feliz Natal! *interj.* Merry Christmas!

fêmea *n.f* female

feminino(a) *adj.m(f)* feminine, female

feno *n.m* hay

feriado *n.m* holiday

férias *n.f.pl* vacation

ferida *n.f* wound

ferimento *n.m* injury

ferir *v.* to injure, wound

ferramenta *n.f* tool

ferro *n.m* iron

ferrugem *n.f* rust

ferver *v.* to boil

festa *n.f* party, feast

festejar *v.* to celebrate

fevereiro *n.m* February

fezes *n.f* feces

fiança *n.f* guarantee, surety, bail

fibra *n.f* fiber

ficar *v.* to remain, stay

fiel *adj.* faithful, loyal

fígado *n.m* liver

figura *n.f* figure, picture

fila *n.f* queue, line, row

fileira *n.f* row

filha *n.f* daughter

filho *n.m* son

filmar *v.* to film, to record (on video)

filme *n.m* film, movie

filtrar *v.* to filter

filtro *n.m* filter

fim *n.m* end

final *adj.* final

finalidade *n.f* purpose

finalizar *v.* to finalize, finish, end

financeiro(a) *adj.m(f)* financial

fingir *v.* to fake

fino(a) *adj.m(f)* thin

fio *n.m* wire, cord, cable

firma *n.f* firm, company, business

firmar *v.* to sign, secure, make firm

firme *adj.* steady, stable

fiscal *adj.* fiscal

fiscalizar *v.* to inspect, check, supervise

fisgar *v.* to catch

física *n.f* physics

físico *n.m* physique (body); *adj.* physical

físico(a) *n.m(f)* physicist

fita *n.f* ribbon, tape

fitar *v.* to stare, gaze at

fixar *v.* to fix, set

fixo(a) *adj.m(f)* fix, set

flash *n.m* flash

flecha *n.f* arrow

flertar *v.* to flirt

flerte *n.m* flirt

flexível *adj.* supple

floco *n.m* flake

flor *n.f* flower

floresta *n.f* forest

florista *n.f* florist

fluente *adj.* fluent

flutuar *v.* to float

fluxo *n.m* flow

fofo(a) *adj.m(f)* soft, cute

fofocar *v.* to gossip

fogão *n.m* cooker, stove

fogo *n.m* fire
fogos de artifício *n.m.pl* fireworks
folga *n.f* rest, break
folgar *v.* to loosen, slack, rest, relax
folha *n.f* leaf, sheet
folha solta *n.f* insert
folhear *v.* to leaf through, read quickly
fome *n.f* hunger
fonte *n.f* fountain, source, font
fora *adv.* out, outside
forasteiro(a) *n.m(f)* outsider
força *n.f* force, strength
forçar *v.* to force, strain
forma *n.f* shape, form
formal *adj.* formal
formar *v.* to shape, form
fórmula *n.f* formula
formular *v.* to formulate
formulário *n.m* form
fornecer *v.* to provide, supply
fornecimento *n.m* supply
forno *n.m* oven
forte *adj.* strong
fosco(a) *adj.m(f)* tarnished, matted, opaque
fósforo *n.m* match
fossa *n.f* pit
foto *n.f* photo
fotografar *v.* to photograph, take a picture
fracassar *v.* to flop
fracasso *n.m* flop
fraco(a) *adj.m(f)* frail, weak
frágil *adj.* fragile, breakable
fralda *n.f* diaper
França *n.f* France
francês(~a) *n.m; adj.m(f)* French

franquia *n.f* franchise, deductible, levy
fraqueza *n.f* weakness
frasco *n.m* vial, bottle
frase *n.f* phrase
fraudar *v.* to cheat, steal
fraude *n.f* fraud
freguês(~a) *n.m,f* client, patron
freira *n.f* nun
freqüentar *v.* to frequent
freqüente *adj.* frequent
freqüentemente *adv.* often
fresco(a) *adj.m(f)* fresh
fricção *n.f* friction
friccionar *v.* to rub
frigideira *n.f* frying pan
frio(a) *n.m; adj.m(f)* cool, cold
fritar *v.* to fry
fronha *n.f* pillowcase
fronteira *n.f* border
fruta(o) *n.f(m)* fruit, berry
fuga *n.f* escape, flight
fugir *v.* to flee, escape
fumaça *n.f* smoke, fume
fumar *v.* to smoke, fume
função *n.f* function
funcionamento *n.m* functioning, working
funcionar *v.* to function
funcionário(a) *n.m(f)* officer
fundação *n.f* foundation
funeral *n.m* funeral
funil *n.m* funnel
furacão *n.m* hurricane
fusão *n.f* merger
fusível *n.m* fuse
futebol *n.m* soccer
futuro(a) *n.m; adj.m(f)* future

G

gaiola n.f cage
galão n.m gallon
galeria n.f gallery
galinha n.f hen
ganância n.f greed
gancho n.m hook
ganhar v. to earn, win, gain
ganho n.m gain, earnings
ganso n.m goose
garagem n.f garage
garantia n.f warranty
garantir v. to guarantee
garçom n.m waiter
garçonete n.f waitress
garfo n.m fork
garganta n.f throat
garrafa n.f bottle
gás n.m gas
gasolina n.f petrol, gasoline, gas
gastar v. to spend
gasto n.m expense
gato n.m cat
gay adj. gay
geada n.f frost
geladeira n.f refrigerator
gelado(a) adj.m(f) cold, icy
geléia n.f jam, jelly
gelatina n.f gelatin
gelar v. to freeze, chill
gelo n.m ice
gêmeos(as) n.m; adj.m(f)pl twin
gemer v. to moan
gemido n.m moan
general n.m army general
gengiva n.f gum
genro n.m son-in-law
geografia n.f geography
geral n. general
geralmente adv. usually
gerente n. manager
germe n.m germ

gesto n.m gesture
gigante n. giant
ginecologista n. gynecologist
girassol n.m sunflower
gíria n.f slang
global adj. total, global, worldwide
golpe n.m blow, ploy, stroke, trick; coup d'état
golpear v. hit, punch
gordo(a) adj.m(f) fat
gordura n.f fat
gorduroso(a) adj.m(f) oily
gorjeta n.f tip, gratuity
gostar v. to like
gosto n.m taste
gota n.f drop
gotejar v. to drip
governar v. to govern
governo n.m government
gozar v. to enjoy; make fun of; have an orgasm
Grã Bretanha n.f Great Britain
gracinha adj. cute
grade n.m grid
graduado(a) n.m(f) graduate
graduar v. to graduate
grama¹ n.f grass (plant)
grama² n.m gram (weight)
gramado n.m lawn
gramática n.f grammar
grampear v. to staple; tap (telephone)
grampo n.m staple; hairgrip; tap (telephone); bobby pin
grande adj. big, great, large
granizo n.m hail
grão n.m grain
grão de areia n.m grit
grau n.m degree, grade

graduar *v.* to graduate

grátis *adj.* free of charge

gravador *n.m* recorder

gravar *v.* to engrave

grávida *adj.f* pregnant

graxa *n.f* shoe polish, grease

grelha *n.f* grill

grêmio *n.m* guild

gripe *n.f* flu

gritar *v.* to scream, shout, cry

grito *n.m* scream, shout, cry

grosseiro(a) *adj.m(f)* rough, rude, brutish

grosso(a) *adj.m(f)* thick, rude, gross

grupo *n.m* group

guarda-chuva *n.m* umbrella

guardanapo *n.m* napkin

guardar *v.* to keep, watch

guardiã(~o) *n.f (m)* keeper, guardian

guerra *n.f* war

guia *n.* guide, guidance, permit

guiar *v.* to drive, orientate

gula *n.f* greed

guri(a) *n.m(f)* child, kid

H

há *v.* there is, there are

hábil *adj.* able

habilidade *n.f* ability

habilitar *v.* to enable

habitante *n.* inhabitant

habitar *v.* to inhabit, live in

hábito *n.m* habit, custom

haver *v.* to have

haxixe *n.* hashish, cannabis

helicóptero *n.m* helicopter

herdar *v.* to inherit

herdeiro(a) *n.m(f)* heir

herói *n.m* hero

heroína *n.f* heroine, heroin

hesitar *v.* to hesitate

hífen *n.m* hyphen

higiene *n.f* hygiene

hipismo *n.m* horse riding

hipoteca *n.f* mortgage

história *n.f* history

histórico(a) *n.m* history; *adj.m(f)* historic

hobby *n.m* hobby

hoje *n.m* today

holocausto *n.m* holocaust

holofote *n.m* searchlight, floodlight

homem *n.m* man

homenagear *v.* to honor, pay homage

homenagem *n.f* tribute, homage

honesto(a) *n.m; adj.m(f)* honest

honra *n.f* honor

honradez *n.f* honesty, integrity, decency

honrar *v.* to honor

hóquei *n.m* hockey

hora *n.f* hour

horário *n.m* timetable, working hours

horizonte *n.m* horizon

horrível *adj.* horrible, awful

horror *n.m* horror

horrorizar *v.* to horrify

horta *n.f* vegetable garden

hortelã *n.f* mint

horto *n.m* botanical garden, reserve

hospício *n.m* asylum, mental hospital

hospital *n.m* hospital

hospitalidade *n.f*
hospitality

hospitalizar *v.* to
hospitalize

hostil *adj.* hostile

hostilidade *n.f* hostility

hostilizar *v.* to antagonize

hotel *n.m* hotel

humanidade *n.f* mankind

humano(a) *adj.m(f)*
human, humane

humilde *adj.* humble

humor *n.m* humor, mood

I

iate *n.m* yacht

icterícia *n.f* jaundice

ida *n.f* going

ida-e-volta *n.f* round-trip
ticket

idade *n.f* age

ideal *adj.* ideal

idealizar *v.* to idealize,
devise, create

idéia *n.f* idea

idêntico(a) *adj.m(f)*
identical

identidade *n.f* identity

identificar *v.* to identify

idioma *n.f* language, idiom

idiota *adj.m(f)* moron,
stupid

idoso(a) *adj.* old person

ignição *n.f* ignition

ignorância *n.f* ignorance

ignorar *v.* to ignore

igreja *n.f* church

igual *adj.* equal, alike

igualar *v.* to equalize

igualdade *n.f* equality

ilegal *adj.* illegal, unlawful

ilha *n.f* island

ilimitado(a) *adj.m(f)*
unlimited

iluminação *n.f* lighting

iluminar *v.* to light up,
enlighten

ilustração *n.f* illustration

ilustrar *v.* to illustrate,
inform

ímã *n.f* magnet

imagem *n.f* image, picture

imaginação *n.f*
imagination

imaginar *v.* to imagine

imaturo(a) *adj.m(f)*
immature

imediatamente *adv.*
immediately

imenso(a) *adj.m(f)*
immense

imitar *v.* to imitate, copy

imóveis *n.m.pl* real estate

impagável *adj.* priceless

ímpar *adj.* odd number

imparcial *adj.* impartial

impedir *v.* to impede,
obstruct, block, prevent

impensado(a) *adj.m(f)*
thoughtless

imperdoável *adj.*
unforgivable,
inexcusable

imperfeito(a) *adj.m(f)*
imperfect

impermeável *adj.*
waterproof

ímpeto *n.m* impetus, fury

implacável *adj.* unforgiving

implicar *v.* to involve

implorar *v.* to beg, implore

impor *v.* to impose

importação *n.f* import

importância *n.f*
importance

importante *adj.* important

importar *v.* to import
impossível *adj.* impossible
imposto *n.m* levy, tax, duty
impostor(~a) *n.m(f)* impostor
impreciso(a) *adj.m(f)* vague
imprensa *n.f* press machine
impressão *n.f* print
imprimir *v.* to print
impróprio(a) *adj.m(f)* inappropriate
improvável *adj.* unlikely
impugnar *v.* to impeach
imundo(a) *adj.m(f)* filthy
inacabado(a) *adj.m(f)* unfinished
inacreditável *adj.* unbelievable
incapacidade *n.f* inability, handicap
incapacitar *v.* to disable
incapaz *adj.; n.* unable
incendiar *v.* to set on fire
incêndio *n.m* fire
incentivar *v.* to stimulate, encourage
incentivo *n.m* inducement
inchaço *n.m* swelling
inchar *v.* to swell
incidente *n.m* incident
inclinação *n.f* tendency
inclinar *v.* to incline, tend
incluir *v.* to enclose, include
incluso(a) *adj.m(f)* included
incomodar *v.* to bother, disturb
incômodo(a) *n.m; adj.m(f)* inconvenience; uncomfortable
incomparável *adj.* matchless, incomparable

incomum *adj.* unusual, rare
inconsciente *adj.* unaware, unconscious
inconveniente *adj.* inconvenient
incorrer *v.* to incur
incrível *adj.* incredible, unbelievable
inculpar *v.* to blame, accuse
indeferir *v.* to reject, refuse
indenizar *v.* to compensate
indevido(a) *adj.m(f)* undue
indiano(a) *adj.m(f)* Indian (from India)
indicar *v.* to indicate
índice *n.m* index
indício *n.m* sign, clue
indiferente *adj.* indifferent
indigestão *n.f* indigestion
índio(a) *n.m(f)* native, indigenous people
indireta *n.f* insinuation, hint
indireto(a) *adj.m(f)* indirect
indispor *v.* to upset
índole *n.f* nature
indulgente *adj.* indulgent, lenient
indústria *n.f* industry
industrializar *v.* to industrialize
induzir *v.* to induce, lead
inesquecível *adj.* unforgettable
infância *n.f* childhood
infarto *n.m* heart attack
infecção *n.f* infection
infeccionar *v.* to infect
infectar *v.* to infect
infeliz *adj.* unhappy, unfortunate
inferior *adj.* inferior
inferno *n.m* hell

infiel *adj.* disloyal
infinito(a) *adj.m(f)* endless
influência *n.f* influence
informação *n.f* information
informar *v.* to inform
infração *n.f* breach, infringement, offense
infrator(~a) *adj.m(f)* offender
ingênuo(a) *adj.m(f)* ingenuous, naive
Inglaterra *n.f* England
inglês(a) *n.m; adj.m(f)* English
ingressar *v.* to enter
ingresso *n.m* entry, ticket
inicial *adj.* initial
inicializar *v.* to initialize
iniciar *v.* to initiate, begin, start
início *n.m* outset
inimigo(a) *n.m(f)* enemy
inimizade *n.f* feud
injeção *n.f* injection, jab
injetar *v.* to inject
injetor *n.m* gun
injunção *n.f* court order
injustiça *n.f* injustice
injusto(a) *adj.m(f)* unfair, unjust, wrong
inocente *adj.* innocent, naïve, not guilty
inócuo(a) *adj.m(f)* harmless
inquérito *n.m* inquiry
inquieto(a) *adj.m(f)* uneasy, restless
inquilino(a) *n.m(f)* tenant
insalubre *adj.* unhealthy
inscrever *v.* to inscribe, enroll
insensato(a) *adj.m(f)* unreasonable
insensível *adj.* insensitive, numb

inseto *n.m* insect
insignificante *adj.* negligible, insignificant
insistir *v.* to insist
insolação *n.f* sunstroke
insolente *adj.* cheeky
insônia *n.f* insomnia
inspecionar *v.* to inspect
inspetor(~a) *n.m(f)* inspector
instalação *n.f* installation
instalar *v.* to install, put up, settle
instante *n.m* moment; *adj.* urgent
instruir *v.* to brief, instruct
instrumento *n.m* instrument
insuficiência *n.f* insufficiency, lack
insultar *v.* to insult
insulto *n.m* insult
insuportável *adj.* unbearable
inteiro(a) *adj.m(f)* entire, whole
intelectual *n.; adj.* intellectual
inteligência *n.f* intelligence
inteligente *adj.* clever, intelligent
interessante *adj.* interesting
interessar *v.* to interest
interesse *n.m* concern, interest
interferência *n.f* interference
interferir *v.* to meddle
interior *n.m* inland, inside
intermediário(a) *adj.* intermediate; *n.m(f)* intermediary

internacional *adj.* international

internar *v.* to confine

internato *n.m* boarding school

Internet *n.f* Internet

interno(a) *adj.m(f)* inside, inward

interpretar *v.* to interpret

interruptor *n.m* switch

intersecção *n.f* intersection

intervenção *n.f* intervention

intervir *v.* to intervene

intestino *n.m* gut, intestine

intimação *n.f* subpoena, summon

intimar *v.* to summon, subpoena

intimidade *n.f* intimacy, closeness

íntimo(a) *adj.m(f)* intimate, close

intoxicado(a) *adj.m(f)* intoxicated, poisoned

intoxicar *v.* to poison

intraduzível *adj.* untranslatable

introdução *n.f* introduction

introduzir *v.* to introduce, insert

intrometer *v.* to meddle, interfere

intrometido(a) *adj.m(f)* nosy

inundação *n.f* flood

inundar *v.* to flood

inútil *adj.* useless

inutilizar *v.* to break, disable

inveja *n.f* envy

invejar *v.* to envy

invenção *n.f* invention

inventar *v.* to invent, fabricate

inverno *n.m* winter

invés *n.m* instead

investigar *v.* to investigate

ir *v.* to go

irmã *n.f* sister

irmão *n.m* brother

irritar *v.* to annoy, irritate

isca *n.f* bait

iscar *v.* to bait

isenção *n.f* exemption

isentar *v.* to exempt

Islã *n.m* Islam

islamico(a) *adj.m(f)* Islamic

isolamento *n.m* insulation

isolar *v.* to insulate, isolate

isqueiro *n.m* lighter

isso *pron.* that

isto é *conj.* i.e., that is

Itália *n.f* Italy

italiano(a) *n.m; adj.m(f)* Italian

item *n.m* item

J

já *adv.* already, now

jamais *adv.* never

janeiro *n.m* January

janela *n.f* window

jangada *n.f* raft

jantar¹ *n.m* dinner

jantar² *v.* to dinner

Japão *n.m* Japan

japonês(~a) *n.m; adj.m(f)* Japanese

jardim *n.m* garden

jardim da infância *n.m* kindergarten

jardim zoológico *n.m* zoo

jardineiro(a) *n.m(f)* gardener

jarro(a) *n.m(f)* jug, jar
jato *n.m* jet
jaula *n.f* cage
jeito *n.m* way, manner, knack
jeitoso(a) *adj.m(f)* skillful
jejuar *v.* to fast
jejum *n.m* fast, fasting
joalheiro *n.m* jeweler
joalheria *n.f* jewelry store
joelho *n.m* knee
jogador(~a) *n.m(f)* player
jogar *v.* to play
jogo *n.m* game, match, play
jóia *n.f* jewel
jornada *n.f* journey
jornal *n.m* newspaper
jornaleiro(a) *n.m(f)* news vendor; journeyman
jornalismo *n.m* journalism
jornalista *n.* journalist
jorrar *v.* to gush, spurt out
jorro *n.m* jet, spurt
jovem *n.* youngster, young
judaico(a) *adj.m(f)* Jewish
judeu, judia *adj.m,f* Jewish, Jew
juiz(~a) *n.m(f)* judge
juízo *n.m* judgment, wisdom
julgamento *n.m* judgment
julgar *v.* to judge
julho *n.m* July
junho *n.m* June
junta *n.f* joint, council, commission
juntar *v.* to join
juntos(as) *adj.m(f)pl* together
juramento *n.m* oath
jura *n.f* vow
jurado(a) *adj.m(f)* sworn; *n.m(f)* juror

jurar *v.* to swear
júri *n.m* jury
juros *n.m.pl* interest (finances)
justamente *adv.* fairly, justly
justiça *n.f* justice
justificar *v.* to justify
justo(a) *adj.m(f)* just, fair
juvenil *adj.* young, juvenile
juventude *n.f* youth

K
karaoke *n.m* karaoke
kart *n.m* go-kart
kilo *n.m* kilogram (thousand grams = 32.26 oz)
kit *n.m* kit, set
kitchenette *n.m* studio apartment
kg *n.m* kilogram
km *n.m* kilometer (thousand meters = 0.62 mile)
know-how *n.m* know-how

L
lã *n.f* wool
lá *adv.* there, over there
lábio *n.m* lip
labirinto *n.m* maze
laboratório *n.m* laboratory
laço *n.m* tie
lacre *n.m* seal
lacticínios *n.m* dairy products
lacuna *n.f* gap, omission, blank
lado *n.m* side

ladrão, ladra *n.m,f* burglar, thief, robber

lago *n.m* lake, pond

lagosta *n.f* lobster

lagostim *n.f* scampi, crayfish

lágrima *n.f* tear

laia *n.f* kind, sort, type, deceptive talk

lama *n.f* mud

lamber *v.* to lick

lambida *n.f* lick

lambuja *n.f* head start, advantage

lâmina *n.f* blade

lâmpada *n.f* lamp, bulb

lançamento *n.m* launching; throw

lançar *v.* to launch, throw

lancha *n.f* motorboat

lanche *n.m* snack, sandwich, small meal

lanterna *n.f* lantern, torch

lápide *n.f* gravestone, tombstone

lápis *n.m* pencil

laptop (computador) *n.m* laptop (computer)

lar *n.m* home

laranja *n.f* orange

lareira *n.f* fireplace

largar *v.* to release, let go

largo[1] *n.m* square (place)

largo(a)[2] *adj.m(f)* wide

lasca *n.f* splinter, chip

lascar *v.* to chip

lástima *n.f* pity, compassion

lastimar *v.* to lament, be sorry

lata *n.f* can, tin

latir *v.* to bark

lavar *v.* to wash

lavagem *n.f* wash, laundry

lavanderia *n.f* laundromat, launderette

laxante *n.m* laxative

lazer *n.m* leisure

leal *adj.* loyal

legal *adj.* legal, lawful

legalizar *v.* to legalize

legitimar *v.* to legitimate

legítimo(a) *adj.m(f)* legitimate, genuine

lei *n.f* law

leigo(a) *adj.* lay

leilão *n.m* auction

leite *n.m* milk

leiteria *n.f* dairy

leitor(~a) *n.m(f)* reader

lema *n.m* logo, motto

leme *n.m* helm, control

lembrança *n.f* remembrance, souvenir, recall

lembrar *v.* to remember, recall, remind

lenço *n.m* handkerchief

lençol *n.m* bedding sheet

lenda *n.f* legend, myth

lente *n.f* lens

lento(a) *adj.m(f)* slow

ler *v.* to read

lesar *v.* to harm, damage

leste *n.m* east

letra *n.f* letter (of the alphabet), handwriting

levantar *v.* to lift, raise

levar *v.* to take away, carry, lead

leve *adj.* light, not heavy

lhe *pron.* to him, to her

lhes *pron.pl* to them

liberar *v.* to free, liberate, deregulate

liberdade *n.f* freedom, liberty

libra *n.f* pound

lição *n.f* lesson
lição de casa *n.f* homework
licença *n.f* license
licor *n.m* liqueur
lidar *v.* to deal, struggle, work
liderança *n.f* leadership
liga *n.f* league
ligação *n.f* liaison, link, connection, phone call
ligar *v.* to link, connect, liaise, switch on
lima *n.f* bitter orange; file (tool)
limão *n.m* lemon
limão galego *n.m* lime
limitar *v.* to limit, restrict
limite *n.m* limit
limpar *v.* to clean, sweep, brush, wash, wipe
limpeza *n.f* sweep
limpo(a) *adj.m(f)* clean
lindo(a) *adj.m(f)* beautiful; nice
língua *n.f* tongue; language
linguagem *n.f* language
lingüiça *n.f* sausage
linha *n.f* line, thread
linha aérea *n.f* airline
linho *n.m* linen tissue
liquidação *n.f* sale
liquidar *v.* to liquidate, settle, destroy
líquido(a) *n.m*; *adj.m(f)* liquid
liso(a) *adj.m(f)* smooth, soft
lisonjear *v.* to flatter
lista *n.f* list
listar *v.* to list
literatura *n.f* literature
litígio *n.m* lawsuit
litoral *n* shore, coast; *adj.m* coastal

litro *n.m* liter (approx. 1 quarter U.S. gallon)
livrar *v.* to release
livraria *n.f* bookstore
livre *adj.* free
livro *n.m* book
lixar *v.* to sand, file
lixeira *n.f* dustbin, garbage can
lixo *n.m* garbage, trash, rubbish; litter
lobo *n.m* wolf
local *n.m* site, place; *adj.m* local
localizar *v.* to locate, place
loção *n.f* lotion
lodo *n.m* mud
logo *adv.* right away, soon
lograr *v.* to achieve, get, cheat
loiro(a) *adj.m(f)* blond
loja *n.f* shop, store
lombo *n.m* back, loin
lona *n.f* canvas
longe *adv.* far, distant
longo(a) *adj.m(f)* long
lotação *n.f* minibus taxi, capacity
lotar *v* to fill with people
lote *n.m* plot, lot, portion, share
louça *n.f* china, crockery
louco(a) *adj.m(f)* insane, crazy; lunatic
loucura *n.f* madness, folly
lua *n.f* moon
lucrar *v.* to profit
lucro *n.m* profit
lugar *n.m* place, site
lupa *n.f* magnifying glass
luta *n.f* fight
lutar *v.* to fight
luva *n.f* glove

luxação *n.f* bone dislocation
luxo *n.m* luxury
luxuoso(a) *adj.m(f)* lavish
luxúria *n.f* lust
luz *n.f* light

M

má *n.f* bad, nasty, vile
maçã *n.f* apple
macaco *n.m* monkey; jack (car)
maçaneta *n.f* knob, handle
macho *n.m* male
machucado(a) *adj.m(f)* hurt; *n.m* bruise, injury
machucar *v.* to hurt, harm
macio(a) *adj.m(f)* soft, smooth, fluffy
maconha *n.f* marijuana, dope; joint
madeira *n.f* wood
madrasta *n.f* stepmother
madre *n.f* senior nun
madrinha *n.f* godmother
madrugada *n.f* night (from midnight to 6 am)
maduro(a) *adj.m(f)* ripe, mature
mãe *n.f* mother
mágica *n.f* magic, trick
mágico(a) *n.m(f)* magician; *adj.* magic
mágoa *n.f* sorrow, grief, hurt
magoar *v.* to hurt, cause sorrow
magro(a) *adj.m(f)* slim, lean
maio *n.m* May
maior *adj.* bigger, larger, greater
maioria *n.f* majority

mais *adv.* more, else, plus
mais elevado(a) *adj.m(f)* uppermost
mais íntimo(a) *adj.m(f)* inmost
mais tarde *adv.* later
mais velho(a) *adj.m(f)* older
mal *n.m* evil, harm, illness
mal- *pref.* badly
mala *n.f* suitcase
malandro(a) *n.m(f)* crook, idle, wily, cunning
malcriado(a) *adj.m(f)* rude
maldade *n.f* cruelty
malha *n.f* sweater, leotard
malícia *n.f* cleverness, double meaning
mamãe *n.f* mom
mancar *v.* to limp, cripple
mancha *n.f* stain
manchar *v.* to stain
manchete *n.f* headline
manco(a) *adj.m(f)* lame, limp
mandar *v.* to order, send
maneira *n.f* manner, way
manga *n.f* sleeve, mango
mangue *n.m* swamp area
mangueira *n.f* hose, mango tree
manhã *n.f* morning
maníaco(a) *n.m(f)* maniac, agitated
manjar[1] *n.m* sweet cake, pudding
manjar[2] *v.* to grasp, understand
manobra *n.f* maneuver
manobrar *v.* to maneuver, move
manso(a) *adj.m(f)* tame, docile, gentle, calm
manter *v.* to maintain

mantimentos *n.m.pl* groceries

manual *adj*; *n.m* manual

manutenção *n.f* maintenance, upkeep

mão *n.f* hand

mapa *n.m* map

maquiagem *n.f* make up

maquiar, maquilar *v.* to make up (face)

máquina *n.f* machine

maquinário *n.m* hardware, machinery

mar *n.m* sea

maravilhoso(a) *adj.m(f)* wonderful

marca *n.f* brand, mark, hallmark

marca-passo *n.m* pacemaker

marcar *v.* to mark, fix, set

marcha de carro *n.f* gear

marco *n.m* milestone

março *n.m* March

maré *n.f* tide

margem *n.f* margin

marido *n.m* husband

marinha *n.f* navy

marinheiro *n.m* sailor

marinho(a) *adj.m(f)* marine

marrom *adj.m* brown

martelar *v.* to hammer

martelo *n.m* hammer

mas *conj*; *prep.* but

máscara *n.f* mask

mascarar *v.* to mask

masculino(a) *adj.m(f)* masculine, male

massa *n.f* pasta, dough

mastigar *v.* to chew

mata *n.f* forest

matar *v.* to kill

matéria *n.f* matter, topic, subject-matter

material *n.m* stuff, material, substance

maternidade *n.f* maternity

matriz *n.f* headquarters, head office

maturidade *n.f* maturity

mau, má *adj.m,f* bad, nasty

máximo (a) *n*; *adj.m(f)* maximum

me, mim *pron.* me, myself, to me

mecânico(a) *n.m* mechanic; *adj.* mechanical

medalha *n.f* medal

média(o) *adj. f(m)* average, mean

mediar *v.* to mediate

medicação *n.f* medication, remedy

medicar *v.* to treat, practice medicine

medicina *n.f* medicine (profession)

médico(a) *n.m(f)* doctor, physician; *adj.* medical

medida *n.f* measure

médio(a) *adj.m(f)* middle, midst

mediocre *adj.* mediocre

medir *v.* to measure

medo *n.m* fear

meia calça *n.f* stocking

meia-noite *n.f* midnight

meia soquete *n.f* sock

meio *n.m* middle, midst

meio expediente *adj.m* part-time

meio-dia *n.m* noon

meio-fio *n.m* curb

meio-irmã *n.f* half-sister, stepsister

meio-irmão *n.m* half-brother, stepbrother
meios *n.m.pl* means
mel *n.m* honey
melhor *adj.* better, best
melodia *n.f* tune, melody
membro *n.* limb, member
memória *n.f* memory
memória RAM *n.f* RAM
memorizar *v.* to memorize
menção *n.f* mention
mencionar *v.* to mention
mendigo(a) *n.m(f)* tramp
menina, moça *n.f* girl
menor *adj.* smaller, shorter
menor de idade *n.* minor
menos *adv, prep.* less, minus
mensageiro(a) *n.m(f)* messenger
mensagem *n.f* message
menstruação *n.f* menstruation, period
mente *n.f* mind
mentir *v.* to lie
mentira *n.f* fib, lie
mentiroso(a) *n.m(f)* liar
menu *n.m* menu
mercado *n.m* market
mercadoria *n.f* merchandise, goods
mercearia *n.f* grocery store
merecedor(~a) *adj.m(f)* worthy
merecer *v.* to deserve
mergulhador(~a) *n.m(f)* diver
mergulhar *v.* to dive
mergulho *n.m* dive
mero(a) *adj.m(f)* mere
mês *n.m* month
mesa *n.f* table, desk
mesmo(a) *adj.m(f)* same; *adv.* even

mesquinho(a) *adj.m(f)* petty, mean, stingy
mesquita *n.f* mosque
mestre *n.* master
metade *n.f* half
metal *n.m* metal
métrico(a) *adj.m(f)* metric
metro *n.m* meter
mexer *v.* to tamper
microondas *n.m* microwave
migalha *n.f* crumb
migração *n.f* migration
mil *num.* thousand
milha *n.f* mile
milhão *num.* million
milho *n.m* sweet corn, maize
militar *adj.* military
mina *n.f* source, mine
mínimo(a) *adj.m(f)* minimum
ministro(a) *n.m(f)* minister
minoria *n.f* minority
minuto *n.m* minute
miolo *n.m* core, inside, pulp, brain
missa *n.f* mass
missão *n.f* mission
mistura *n.f* mixture, blend
misturar *v.* to mix, blend
miúdo(a) *n.m(f)* tiny, minute, very small
mobília *n.f* furniture
mobilizar *v.* to mobilize
moça *n.f* girl, young woman
mochila *n.f* backpack
moda *n.f* fashion, fad
modelar *v.* to model, shape
modelo *n.* model
modem *n.m* modem
moderado(a) *adj.m(f)* moderate

moderno(a) *adj.m(f)*
modern, up-to-date
modesto(a) *adj.m(f)*
modest, humble
modificar *v.* to modify
modo *n.m* way, manner
modo de andar *n.m* gait,
manner of walking
moeda *n.f* coin
moeda corrente *n.f*
currency, legal tender
moinho *n.m* mill
mola *n.f* spring
moldar *v.* to mold
molde *n.m* mold
moldura *n.f* frame
molestar *v.* to molest
molhado(a) *adj.m(f)* wet
molhar *v.* to wet
molho *n.m* sauce
momento *n.m* moment
monastério *n.m* monastery
monge *n.m* monk
monitor *n.m* video monitor
monstro *n.m* monster
montagem *n.f* assembly,
editing film
montanha *n.f* mountain
montar *v.* to assemble,
mount
monte *n.m* hill, lump, heap
monumento *n.m*
monument
morar *v.* to dwell, reside,
live
morder *v.* to bite
mordida *n.f* bite
morno(a) *adj.m(f)* warm
morrer *v.* to die
morro *n.m* hill
mortal *adj.* deadly
morte *n.f* death
morto(a) *adj.m(f)* dead

mosca *n.f* fly
mosquito *n.m* mosquito
mostarda *n.f* mustard
mostrar *v.* to show, display
motim *n.m* riot
motivar *v.* to motivate,
cause
motivo *n.m* reason, cause,
motive, sake
motocicleta *n.f* motorbike
motor *n.m* engine
motorista *n.* driver
móveis *n.m.pl* furniture
movimentar *v.* to move
movimento *n.m* motion
mudança *n.f* change, shift,
removal
mudar *v.* to shift, change,
move
mudo(a) *adj.m(f)* dumb,
mute
muito *adv.* very, much,
a lot, many
muito(a)(os)(as)
adj.m(f)(pl);
pron. many
muleta *n.f* crutch
mulher *n.f* woman
mulherengo *n.m*
womanizer
multa *n.f* fine, penalty
multidão *n.f* crowd, mob
multiplicar *v.* to multiply
múltiplo(a) *adj.m(f)*
manifold, multiple
mundial *adj.* worldwide,
world, global
mundo *n.m* world
muro *n.m* wall
músculo *n.m* muscle
museu *n.m* museum
música *n.f* music
músico *n.m* musician

N

na *prep. + art.f* in the
nação *n.f* nation
nacionalidade *n.f*
    nationality
nada *n.m* nothing
nadar *v.* to swim
namorada *n.f* girlfriend
não *adv.* no, not
não-, anti-, des-, in-, un-
    pref. non-
narina *n.f* nostril
nariz *n.m* nose
nascer *v.* to be born
nascer do sol *n.m* sunrise
nascido(a) *adj.m(f)* born
nascimento *n.m* birth
Natal *n.m* Christmas
nativo(a) *n.m(f); adj.* native
natural *adj.* natural
naturalmente *adv.* of
    course
natureza *n.f* nature
naufragar *v.* to be wrecked
naufrágio *n.m* wreck
náusea *n.f* nausea
navalha *n.f* razor
navegar *v.* to navigate, sail
navio *n.m* ship
neblina *n.f* mist, fog
necessário(a) *adj.m(f)*
    necessary
necessidade *n.f* necessity,
    need
necessitar *v.* to need
negar *v.* to deny
negativo(a) *adj.m(f)*
    negative
negligência *n.f* negligence
negociante *n.* dealer
negociar *v.* to negotiate,
    trade, deal
negócio *n.m* business, deal

negro(a) *n.m; adj.m(f)*
    black
nem *conj.* no, neither
nenhum(~a) *adj.m(f)* no;
    pron. none
nervo *n.m* nerve
nervoso(a) *adj.m(f)*
    nervous, jumpy
neta *n.f* granddaughter
neto *n.m* grandson
netos *n.pl* grandchildren
neutro(a) *adj.m(f)* neutral
nevar *v.* to snow
neve *n.f* snow
ninguém *pron.* nobody
ninho *n.m* nest
nisso, nisto *adv.* in that,
    in this
nítido(a) *adj.m(f)* clear,
    sharp
nível *n.m* level, standard
nivelar *v.* to level, be equal
no *prep. + art.m* in the
nó *n.m* knot
nobreza *n.f* nobility
noite *n.f* evening, night
noivo(a) *n.m(f)* groom,
    bride, fiancé(ée)
nojo *n.m* nausea,
    repugnance, disgust
nome *n.m* name
nome de solteira *n.m*
    maiden name
nomeação *n.f* appointment
nomear *v.* to name
nono(a) *num.m(f)* ninth
nora *n.f* daughter-in-law
normal *adj.* normal
normalizar *v.* to normalize
norte *n.m* north
nos, nós *pron.* us
nós mesmos *pron.*
    ourselves
nosso(a) *adj.m(f)* our

nota *n.f* note
notar *v.* to note
notícia *n.f* news
noticiar *v.* to announce, report
notificar *v.* to notify
nove *num.* nine
novembro *n.m* November
novo(a) *adj.m(f)* new
nozes *n.f.pl* nuts
nú *n.m* nude; *adj.* naked, bare
nua *adj.f* naked, bare
nublado(a) *adj.m(f)* hazy, overcast, dark
núcleo *n.m* core
nulo(a) *adj.m(f)* null
numerar *v.* to number
número *n.m* number
nunca *adv.* never
nutritivo(a) *adj.m(f)* nourishing
nuvem *n.f* cloud

O

o(~s), a(~s) *art.m(pl), f(pl)* the
oba! *interj. excl.* wow! great!
obedecer *v.* to obey
óbito *n.m* death
objeção *n.f* objection
objetar *v.* to object
objetivo(a) *adj.m(f)* objective; *n.m* aim, purpose
objeto *n.m* object
obra *n.f* work, construction
obrigação *n.f* duty, obligation, bond
obrigado(a) *adj.m(f)* obliged
obrigado(a)! *interj. excl.* thanks, thank you!

obrigar *v.* to compel, oblige
obrigatório(a) *adj.m(f)* compulsory, obligatory
obsceno(a) *adj.m(f)* obscene
obscuro(a) *adj.m(f)* obscure, dark
observação *n.f* observation, remark, comment
observar *v.* to observe, notice
obsessão *n.f* obsession
obsoleto(a) *adj.m(f)* obsolete
obstáculo *n.m* obstacle, hindrance, drawback
obstinado(a) *adj.m(f)* obstinate, stubborn
obstruir *v.* to obstruct, impede
obter *v.* to obtain, get, gain
obturador *n.m* shutter
óbvio(a) *adj.m(f)* obvious
ocasião *n.f* chance, opportunity, moment, time
ocasional *adj.* chance
ocasionar *v.* to cause, bring about
oceano *n.m* ocean
ocidente *n.m* west
ócio *n.m* idleness, laziness, leisure
oco(a) *adj.m(f)* hollow, empty
ocorrer *v.* to happen, occur
oculista *n.* optician, ophthalmologist
óculos *n.m* spectacles, eyeglasses
ocultar *v.* to hide, conceal
oculto(a) *adj.m(f)* hidden

ocupação *n.f* occupation, job

ocupado(a) *adj.m(f)* busy, occupied

ocupar *v.* to occupy

odiar *v.* to hate, loathe

ódio *n.m* hatred

odor *n.m* smell, odor, stink

ofegar *v.* to pant, puff

ofender *v.* to offend

ofensa *n.f* insult, offense

ofensivo(a) *adj.m(f)* offensive

oferecer *v.* to offer, dedicate

oferta *n.f* offer, offering; gift; bid, supply

ofertar *v.* to offer

oficial *n; adj.* official

oficializar *v.* to make official

ofício *n.m* profession, trade

oi! *interj. excl.* hi!

oitavo(a) *num.m(f)* eighth

oito *num.* eight

olá! *interj. excl.* hi!

óleo *n.m* oil

olhar[1] *n.m* look, gaze

olhar[2] *v.* to look

olho *n.m* eye

ombro *n.m* shoulder

omelete *n.f* omelet

omissão *n.f* omission, negligence

omitir *v.* to omit, overlook

onça[1] *n.f* ounce (28 grams or 31 grams)

onça[2] *n.f* small leopard

onda *n.f* wave, fashion, commotion

onde *conj.* where, in which; *adv.* where

onde quer que *adv.* wherever

ônibus *n.m* bus, coach

ontem *adv.* yesterday

onze *num.* eleven

opa! *interj. excl.* oops! wow! hi!

opção *n.f* option

operação *n.f* operation

operador(~a) *n.m(f)* operator, provider; company

operar *v.* to operate, effect

opinar *v.* to give an opinion, suggest

opinião *n.f* opinion, judgment

oponente *adj.* opposing; *n.* opponent

opor *v.* to oppose

oposto(a) *adj.m(f)* opposite, facing; *n.m* opposite

optar *v.* to opt, choose

oral *adj.* oral

orar *v.* to pray

orçamento *n.m* budget, estimate

orçar *v.* to estimate, value

ordem *n.f* order

ordenar *v.* to arrange, put in order, decree

ordinal *adj.* ordinal

ordinário(a) *adj.m(f)* ordinary, usual; coarse

orelha *n.f* ear; flap

orelhão *n.m* public telephone

órfã(~o) *adj.f(m)* orphan

organização *n.f* organization

organizar *v.* to organize

órgão *n.m* organ

orgulhar *v.* to be proud

orgulho *n.m* pride

orgulhoso(a) *adj.m(f)* proud

orientação *n.f* orientation, tendency, guidance

orientar *v.* to orientate, direct, guide

origem *n.f* origin, descent

original *adj.* original, manuscript, legitimate

originar *v.* to give rise, originate

orla *n.f* edge, border, margin

ornamento *n.m* adornment, decoration

ornar *v.* to adorn, decorate

orquestra *n.f* orchestra

orvalho *n.m* dew

osso *n.m* bone

ostentação *n.f* ostentation

ostentar *v.* to show off

ostra *n.f* oyster

ótimo(a) *adj.m(f)* excellent, splendid, optimum

ou seja *conj.* i.e, that is

ouro *n.m* gold

ousar *v.* to dare

outra vez *adv.* again

outro(a) *adj.m(f); pron.* another

outubro *n.m* October

ouvir *v.* to hear, listen

ovo *n.m* egg

oxigênio *n.m* oxygen

P

pá *n.f* blade, spade, shovel

pacato(a) *adj.m(f)* quiet, peaceful

pacto *n.m* pact, agreement

paciente *n.* patient

pacífico(a) *adj.m(f)* peaceful, undisputed

pacote *n.m* parcel; packet, package

padaria *n.f* bakery, baker's shop

padeiro(a) *n.m(f)* baker

padrão *n.m* standard, yardstick, pattern

padre *n.m* priest

padrinho *n.m* godfather

pagamento *n.m* payment

pagar *v.* to pay

página *n.f* page

pago(a) *adj.m(f)* paid

pago(a) antecipadamente *adj.m(f)* prepaid

pai *n.m* father

painel *n.m* panel

país *n.m* country

pais *n.m.pl* parents

paisagem *n.f* landscape, scenery

paisano(a) *adj.* civilian, plain clothes

paixão *n.f* passion

palácio *n.m* palace

palavra *n.f* word

palavras cruzadas *n.f.pl* crossword

palco *n.m* stage

palestra *n.f* talk, lecture

paletó *n.m* jacket

paletó smoking *n.m* tuxedo

palha *n.f* straw

pálido(a) *adj.m(f)* pale

palito *n.m* toothpick

palmeira *n.f* palm tree

pálpebra *n.f* eyelid

palpitar *v.* to beat (heart); give opinion

palpite *n.m* hunch, tip, unsolicited opinion

pamonha[1] *n.f* sweet corn pie

pamonha[2] *adj.* weak person, idiotic
pancada *n.f* hit, blow, punch, stroke
panela *n.f* pan
pânico *n.m* panic
pano *n.m* cloth
pantanal *n.m* swampland
pântano *n.m* swamp
pão *n.m* bread
Papa *n.m* Pope
papagaio *n.m* parrot, kite
papai *n.m* daddy
Papai Noel *n.m* Santa Claus
papel *n.m* paper; role
papel higiênico *n.m* toilet paper
papo *n.m* chat, talk
papo-furado *n.m* meaningless talk, useless chat, nonsense
par *n.m* pair, couple; *adj.* even *(num.)*
para *prep.* for, to, toward
para diante *adv.* forward, onto
para sempre *adv.* forever
para trás *adv.* backwards
pára-brisa *n.m* windshield
parabens! *interj. excl.* congratulations!
parada *n.f* stop
parafusar *v.* to screw
parafuso *n.m* bolt, screw
paralisar *v.* to paralyze
paralisia *n.f* paralysis
parapeito *n.m* parapet, window sill
parar *v.* to stop
parcela *n.f* installment
parcelar *v.* to schedule in installments
parceria *n.f* partnership
parecer *v.* to seem, look like

parede *n.f* wall
parente(a) *n.m(f)* relative, kin
parentes por casamento *n.m.pl* in-laws
parque *n.m* park
parte *n.f* part, section, share
parteira *n.f* midwife
particular *adj.* private, particular
partida *n.f* departure
partido *n.m* party (political)
Páscoa *n.f* Easter
pasmar *v.* to amaze, astonish
passado(a) *n.m; adj.m(f)* past
passageiro(a) *n.m(f)* passenger
passagem *n.f* ticket
passagem subterrânea *n.f* subway
passaporte *n.m* passport
passar *v.* to pass, cross; iron; send; die
passar a ferro *v.* to iron clothes
passar fome *v.* to starve
pássaro *n.m* bird
passeio *n.m* walk, excursion, outing; sidewalk
passear *v.* to walk around; ride
passo *n.m* step; pace
pasta *n.f* paste
pasta de dente *n.f* toothpaste
pasto *n.m* pasture, grass
pastor *n.m* shepherd
pata de animal *n.f* animal paw

patim *n.m* skate
patinar *v.* to skate
pátio *n.m* courtyard
pato(a) *n.m(f)* duck
patrão, patroa *n.m, f* boss
pátria *n.f* homeland
patrimônio *n.m* estate
patrocinador(~a) *n.m(f)* sponsor
patrocinar *v.* to sponsor
pau *n.m* stick, wood; penis (*coll.*)
pausa *n.f* pause
pausar *v.* to pause
pavimentar *v.* to pave
pavio *n.m* wick
pavor *n.m* dread, fear
paz *n.f* peace
pé *n.m* foot
pecado *n.m* sin
pecar *v.* to sin
peça de reposição *n.f* spare part
pechinchar *v.* to haggle, bargain
pedaço *n.m* bit, piece, slice
peça *n.f* piece
pecuária *n.f* cattle raising
pecúlio *n.m* savings, wealth
pedaço *n.m* piece, bit
pedágio *n.m* toll
pedal *n.m* pedal
pedalar *v.* to pedal
pedestre *n.* pedestrian
pedido *n.m* a request
pedir *v.* to request, ask, beg
pedra *n.f* stone
pedregulho *n.m* gravel, pebble
pedreira *n.f* quarry
pedreiro *n.m* mason
pedrinha *n.f* pebble
pegar *v.* to catch, grab, take, get

pegar carona *v.* to hitchhike, get a lift
peito *n.m* breast, chest
peixe *n.m* fish
pelado(a) *adj.m(f)* naked
pele *n.f* skin, fur
pelo(a) *prep. + art.m(f)* by the
pena *n.f* feather, pity, punishment
pendurar *v.* to hang
penhasco *n.m* cliff
penhor *n.m* pledge; pawnshop
pensamento *n.m* thought
pensão *n.f* boarding house, pension; alimony
pensar *v.* to think
pente *n.m* comb
pentear *v.* to comb
pequeno(a) *adj.m(f)* small
porcento *n.m* percent
pêra *n.f* pear
perambular *v.* to wander
perante *prep.* before, in the presence
perceber *v.* to realize
percorrer *v.* to travel, cover distance, traverse
perda *n.f* loss, waste
perdão *n.m* pardon
perdedor(~a) *n.m(f)* loser
perder *v.* to lose
perdido(a) *adj.m(f)* lost
perdoar *v.* to forgive, pardon
perfeito(a) *adj.m(f)* perfect
perfil *n.m* profile
perfume *n.m* perfume
pergunta *n.f* question
perguntar *v.* to inquire, ask
perigo *n.m* danger, peril
perigoso(a) *adj.m(f)* dangerous, unsafe, risky

período *n.m* period, era, phase

perito(a) *n.m(f); adj.m(f)* expert

permanecer *v.* to remain, stay

permanente *adj.* constant, permanent

permissão *n.f* permit, license, authorization

permitir *v.* to permit, allow

permutar *v.* to swap

perna *n.f* leg

pérola *n.f* pearl

perseguição *n.f* persecution, harassment

perseguir *v.* to pursue, chase

personalizar *v.* to personalize

perspectiva *n.f* perspective, outlook

pertencer *v.* to belong

pertences *n.m.pl* belongings

perto *adv.* near; *adj.m* nearby

perturbar *v.* to disturb, harass

peruca *n.f* wig

perverter *v.* to pervert, corrupt

pervertido(a) *adj.m(f)* perverted

pesadelo *n.m* nightmare

pesado(a) *adj.m(f)* heavy

pesar *v.* to weigh

pesca *n.f* fishing

pescador *n.m* fisherman

pescar *v.* to fish

pescoço *n.m* neck

peso *n.m* weight; Hispanic currencies

pesquisa *n.f* research

pesquisar *v.* to research

pessoa *n.f* person

pessoal *adj.* personal; *n.m* personnel, staff

povo *n.m* people

petiscar *v.* to nibble

petisco *n.m* snack

pia *n.f* sink

piada *n.f* gag, joke

picada *n.f* bite, prick, sting

picar *v.* to prick, sting, bite

piche *n.m* tar, pitch

pico *n.m* peak

piedade *n.f* mercy

pijama *n.m* pajamas

pilha *n.f* battery

pilotar *v.* to pilot

piloto(a) *n.m(f)* pilot

pílula *n.f* pill

pílula anticoncepcional *n.f* birth control pill

pimenta *n.f* pepper

pimentão *n.m* sweet pepper

pinça *n.f* tweezers

pinheiro *n.m* pine tree

pinta *n.f* spot

pinta *n.f* pint (568ml)

pintar *v.* to paint

pinto *n.m* baby hen; penis *(coll.)*

pintura *n.f* painting

pior *adj.* worse

pipi *n.m* pee, urinate

piquenique *n.m* picnic

pisada *n.f* tread

pisar *v.* to tread

piscar *v.* to blink

piscina *n.f* swimming pool

piso superior *n.m* upstairs

pista *n.f* track, path, lane

placa *n.f* board, plate

placa de carro *n.f* license
plate
planejar *v.* to plan
planeta *n.m* planet
plano *n.m* plan, project;
plane
plano(a) *adj.m(f)* flat, level
planta *n.f* plant
plantar *v.* to plant, sow
plástico(a) *n.m(f)* plastic
plataforma *n.f* platform,
deck
pleno(a) *adj.m(f)* full,
complete
plural *n.m*; *adj.* plural
pneu *n.m* car tire
pó *n.m* powder
pobre *adj.* poor
poça *n.f* puddle, pool
poço *n.m* well
poder[1] *v.* to be able to
poder[2] *n.m* power,
authority, might
podre *adj.* rotten
poeira *n.f* dust
poesia *n.f* poetry
pois *adv.* so; *conj.* since, as
pois não *adv. idiom* yes;
how can I help you?
pois sim *adv. idiom* no;
no way, absolutely not
polegada *n.f* inch
polegar *n.m* thumb
polêmica *n.f* controversy
polícia *n.f* police
policiar *v.* to police,
control, watch
policial *n.* police officer
política *n.f* policy, politics
político(a) *adj.m(f)*
political; *n.m(f)*
politician
pólo *n.m* pole

poltrona *n.f* armchair
pônei *n.m* pony
ponta *n.f* tip, end, extremity
ponta-pé *n.m* kick
ponte *n.f* bridge
ponte aérea *n.f* shuttle
ponto *n.m* dot, point,
stitch, suture
população *n.f* population
popular *adj.* popular
por[1] *prep.* for, by
pôr[2] *v.* to put
por favor *interj.* please
por correio *v.* to mail
porão *n.m* basement
porção *n.f* portion, lot
porcelana *n.f* china
porco *n.m* pig, pork
porém *conj.* however, yet
porque *conj.* because
porque? *interrog.* why?
porra *n.f* useless thing;
interj. hell! *(coll.)*
porta *n.f* door
portanto *adv.* therefore, so,
hence
portão *n.m* gate
porte *n.m* costs of
transport, charge
porteiro(a) *n.m(f)* porter,
caretaker
porto *n.m* harbor, port
posição *n.f* position
posicionar *v.* to position
positivo(a) *adj.m(f)*
positive
posse *n.f* possession
possível *adj.* possible
possuir *v.* to own
poste *n.m* pole, post
posto avançado *n.m*
outpost
pote *n.m* pot, vase

potência *n.f* power, potency

pouco(a) *adj.m(f)* little, few

pousada *n.f* lodging, hostel, country hotel

povo *n.m* folk, people

poxa! *interj. excl.* gosh!

praia *n.f* beach

prata *n.f* silver

prateleira *n.f* shelf

prática *n.f* practice

praticar *v.* to practice

prático(a) *adj.m(f)* practical, handy, useful,

prato *n.m* dish, plate

prazer *n.m* pleasure

prazo *n.m* term, period

precaução *n.f* precaution

precaver *v.* to warn

precedente *n.m* precedent; *adj.* preceding

preceder *v.* to precede

precioso(a) *adj.m(f)* precious

precipitação *n.f* haste, rashness, rush

precipitar *v.* to precipitate, rush, hurl

precisar *v.* to need

preço *n.m* price

prédio *n.m* building

predizer *v.* to predict

prefeito(a) *n.m(f)* mayor

preferir *v.* to prefer

pregador de roupa *n.m* peg

pregar *v.* to nail; preach

prego *n.m* nail, pin

preguiçoso(a) *adj.m(f)* lazy, idle

prejudicar *v.* to harm

premiar *v.* to award a prize, reward

prêmio *n.m* prize

prender *v.* to arrest, jail

preocupação *n.f* worry, pre-occupation, concern

preocupar *v.* to worry, preoccupy

preparar *v.* to prepare

presença *n.f* presence

presença de espírito *n.f* wit

presenciar *v.* to witness, be present

presente *n.m; adj.* present

presentear *v.* to present

presidente *n.m* president

presidiário(a) *n.m(f)* prisoner

preso(a) *adj.m(f)* prisoner

pressa *n.f* hurry, rush

presságio *n.m* omen

pressão *n.f* pressure

prestação *n.f* installment

prestar *v.* to render, supply, give, be good for

presunto *n.m* ham

preto(a) *n.m; adj.m(f)* black

prevenir *v.* to warn

previsão *n.f* preview, forecast, premonition

previsão do tempo *n.f* weather forecast

primavera *n.f* spring season

primeiro(a) *num.m(f)* first

primeiro ministro *n.m* prime minister

primo(a) *n.m(f)* cousin

principal *adj.* main, principal

principiante *n.* beginner

princípio *n.m* principle, start, beginning

prisão *n.f* prison, jail

prisão de ventre *n.f* constipation

privacidade *n.f* privacy
privilegiar *v.* to privilege
privilégio *n.m* privilege
probabilidade *n.f* odds, chances, probability
problema *n.m* problem, trouble
processar *v.* to sue, process
processo *n.m* lawsuit, procedure, process
procura *n.f* search
procurar *v.* to search
produção *n.f* production, output
produto *n.m* product
produto químico *n.m* chemical product
produzir *v.* to produce
professor(~a) *n.m(f)* teacher
profissão *n.f* profession, occupation
profundidade *n.f* depth
profundo(a) *adj.m(f)* deep
programa *n.m* program, love encounter
programação *n.f* schedule
programar *v.* to program, plan, schedule
progredir *v.* to progress
progresso *n.m* progress
proibição *n.f* ban
proibido(a) *adj.m(f)* prohibited, forbidden
proibir *v.* to ban, forbid
projetar *v.* to project
projeto *n.m* project
prolongar *v.* to extend
promessa *n.f* pledge, promise
prometedor(~a) *adj.m(f)* promising
prometer *v.* to pledge, promise

promover *v.* to promote
pronto(a) *adj.m(f)* ready
propaganda *n.f* advertisement
propor *v.* to propose
proposta *n.f* proposal
propriedade *n.f* property
proprietário(a) *n.m(f)* owner, landlord
próprio(a) *adj.m(f)* one's own, proper, suitable
proteção *n.f* protection
proteger *v.* to protect
protestante *n; adj.* Protestant
protestar *v.* to protest
protesto *n.m* outcry, protest
protetor(~a) *n.m(f)* protector, protective
prova *n.f* proof, test, evidence
provação *n.f* ordeal
provar *v.* to prove
provável *adj.* probable
proveito *n.m* advantage, enjoyment
proveitoso(a) *adj.m(f)* profitable, useful
provérbio *n.m* proverb
providenciar *v.* to provide, arrange
província *n.f* province
provocar *v.* to provoke, tempt; attract; cause,
próximo(a) *n.m* fellow man; *adj.* close, next; *adv.* near
prudente *adj.* cautious, prudent
psiu! *interj. excl.* quiet! Hey!
publicar *v.* to publish

publicidade *n.f* publicity

público(a) *n.m; adj.m(f)* public

pular *v.* to jump

pulga *n.f* flea

pulmão *n.m* lung

pulseira *n.f* bracelet

pulso *n.m* pulse; wrist

punhado *n.m* handful, bunch

punho *n.m* fist

puro(a) *adj.m(f)* neat, pure, sheer

puta *n.f* whore, prostitute

puto(a) *adj.m(f)* furious, nasty, enormous

puxar *v.* to pull, draw

puxa-saco *n.m* creep, crawler, yes-man

Q

quadra *n.f* street block; sports court, field

quadrado *n.m* square

quadril *n.m* hip

quadrilha *n.f* gang

quadro *n.m* painting, picture; board

qual *pron.* which; *conj.* as, like

qualidade *n.f* quality

qualificar *v.* to qualify

qualquer *adj.* whatever

qualquer um(a)[1] *pron.m(f)* anybody

qualquer um(a)[2] *adj.m(f)* either

quando *adv, conj.* when

quantidade *n.f* quantity, amount

quanto? *pron.interrog.* how much?

quarenta *num.* forty

quarentena *n.f* quarantine

quaresma *n.f* Lent

quarta-feira *n.f* Wednesday

quartel *n.m* barracks

quartel-general *n.m* headquarters

quarto(a) *num.m(f)* fourth

quarto *n.m* room

quase *adv.* almost, nearly

quatro *num.* four

que *pron.* what, which, that

quebra *n.f* break

quebrar *v.* to break

queda *n.f* fall

queijo *n.m* cheese

queimado(a) *adj.m(f)* burnt

queimadura *n.f* burn

queimar *v.* to burn

queixa *n.f* complaint

queixar *v.* to complain

queixo *n.m* chin

quem *pron.* who

quem quer que *pron.* whoever

quente *adj.* hot

querer *v.* to want, wish

querido(a) *adj.m(f)* dear, darling

questão *n.f* question, inquiry, matter

quieto(a) *adj.m(f)* quiet, still, calm

quilo *n.m* kilo

quilômetro *n.m* kilometer

químico(a) *n.m(f)* chemist; *adj.* chemical

quinta-feira *n.f* Thursday

quintal *n.m* backyard

quinto(a) *num.m(f)* fifth

quinzena *n.f* fortnight, two weeks, 15 days

R

rã *n.f* toad
rabino *n.m* rabbi
rabo *n.m* tail
raça *n.f* race
ração *n.f* ration
racho *n.m* crack, split
racismo *n.m* racism
rádio *n.m* radio
raínha *n.f* queen
raio *n.m* ray, beam; range; lightning
raio-X *n.m* X-ray
raiva *n.f* rage, rabies
raiz *n.f* root
rajada *n.f* gust
ramo *n.m* branch, business area
rampa *n.f* ramp, slope
rançoso(a) *adj.m(f)* rancid
rapaz *n.m* boy, guy, lad
rápido(a) *adj.m(f)* quick, fast
raposa *n.f* fox
raquete *n.f* racket
raramente *adv.* seldom
raro(a) *adj.m(f)* rare
rascunhar *v.* to draft, sketch, outline
rascunho *n.m* draft, rough copy, sketch, outline
rasgado(a) *adj.* torn, ripped
rasgar *v.* to tear, rip, cut
raspar *v.* to scrape, scratch
raso(a) *adj.m(f)* shallow, flat
rastejar *v.* to crawl
rastro *n.m* trail
rato *n.m* mouse, rat
razão *n.f* reason
ré *n.f* reverse
re- *pref.* again, repeat, against
reação *n.f* reaction

reagir *v.* to react
reajustar *v.* to reset
real *adj.* real, royal
realidade *n.f* reality
realizar *v.* to fulfill, achieve
realmente *adv.* indeed
rebaixar *v.* to lower
rebentar *v.* to break out, smash
rebocar *v.* to tow
reboque *n.m* trailer
rebuliço *n.m* hubbub, commotion
receber *v.* to receive, get
receita *n.f* recipe, income
receita médica *n.f* prescription
receitar *v.* to prescribe
recém- *adv. pref.* recently
recente *adj.* recent
receoso(a) *adj.m(f)* afraid
recepção *n.f* reception
recepcionar *v.* to receive
receptor(~a) *n.m(f)* receiver
rechear *v.* to stuff
recheio *n.m* stuffing, filling
recibo *n.m* receipt
recipiente *n.m* container
reclamar *v.* to complain
reclame *n.m* advertisement, publicity
recolher *v.* to collect, gather
recommendar *v.* to recommend
recompensa *n.f* reward
recompensar *v.* to reward
reconhecer *v.* to recognize
reconhecimento *n.m* acknowledgement
recorrer *v.* to turn to, resort, appeal
recuperar *v.* to recover

recurso *n.m* resource, appeal

recusar *v.* to refuse, deny, decline

rede *n.f* net, network

redigir *v.* to write

redondo(a) *adj.m(f)* round

redução *n.f* reduction

reduzir *v.* to reduce

reembolsar *v.* to refund

reembolso *n.m* refund

refeição *n.f* meal

refém *n.* hostage

refletir *v.* to reflect, think

reflexão *n.f* reflection, thought

reforma *n.f* reform, renovation

reformar *v.* to reform, renovate

refrescar *v.* to refresh

refrigerante *n.m* soft drink

regar *v.* to water

região *n.f* region

registrar *v.* to record, register

registro *n.m* record, register

regra *n.f* rule

régua *n.f* ruler

regulamento *n.m* regulation

regular *adj.* regular

rei *n.m* king

reinar *v.* to reign

reino *n.m* kingdom

relação *n.f* relation, connection

relacionamento *n.m* relationship

relacionar *v.* to relate, make a list

relâmpago *n.m* lightning

relance *n.m* glance

relatar *v.* to report

relatório *n.m* report

relaxado(a) *adj.m(f)* relaxed, complacent

relaxar *v.* to relax, be complacent

relevo *n.m* relief

religião *n.f* religion

religioso(a) *adj.m(f)* religious

relógio *n.m* clock, watch

remédio *n.m* medicine, remedy

remendar *v.* to mend, patch up

remendo *n.m* patch

remessa *n.f* dispatch

remeter *v.* to send

remetente *n.* sender

remoto(a) *adj.m(f)* remote

remover *v.* to remove

renda *n.f* income; lace

render *v.* to yield, profit, produce

renovação *n.f* renovation

renovar *v.* to renew

repelente *n.* repellent

repelir *v.* to repel, reject, repudiate

repetição *n.f* repeat

repetir *v.* to repeat

reportagem *n.f* report, news

representante *n.* representative

representar *v.* to represent

república *n.f* republic

reputação *n.f* reputation, prestige

requerer *v.* to require, ask

requintado(a) *adj.m(f)* exquisite

reserva *n.f* reservation
reservar *v.* to reserve
resfriar *v.* to cool, chill, catch a cold
resgatar *v.* to redeem
resgate *n.m* rescue, first aid, ransom
residência *n.f* residence
residência temporária *n.f* lodge
residir *v.* to live, reside
resistência *n.f* resistance
resistente *adj.* resistant
resistir *v.* to resist
resmungar *v.* to mumble, mutter, complain
resmungo *n.m* mumble
resolução *n.f* resolution
resolver *v.* to solve, sort out, decide
respeitar *v.* to regard, respect
respeito *n.m* regard, respect
respiração *n.f* breath
respiradouro *n.m* vent
respirar *v.* to breathe
responder *v.* to answer, respond, reply
responsabilidade *n.f* responsibility, liability
responsabilizar *v.* to hold responsible
responsável *adj.* responsible, liable
resposta *n.f* answer, response
ressaca *n.f* hangover, rough sea
restar *v.* to remain, be left
restaurante *n.m* restaurant
restaurar *v.* to restore
restringir *v.* to restrict

resultado *n.m* result, outcome
resultar *v.* to result
resumo *n.m* summary
retalhar *v.* to divide
retalho *n.m* patch, small piece of fabric
retaliar *v.* to repay, retaliate
reter *v.* to hold, keep, detain, stop
retirar *v.* to withdraw
reto *n.m* rectum
reto(a) *adj.m(f)* straight
retornar *v.* to return
retratar *v.* to depict
retrato *n.m* portrait
réu, ré *n.m,f* defendant, culprit, accused
reunião *n.f* meeting
revelador(~a) *adj.m(f)* tell-tale, revealer, discloser
revelar *v.* to reveal, develop, show
reverso *n.m* reverse
revestimento *n.m* coat
revestir *v.* to cover; line; assume
revisão *n.f* review, revision
revista *n.f* magazine, inspection
revistar *v.* to search, frisk
reza *n.f* prayer
rezar *v.* to pray
riacho *n.m* stream, brook
rico(a) *adj.m(f)* rich, wealthy
rifa *n.f* raffle
rigor *n.m* rigidity, severity
rim *n.m* kidney
rio *n.m* river
riqueza *n.f* wealth
rir *v.* to laugh
riscar *v.* to scratch

risco *n.m* hazard, danger, risk
riso *n.m* laugh
riso sardônico *n.m* grin
ritmo *n.m* rhythm
roça *n.f* plantation, countryside
rocha *n.f* rock
roda *n.f* wheel
rodar *v.* to turn, spin
rolar *v.* to roll
rolha *n.f* cork
rolo *n.m* roll
romance *n.m* romance
romance literário *n.m* novel
rombo *n.m* hole
roncar *v.* to snore
ronco *n.m* snore
rosto *n.m* face
roteiro de cinema *n.m* script
rótula *n.f* kneecap
rotular *v.* to label
rótulo *n.m* label
roubar *v.* to rob, steal
roubo *n.m* theft, robbery
rouco(a) *adj.m(f)* hoarse
roupa *n.f* clothes, outfit
roupa de baixo *n.f* underwear
roupa de banho *n.f* swimsuit
roupão *n.m* bathrobe, gown, robe
roupas *n.f.pl* clothes
roxo(a) *adj.m(f)* purple
rua *n.f* street, road
rude *adj.* rude
ruga *n.f* wrinkle
ruim *adj.* bad
rumo *n.m* course, way, direction
ruína *n.f* ruin

S

sábado *n.m* Saturday
sabão *n.m* soap
saber *v.* to know
sábio(a) *adj.m(f)* wise
sabor *n.m* flavor
saboroso(a) *adj.m(f)* tasty
sacar *v.* to withdraw, take out
saco *n.m* bag, sack
sacudida *n.f* jolt
sadio(a) *adj.m(f)* sane, healthy
safra *n.f* crop, harvest
saguão *n.m* lobby, hall
saguão de shopping *n.m* mall
saia *n.f* skirt
saída *n.f* exit, way out
sair *v.* to leave, go out, quit
sal *n.m* salt
sala *n.f* room, hall
sala de espera *n.f* waiting room
sala de estar *n.f* living room, lounge
sala de inspeção *n.f* checkroom
sala de jantar *n.f* dining room
salada *n.f* salad
salão *n.m* hall
salão de baile *n.m* ballroom
salário *n.m* wages, salary, earnings
saldar *v.* to pay a debt
saldo *n.m* balance
saldo negativo *n.m* overdraft
saliva *n.f* saliva
salgadinho *n.m* savory snack

salgado(a) *adj.m(f)* salty, pricey *(coll)*, expensive
salgar *v.* to salt
salmão *n.m* salmon
salsicha *n.f* sausage
saltar *v.* to jump, skip
salto *n.m* jump, skip
salvamento *n.m* rescue
salvar *v.* to save
salvo(a) *adj.m(f)* save
sandália *n.f* sandal
sanduíche *n.m* sandwich
sangrar *v.* to bleed
sangrento(a) *adj.m(f)* gory
sangue *n.m* blood
sanha *n.f* desire, enthusiasm
santo(a) *adj.m(f)* holy
sapataria *n.f* shoemaker, shoe store
sapateiro *n.m* shoemaker, cobbler
sapato *n.m* shoe
saque *n.m* withdrawal, loot
saquear *v.* to withdraw, loot
sarna *n.f* scabies
satisfazer *v.* to satisfy
saudades *n.f.pl* longing, nostalgia, homesickness
saudar *v.* to greet, welcome
saudável *adj.* healthy
saúde *n.f* health
saúde! *interj. excl.* cheers! To your health!
se *conj.* if, whether; *pron.* oneself
secador *n.m* dryer
seção *n.f* section
secar *v.* to dry
seco(a) *adj.m(f)* dry
secretário(a) *n.m(f)* secretary
secreto(a) *adj.m(f)* secret

século *n.m* century
seda *n.f* silk
sede *n.f* thirst
segredo *n.m* secret
seguir *v.* to follow
segunda-feira *n.f* Monday
segundo(a) *num.m(f)* second
segurança *n.f* safety, security
segurar *v.* to hold
seguro *n.m* insurance
seguro(a) *adj.m(f)* safe
seis *num.* six
sela *n.f* saddle
selar *v.* to stamp, seal, mark
seleção *n.f* selection
selecionar *v.* to select
seleto(a) *adj.m(f)* select
selo *n.m* stamp, seal, mark
selvagem *adj.* wild
sem *prep.* without
semana *n.f* week
semente *n.f* seed
semestre *n.m* semester
sempre *adv.* always, ever
senão *conj.* otherwise, but
senhor, Sr. *(abbrev.) n.m* mister, Mr. *(abbrev.)*
Senhor *n.m* Sir; Lord (God)
senhora, Sra. *(abbrev.) n.f* Mrs., Ms. *(abbrev.)*
senhorita *n.f* Miss
sensação *n.f* sensation, feel
sentar *v.* to sit
sentença *n.f* sentence
sentenciar *v.* to sentence, pass judgment
sentido *n.m* meaning, direction, sense
sentimento *n.m* feeling
sentir *v.* to feel
separação *n.f* separation

separado(a) *adj.m(f)* separate

separar *v.* to separate

sepultura *n.f* grave

sequer *adv.* not even

seqüestrar *v.* to kidnap, hijack

seqüestro *n.m* kidnap, hijack

ser *v.* to be

série *n.f* series

seringa *n.f* syringe

sério(a) *adj.m(f)* serious

serviço *n.m* service

sessão *n.f* session, showing, meeting

sessenta *num.* sixty

sete *num.* seven

setenta *num.* seventy

setembro *n.m* September

sétimo(a) *num.m(f)* seventh

seu, sua *pron.m,f* your, his, her

severo(a) *adj.m(f)* severe, harsh

sexo *n.m* sex, gender

sexta-feira *n.f* Friday

sexto(a) *num.m(f)* sixth

show *n.m* show, concert

significado *n.m* meaning

significar *v.* to signify, mean

silenciar *v.* to silence, shut up, hush up

silêncio *n.m* silence

silencioso(a) *adj.m(f)* silent

si *pron.* for oneself

sim *adv.* yes

simbolizar *v.* to symbolize

símbolo *n.m* symbol, token

similar *adj.* similar

simpático(a) *adj.m(f)* nice, pleasant

simples *adj.* simple, plain, modest

sinagoga *n.f* synagogue

sinal *n.m* sign

sinalizar *v.* to signal

sincero(a) *adj.m(f)* sincere

sino *n.m* bell

sintoma *n.m* symptom

sintonizar *v.* to tune, get on with

siri *n.m* crab

sitiar *v.* to besiege

sítio *n.m* small farm, siege

só *adj.* alone; *adv.* only

sob *prep; adv.* under

sobra *n.f* remains, leftovers

sobrancelha *n.f* eyebrow

sobrar *v.* to remain, be left out

sobre *prep.* on, about, over

sobremesa *n.f* dessert

sobrepor *v.* to overlap

sobreposição *n.f* overlap

sobreviver *v.* to survive

sobrinha *n.f* niece

sobrinho *n.m* nephew

sociedade *n.f* partnership, society

sócio(a) *n.m(f)* partner, member

sofá *n.m* sofa, couch

sofrer *v.* to suffer

sofrimento *n.m* suffering, pain, hardship

sogra *n.f* mother-in-law

sogro *n.m* father-in-law

soja *n.f* soy

sol *n.m* sun

soletrar *v.* to spell, read out

sola *n.f* sole

solidão *n.f* loneliness

sólido(a) *adj.m(f)* solid, sound

solitário(a) *adj.m(f)* lonely

solo *n.m* soil, ground
soltar *v.* to set free
solteira *n.f* maid
solteiro *n.m* bachelor
solto(a) *adj.m(f)* loose
soluçar *v.* to sob, hiccup
soluço *n.m* hiccup
soma *n.f* sum, total, amount
somar *v.* to add up
sombra *n.f* shadow, shade
somente *adv.* only
sonhar *v.* to dream
sonho *n.m* dream
sono *n.m* sleep
sopa *n.f* soup
soporífero *n.m* sleeping pill
soprar *v.* to blow
sorrir *v.* to smile
sorriso *n.m* smile
sorte *n.f* luck
sorvete *n.m* ice cream
sósia *n.* double, look alike
sossegado(a) *adj.m(f)* calm, quieted, tranquil
sossegar *v.* to calm
sossego *n.m* peace, tranquility
sótão *n.m* attic, loft
sotaque *n.m* accent
sozinho(a) *adj.m(f)* alone
suar *v.* to sweat
suave *adj.* mild, gentle, soft, mellow
sub- *pref.* under-
subestimar *v.* to underestimate
subida *n.f* climb
subir *v.* to go up, rise
subsídio *n.m* grant, subsidy
substantivo *n.m* noun
substituir *v.* to replace, substitute

subterrâneo(a) *adj.m(f)* underground
subtítulo *n.m* subtitle
subtrair *v.* to subtract
subúrbio *n.m* suburb
sucata *n.f* scrap
sucesso *n.m* success
suco *n.m* juice
suculento(a) *adj.m(f)* juicy
sudeste *n.m.* southeast
sudoeste *n.m.* southwest
sufocar *v.* to suffocate
sufoco *n.m* anxiety, hassle, asphyxiation
suéter *n.m* sweater
Suíça *n.f* Switzerland
suicídio *n.m* suicide
suíço(a) *adj.m(f)* Swiss
sujar *v.* to dirty, sully, make a mess
sujeira *n.f* dirt
sujo(a) *adj.m(f)* dirty
sul *n.m* south
sumário *n.m* summary
suntuoso(a) *adj.m(f)* luxurious
suor *n.m* sweat
superaquecer *v.* to overheat
superar *v.* to overcome
superestimar *v.* to overrate
superior *adj.* upper
supermercado *n.m* supermarket
supervisor(~a) *n.m(f)* supervisor
supor *v.* to suppose
suportar *v.* to bear, tolerate, hold up
suportável *adj.* bearable
suposição *n.f* guess
suprimir *v.* to delete
surdez *n.f* deafness
surdo(a) *adj.m(f)* deaf

surra *n.f* hiding, beating; thrashing

surrar *v.* to beat, wear out

surto *n.m* outbreak, surge, epidemic

suspeitar *v.* to suspect

suspeito(a) *adj.m(f)* suspect

sustar *v.* to stop

susto *n.m* fright

T

tabaco *n.m* tobacco

tabela *n.f* chart, list

tabeliã(~o) *n.f,(m)* notary

tábua *n.f* plank, board, wood

tabuleta *n.f* tablet

taça *n.f* cup, glass

taco *n.m* stick

tal *adj.* such

talher *n.m* cutlery

talvez *adv.* perhaps, maybe

tamanho *n.m* size

também *adv.* also, too, as well

tampa *n.f* lid

tampão *n.m* tampon

tampar *v.* to cover

tanto(a) *adj.m(f); adv.* so much

tão *adv.* so

tapa *n.f* slap

tapete *n.m* carpet

tapete pequeno *n.m* mat, rug

tarde *n.f* afternoon; *adv.* late

tarefa *n.f* chore, task

tato *n.m* tact, diplomacy

tatuagem *n.f* tattoo

taxa *n.f* fee, duty, charge, rate

taxa de câmbio *n.f* exchange rate

taxar *v.* to tax, fix the price

táxi *n.m* cab, taxi

tchau! *interj. excl.* good-bye! bye-bye!

teatro *n.m* theater

tecer *v.* to weave

tecido *n.m* fabric, tissue

teclado *n.m* keyboard

teclar *v.* to key in

teia *n.f* web

teimoso(a) *adj.m(f)* obstinate, willful, stubborn

tela *n.f* screen

tele-conferência *n.f* teleconferencing

telefonar *v.* to phone

telefone *n.m* phone

televisão *n.f* television

televisionar *v.* to televise

telhado *n.m* roof

temperamento *n.m* temper, nature

temperar *v.* to spice, season

temperatura *n.f* temperature

tempestade *n.f* storm

templo *n.m* temple

tempo *n.m* time, weather

tempo integral *n.m* full time

temporada *n.f* season

temporário(a) *adj.m(f)* temporary, provisional

tenda *n.f* tent

tendência *n.f* trend, tendency

tênis *n.m* tennis

tenro(a) *adj.m(f)* soft, tender

tensão *n.f* tension

tenso(a) *adj.m(f)* tense, nervous

tentar *v.* to tempt, try, attempt

tentativa *n.f* attempt

teor *n.m* content, concentration

ter *v.* to have

ter importância *v.* to matter

terça-feira *n.f* Tuesday

terceiro(a) *num.m(f)* third

terminar *v.* to finish

termo *n.m* term, period

termômetro *n.m* thermometer

terno *n.m* suit; formal male dressing

ternura *n.f* tenderness

terra *n.f* earth, land

terraço *n.m* balcony

terremoto *n.m* earthquake

terreno *n.m* plot of land

terrível *adj.* awful, terrible

tesão *n.m (coll.)* horniness, excitement, desire

tese *n.f* theory, thesis

tesoura *n.f* scissors

tesouro *n.m* treasure

testa *n.f* forehead

testar *v.* to test, try

teste *n.m* trial, test, exam

testemunha *n.* witness

testemunhar *v.* to witness

teta *n.f (coll.)* teat, female breast

teto *n.m* ceiling

teu, tua, de vocês *pron.* yours

têxtil *n.* textile

texto *n.m* text

tia *n.f* aunt

tifo *n.m* typhoid, typhus

time *n.m* team

tímido(a) *n.m(f)* shy

tinta *n.f* ink, paint

tio *n.m* uncle

tino *n.m* intuition, talent

típico(a) *adj.m(f)* typical

tipo *n.m* sort, kind, type

tira *n.f* strip, policeman

tirar *v.* to take away, take off

tiro *n.m* shot

titular *n.m* holder, principal

título *n.m* title

titia *n.f* aunty

toa (à toa) *n.f* for no reason, in vain

toalete *n.m* toilet, WC, restroom

toalha *n.f* towel

toalha de mesa *n.f* tablecloth

toalha sanitária *n.f* sanitary pad

toca *n.f* burrow, hole

tocar *v.* to touch

toco *n.m* stub, stump

todo dia *adj.m* everyday

todos(as) *pron.m(f)pl* everybody, everything

toicinho *n.m* fatty bacon

tom *n.m* tone, pitch

tomada *n.f* plug, socket

tomar *v.* to take

topar *v.* to agree, accept

topo *n.m* top

toque *n.m* touch

torcer *v.* to twist, spin, bend

tornar-se *v.* to become

torneio *n.m* tournament

torneira *n.f* tap, faucet

tornozelo *n.m* ankle

torre *n.f* tower

torta *n.f* pie, tort

torto(a) *adj.m(f)* crooked, twisted

tosse *n.f* cough
tossir *v.* to cough
total *adj*; *n.m* total, sum
totalizar *v.* to total up
touro *n.m* bull
trabalhar *v.* to work
trabalho *n.m* labor
traçar *v.* to draw, set out
tradição *n.f* tradition
tradução *n.f* translation
tradutor(~a) *n.m(f)* translator
traduzir *v.* to translate
trafegar *v.* to move, go; drive; walk
tráfego *n.m* traffic
tráfico *n.m* illegal move, illegal trade (drugs)
traição *n.f* treason, betrayal
trair *v.* to betray, be unfaithful
traje *n.m* dress, clothes
trancar *v.* to lock, clam up
transação *n.f* transaction, deal, love act
transferência *n.f* transfer
transferir *v.* to transfer, move, postpone
transmitir *v.* to transmit, broadcast, transfer
transportar *v.* to transport
transporte *n.m* transport
tranqüilo(a) *adj.m(f)* quiet
trapo *n.m* rag
tratamento *n.m* treatment
tratar *v.* to treat
trato *n.m* dealings, agreement
travar *v.* to lock, brake, engage
travesseiro *n.m* pillow
travesso(a) *adj.m(f)* naughty
travessura *n.f* naughtiness

trazer *v.* to bring
trecho *n.m* stretch
treinar *v.* train
trem *n.m* train, railway
trepada *n.f (coll.)* sexual intercourse
trepar *v.* to climb
três *num.* three
tribo *n.m* tribe
tributo *n.m* tribute, homage
tricô *n.m* knit
tricotar *v.* to knit
trigo *n.m* wheat
trilha *n.f* path, track
trimestre *n.m* quarter, three months
tripulação *n.f* crew
triste *adj.* sad
tristeza *n.f* gloom, sadness, sorrow
triturar *v.* to grind
troca *n.f* exchange
trocar *v.* to exchange
troco *n.m* change
trombada *n.f* crash
tronco *n.m* trunk
tropeção *n.m* trip-up
tropeçar *v.* to stumble
trote *n.m* hoax
trovão *n.m* thunder
truque *n.m* trick
tubarão *n.m* shark
tubo *n.m* tube, pipe
tudo *pron.* all
tumor *n.m* tumor
túmulo *n.m* tomb
túnel *n.m* tunnel
turismo *n.m* tourism, sightseeing
turista *n.* tourist
turno *n.m* shift, turn
turvar *v.* to cloud, darken

U

uái!? *interj.* what?!
úlcera *n.f* ulcer
ué!? *interj.* what?! why?!
ui! *interj. excl.* ouch! ow!
  oops!
uísque *n.m* whiskey
ultimamente *adv.* lately
último(a) *adj.m(f)* last,
  latest
ultra- *pref.* ultra-
ultra-mar *n.m* overseas,
  abroad
ultrapassar *v.* to pass, overtake, outdo, outrun
um(a) *art. m(f)* a
um tanto *adv.* rather
uma vez *adv.* once
umbigo *n.m* navel
umedecer *v.* moisten
umidade *n.f* moisture
úmido(a) *adj.m(f)* humid,
  moist, damp
unha *n.f* fingernail, toenail
unhada *n.f* scratch
unhar *v.* to scratch (with
  fingernails)
União Européia *n.f*
  European Union
união *n.f* union
unicamente *adv.* only
único(a) *adj.m(f)* single,
  only, unique
unidade *n.f* unity, unit
unido(a) *adj.m(f)* joined,
  linked
unificar *v.* to unite, join
  together
uniforme *n.m; adj.* uniform
unir *v.* to join together,
  unite
universal *adj.* universal
universidade *n.f* university
universo *n.m* universe

upa! *interj.* whoops!
urbano(a) *adj.m(f)* urban
urgência *n.f* urgency
urgente *adj.* urgent
urina *n.f* urine
urinol *n.m* chamber pot,
  bed pan
urna *n.f* urn
urso(a) *n.m(f)* bear
usado(a) *adj.m(f)* used,
  worn, second hand
usar *v.* to wear
usina *n.f* factory, plant, mill
uso *n.m* use, wear
usual *adj.* usual
usuário(a) *n.m(f)* user
usufruir *v.* to enjoy, profit
utensílio *n.m* utensil
útil *adj.* useful
utilidade *n.f* usefulness,
  advantage, utility
utilização *n.f* use
utilizar *v.* to use
uva *n.f* grape

V

vaca *n.f* cow
vacina *n.f* vaccine, jab
vacinar *v.* to vaccinate
vadiar *v.* to laze
vadio(a) *adj.m(f)* idle, lazy
vaga *n.f* vacancy, free place
vagabundear *v.* to loiter
vagar *v.* to vacate
vagina *n.f* vagina
vago(a) *adj.m(f)* imprecise,
  vague, vacant, free
vaguear *v.* to loiter
vaia *n.f* boo
vaiar *v.* to jeer
vala *n.f* ditch
vale *n.m* valley, voucher
valente *adj.* brave, valiant

valer *v.* to be worth, cost
validade *n.f* validity
validar *v.* to validate
válido(a) *adj.m(f)* valid
valor *n.m* value, merit, worth
vantagem *n.f* advantage
vão[1] *adj.* vain, futile
vão[2] *n.m* space, gap
vapor *n.m* steam, vapor
vaqueiro(a) *n.m(f)* cowboy
vara *n.f* rod, stick
varejo *n.m* retail trade
variar *v.* to vary
vários(as) *adj.m(f) pl* several, various
varrer *v.* to sweep
vaso *n.m* pot, vase, vessel
vassoura *n.f* broom, mop
vasto(a) *adj.m(f)* vast
vazamento *n.m* leak
vazar *v.* to leak
vazio(a) *adj.m(f)* empty
vegetal *n.m* vegetable
vegetariano(a) *adj.m(f)* vegetarian
veia *n.f* vein
veículo *n.m* vehicle
vela *n.f* candle, sail
vela de barco *n.f* sail
velar *v.* to veil
velejar *v.* to sail
velho(a) *adj.m(f)* old
velocidade *n.f* speed
veludo *n.m* velvet
vencedor(~a) *n.m(f)* winner; *adj.* winning
vencer *v.* to win
venda *n.f* general store, bar
vender *v.* to sell
veneno *n.m* venom, poison
venenoso(a) *adj.m(f)* poisonous

ventania *n.f* gale
ventilador *n.m* fan
vento *n.m* wind
ver *v.* to see
verba *n.f* funds, budget
verbo *n.m* verb
verdade *n.f* truth
verdadeiro(a) *adj.m(f)* true
verde *adj.* green
verdura *n.f* greens, vegetables
veredicto *n.m* verdict
vergonha *n.f* shame
verificação *n.f* check
verificar *v.* to verify
vermelho(a) *adj.m(f)* red
versátil *adj.* versatile
vértebra *n.f* vertebra
verter *v.* to translate, pour
vertical *adj.* upright
vertigem *n.f* vertigo
vespa *n.f* wasp
véspera *n.f* eve, day before
vestido *n.m* dress
vestígio *n.m* track, sign, trace
vestir *v.* to clothe, dress
vetar *v.* to veto
veterinário(a) *n.m(f)* veterinarian
veto *n.m* veto
véu *n.m* veil
vexame *n.m* shame, embarrassment
viagem *n.f* journey, travel
viajante *n.* traveler
viajar *v.* to trip, travel
viável *adj.* viable
viciado(a) *adj.m(f)* addicted
viciar *v.* to addict to
vício *n.m* vice, addiction
vida *n.f* life

videira *n.f* vine
vidro *n.m* glass
vigia *n.m* watchman
vigiar *v.* to watch, guard
vil *adj.* vile
vila *n.f* villa
vinagre *n.m* vinegar
vingança *n.f* vengeance
vingar *v.* to avenge
vinhedo *n.m* vineyard
vinho *n.m* wine
vinte *num.* twenty
violação *n.f* rape
violar *v.* to violate
violentar *v.* to rape, force
violento(a) *adj.m(f)* violent
violino *n.m* fiddle
vir *v.* to come
virada 180° *n.f* U-turn
virar *v.* to turn
virgem *adj.* virgin
vírgula *n.f* comma
virilha *n.f* groin
virtual *adj.* virtual
virtude *n.f* virtue
visar *v.* to aim at
visibilidade *n.f* visibility
visita *n.f* visit
visitar *v.* to visit
visitante *n.* visitor
vista *n.f* sight, view
visto *n.m* visa
vital *adj.* vital
vitalício(a) *adj.m(f)* for life
vitalidade *n.f* vitality, energy, drive
vitamina *n.f* vitamin, fruit crush
vítima *n.* victim
viúva *n.f* widow
viúvo *n.m* widower
viver *v.* to live
vivo(a) *adj.m(f)* alive

vizinhança *n.f* neighborhood
vizinho(a) *n.m(f)* neighbor
voar *v.* to fly
vocabulário *n.m* vocabulary
você(s) *pron.* you
vogal *n.f* vowel
volta *n.f* turn
voltagem *n.f* voltage
voltar *v.* to come back
volume *n.m* volume
volume de negócios *n.m* turnover
voluntário(a) *n.m(f)* volunteer
volúpia *n.f* pleasure, ecstasy
volúvel *adj.* changeable
vomitar *v.* to vomit
vômito *n.m* vomit
vontade *n.f* will, wish, urge
vôo *n.m* flight
votação *n.f* poll
votar *v.* to vote
voto *n.m* vow, vote
voz *n.f* voice
vulgar *adj.* common, vulgar

W

watt *n.m* watt
website *n.m* website

X

xadrez *n.m* chess
xampu *n.m* shampoo
xará *n.* namesake
xarope *n.m* syrup, cough syrup; bad thing *(fig)*
xerocar *v.* to photocopy
xerox *n.f* photocopy

xi! *interj. excl.* gee!

xícara *n.f* cup

xingar *v.* to swear at

xixi *n.m* wee, pee, urinate

xodó *n.m* sweetheart, passion, soft spot

Z

zangado(a) *adj.m(f)* angry, annoyed

zangar *v.* to irritate, annoy

zelador(~a) *n.m(f)* caretaker

zelar *v.* to take care, look after

zelo *n.m* zeal

zeloso(a) *adj.m(f)* zealous

zero *num.* zero

ziguezague *n.m* zigzag

-zinho(a), - inho(a) *suffix dimin.* small, little

zíper *n.m* zipper

zombar *v.* to mock

zona *n.f* zone

zonzo(a) *adj.m(f)* dizzy

zumbido *n.m* buzz

zumbir *v.* to buzz, ring

ENGLISH – PORTUGUESE DICTIONARY

A

a *art.* um(~a) *m(f)*
abbreviation *n.* abreviatura *f*
able *adj.* capaz *mf*
aboard *adv.* a bordo de
abortion *n.* aborto *m*
about *prep.* sobre
above *prep.* acima
abroad *adv.* no exterior
absence *n.* ausência *f*
absorb *v.* absorver
abuse *n.* abuso *m; v.* abusar
accelerate *v.* acelerar
accelerator *n.* acelerador *m*
accent *n.* sotaque *m*
accept *v.* aceitar
access *n.* acesso *m*
accessory *n.* acessório *m*
accident *n.* acidente *m*
accommodations *n.* acomodação *f*
account *n.* conta *f*
accountant *n.* contador (~a) *m(f)*
accurate *adj.* exato(a) *m(f)*
accuse *v.* acusar
accustom *v.* acostumar
ache *n.* dor *f*
achieve *v.* conseguir
acknowledgement *n.* reconhecimento *m*

acquaintance *n.* conhecido(a) *m(f)*
across *prep.* através de
act *n.* ato *m; v.* agir
action *n.* ação *f*
active *adj.* ativo(a) *m(f)*
activity *n.* atividade *f*
actor *n.* ator *m*
actress *n.* atriz *f*
adapt *v.* adaptar
add *v.* adicionar
addition *n.* adição *f*
additional *adj.* adicional *mf*
address *n.* endereço *m*
adjective *n. adj.* etivo *m*
adjust *n.* ajuste *m; v.* ajustar
administration *n.* administração *f*
admire *v.* admirar
adolescence *n.* adolescência *f*
adopt *v.* adotar
adult *n.* adulto(a) *m(f)*
adultery *n.* adultério *m*
advance *n.* avanço *m; v.* avançar
advantage *n.* vantagem *f*
adventure *n.* aventura *f*
advertise *v.* anunciar
advertisement *n.* propaganda *f*
advice *n.* conselho *m*
affect *v.* afetar

afford v. ter recursos para
afraid adj. receoso(a) m(f)
Africa n. África
African n.; adj. africano(a)
  m(f)
after prep. depois de;
  adv. depois
afternoon n. tarde f
again adv. outra vez
against prep. contra
age n. idade f; v. envelhecer
agency n. agência f
agent n. agente mf
aggression n. agressão f
aggressive adj. agressivo(a)
  m(f)
ago adv. atrás
agree v. concordar
agreement n. acordo m
ahead adv. à frente
air n. ar m; v. arejar
air-conditioning n. ar
  condicionado m
airline n. linha aérea f
airmail n. correio aéreo m
airplane n. avião m
airport n. aeroporto m
alarm n. alarme m;
  v. alarmar
alcohol n. álcool m
alien n. estrangeiro(a) m(f);
  adj. estranho(a) m(f)
alike adj. igual mf
alive adj. vivo(a) m(f)
all adj. todo(s) m(pl),
  toda(s) f(pl); pron. tudo,
  todos(as) m.pl(f.pl);
  adv. todo
allergic adj. alérgico(a)
  m(f)
allergy n. alergia f
allow v. permitir
almost adv. quase

alone adj. sozinho(a) m(f),
  só mf; adv. somente
aloud adv. alto(a) m(f)
alphabet n. alfabeto m
already adv. já
also adv. também
altitude n. altitude f
always adv. sempre
amaze v. espantar
ambassador n.
  embaixador(~a) m(f)
ambiguous adj.
  ambígüo(a) m(f)
ambition n. ambição f
ambulance n. ambulância f
America n. América f
American n.;
  adj. americano(a) m(f)
among prep. entre
amount n. quantidade f
ancestor n. antepassado(a)
  m(f)
anchor n. âncora f
ancient adj. antigo(a) m(f)
and conj. e
anemia n. anemia f
anesthesia n. anestesia f
angel n. anjo. m
anger n. raiva f; v. enfurecer
angle n. ângulo m
angry adj. enfurecido(a)
  m(f)
animal n. animal m
ankle n. tornozelo m
anniversary n. aniversário
  m
announcement n. anúncio
  m
annual adj. anual mf
another adj. outro(a) m(f)
answer n. resposta f;
  v. responder
antenna n. antena f
antiquity n. antigüidade f

anxiety *n.* ansiedade *f*
any *adj.* algum(~a) *m(f)*
anybody *pron.* qualquer um(~a) *m(f)*
apart *adv.* à parte, à distância
apartment *n.* apartamento *m*
apologize *v.* desculpar-se
appearance *n.* aparência *f*
appendicitis *n.* apendicite *f*
appetite *n.* apetite *m*
appetizer *n.* aperitivo *m*
applaud *v.* aplaudir
applause *n.* aplauso *m*
apple *n.* maçã *f*
appliance *n.* dispositivo *m*
application *n.* aplicação *f*
apply *v.* aplicar
appointment *n.* nomeação *f*
apprentice *n.* aprendiz *mf*
apprenticeship *n.* aprendizagem *f*
approach *n.* aproximação *f*; *v.* aproximar
appropriate *adj.* apropriado(a) *m(f)*
approve *v.* aprovar
April *n.* abril *m*
Arab *n.; adj.* árabe *mf*
arch *n.* arco *m*
architecture *n.* arquitetura *f*
archive *n.* arquivo *m*
area *n.* área *f*
argument *n.* argumento *m*
arm *n.* braço *m*; *v.* armar
armchair *n.* poltrona *f*
armpit *n.* axila *f*
army *n.* exército *m*
around *adv.* em torno; *prep.* ao redor
arrest *n.* apreensão *f*; *v.* prender
arrival *n.* chegada *f*

arrive *v.* chegar
arrow *n.* flecha *f*
art *n.* arte *f*
article *n.* artigo *m*
artificial *adj.* artificial *mf*
artist *n.* artista *mf*
as *conj.; prep.* como
ash *n.* cinza *f*
ashtray *n.* cinzeiro *m*
Asia *n.* Ásia *f*
Asian *n.; adj.* asiático(a) *m(f)*
aside *adv.* de lado
ask *v.* pedir, perguntar
asleep *adj.* adormecido(a) *m(f)*
aspirin *n.* aspirina *f*
assemble *v.* montar
assign *v.* atribuir
assist *v.* dar assistência
assistant *n.* assistente *mf*
association *n.* associação *f*
assure *v.* assegurar
asylum *n.* asilo *m*
at *prep.* em
athlete *n.* atleta *mf*
attempt *n.* tentativa *f*; *v.* tentar
attention *n.* atenção *f*
attentive *adj.* atencioso(a) *m(f)*
attic *n.* sótão *m*
attitude *n.* atitude *f*
attorney *n.* advogado(a) *m(f)*
attract *v.* atrair
attractive *adj.* atraente *mf*
auction *n.* leilão *m*
August *n.* agosto *m*
aunt *n.* tia *f*
authentic *adj.* autêntico(a) *m(f)*
author *n.* autor(~a) *m(f)*
authority *n.* autoridade *f*

authorization n.
autorização f
authorize v. autorizar
automatic adj.
automático(a) m(f)
available adj. disponível mf
avenue n. avenida f
average n. média f
avoid v. evitar
aware adj. ciente mf
away adv. fora
awful adj. terrível mf

B

baby n. bebê m
baby-sit v. cuidar de bebê
baby-sitter n. babá f
bachelor n. solteiro(a) m(f)
back n. costas f.pl;
adv. de volta;
adj. de trás; v. apoiar
backbone n. espinha
dorsal f
backpack n. mochila f
backwards adv. para trás
bacteria n. bactérias f
bad adj. mau m, má f
bag n. saco m
baggage n. bagagem f
bail n. fiança f; v. baldear,
salvar
bait n. isca f; v. iscar
bake v. assar
baker n. padeiro(a) m(f)
bakery n. padaria f
balance n. balanço m
balcony n. balcão m
bald adj. careca mf
ball n. bola f
ballet n. balé m
ballpoint pen n.
esferográfica f

ballroom n. salão de
baile m
ban n. proibição f; v. proibir
band n. banda f, faixa f
bandage n. atadura f
bank n. banco m
banker n. banqueiro(a)
m(f)
banquet n. banquete m
baptism n. batismo m
baptize v. batizar
bar n. bar m, barra f
barber n. barbeiro m
bare adj. nú m, nua f
barefoot adj. descalço(a)
m(f)
bargain n. barato m;
v. pechinchar
barn n. celeiro m
basement n. porão m
basin n. bacia f
basis n. base f
basket n. cesta f
bath n. banho m
bathe v. banhar
bathrobe n. roupão m
bathroom n. banheiro m
bathtub n. banheira f
battery n. pilha f
bay n. baía f
be v. ser, estar
beach n. praia f
beam n. raio de luz m,
viga f
bean n. feijão m, grão m
bear n. urso m; v. agüentar,
carregar, suportar
bearable adj. suportável mf
beard n. barba f
beat n. batida f; v. bater
beautiful adj. bonito(a)
m(f)
beauty n. beleza f
because conj. porque

become *v.* tornar
bed *n.* cama *f*
bedding *n.* lençóis *m.pl*
bedroom *n.* quarto *m*
bee *n.* abelha *f*
beer *n.* cerveja *f*
before *prep.; adv.* antes
beg *v.* implorar
begin *v.* começar
beginner *n.* principiante *mf*
beginning *n.* começo *m*
behave *v.* comportar
behavior *n.*
    comportamento *m*
behind *prep.; adv.* atrás de
Belgian *n.; adj.* belga *mf*
Belgium *n.* Bélgica *f*
belief *n.* crença *f*
believe *v.* acreditar
bell *n.* sino *m*
belly *n.* barriga *f*
belong *v.* pertencer
belongings *n.* pertences *m*
below *prep.; adv.* abaixo
belt *n.* cinto *m*
bench *n.* banco *m*
benefit *n.* benefício *m;*
    v. beneficiar
beret *n.* boina *f*
berry *n.* fruto *m*
beside *prep.* ao lado de
besides *prep.; adv.* além de
best *adj.* o melhor *m*
bet *n.* aposta *f; v.* apostar
better *adj.; adv.* melhor *mf*
between *prep.; adv.* entre
beverage *n.* bebida *f*
beware *v.* ter cautela
beyond *prep.; adv.* além de
bib *n.* babador *m*
Bible *n.* bíblia *f*
bicycle *n.* bicicleta *f*
big *adj.* grande *mf*
bilingual *adj.* bilíngüe *mf*

bill *n.* conta *f*
billion *n.* bilhão *m*
bird *n.* pássaro *m*
birth *n.* nascimento *m*
birth control pill *n.* pílula
    anticoncepcional *f*
birthday *n.* aniversário *m*
bit *n.* pedaço *m*
bite *n.* mordida *f; v.* morder
bitter *adj.* amargo(a) *m(f)*
black *adj.* preto(a) *m(f)*
bladder *n.* bexiga *f*
blade *n.* lâmina *f*
blank *adj.* espaço em
    branco *m*
blanket *n.* cobertor *m*
bleach *n.* descorante *m;*
    v. descorar
bleed *v.* sangrar
blend *n.* mistura *f;*
    v. misturar
bless *v.* abençoar
blind *adj.* cego(a) *m(f)*,
    cortina *f; v.* cegar
blindness *n.* cegueira *f*
blink *v.* piscar
blister *n.* bolha *f*
block *n.* bloco *m*
blond *adj.* loiro(a) *m(f)*
blood *n.* sangue *m*
blouse *n.* blusa *f*
blow-dry *n.* secagem *f*
blue *adj.* azul *mf*
board *n.* placa *f*
boarding pass *n.* cartão de
    embarque *m*
boarding school *n.*
    internato *m*
boat *n.* barco *m*
body *n.* corpo *m*
boil *v.* ferver
boiler *n.* caldeira *f*
bolt *n.* parafuso *m;*
    v. parafusar

bomb *n.* bomba *f;*
  v. bombear, bombardear
bone *n.* osso *m*
book *n.* livro *m; v.* reservar
bookcase *n.* estante de
  livros *f*
bookstore *n.* livraria *f*
boot *n.* bota *f*
border *n.* fronteira *f*
born *adj.* nascido(a) *m(f)*
boss *n.* chefe *mf*
both *adj.* ambos(as) *m(f)*
bother *v.* incomodar
bottle *n.* garrafa *f*
boulevard *n.* alameda *f*
bow *n.* curva *f*
bowl *n.* bacia *f*
box *n.* caixa *f*
boxing *n.* boxe *m*
bracelet *n.* pulseira *f,*
  bracelete *m*
Brazil *n.* Brasil *m*
Brazilian *n.;*
  adj. brasileiro(a) *m(f)*
bread *n.* pão *m*
break *n.* intervalo *m;*
  v. quebrar
breakdown *n.* avaria *f*
breakfast *n.* café da
  manhã *m*
breast *n.* peito *m*
breath *n.* respiração *f*
breathe *v.* respirar
breeze *n.* brisa *f*
bride *n.* noiva *f*
bridge *n.* ponte *f*
brief; *adj.* breve *mf;*
  v. instruir
bright *adj.* brilhante *mf*
bring *v.* trazer
broom *n.* vassoura *f*
brother *n.* irmão *m,* irmã *f*
brother-in-law *n.*
  cunhado(a) *m(f)*

brown *adj.* marrom *mf*
bruise *n.* machucado(a)
  m(f); v. machucar
brush *n.* escova *f; v.* escovar
bubble *n.* bolha *f*
bucket *n.* balde *m*
budget *n.* orçamento *m*
build *v.* construir
building *n.* edifício *m*
bulb *n.* bulbo *m*
bullet *n.* bala *f*
bunch *n.* punhado *m*
buoy *n.* bóia *f*
burglar *n.* ladrão *m,* ladra *f*
burglarize *v.* roubar
burn *n.* queimadura *f;*
  v. queimar
burst *v.* arrebentar
bury *v.* enterrar
bus *n.* ônibus *m*
business *n.* negócio *m*
busy *adj.* ocupado(a) *m(f)*
but *conj.; prep.* mas
butcher *n.* açougueiro(a)
  m(f)
button *n.* botão *m*
buy *v.* comprar
by *prep.* por
bye-bye! *interj.* tchau, até
  logo!

C

cab *n.* táxi *m*
cable *n.* cabo *m*
cage *n.* gaiola *f*
cake *n.* bolo *m*
calculate *v.* calcular
calculator *n.* calculadora *f*
calendar *n.* calendário *m*
call *n.* chamada *f; v.* chamar
calling card *n.* cartão de
  telefone *m*
camera *n.* câmera *f*

camp *n.* campo *m;*
   v. acampar
can *n.* lata *f; v.* poder
Canada *n.* Canadá *m*
Canadian *n.;*
   adj. canadense *mf*
cancel *v.* cancelar
cancellation *n.*
   cancelamento *m*
cancer *n.* câncer *m*
candle *n.* vela *f*
candy *n.* doce *m*
cane *n.* bastão *m*
canoe *n.* canoa *f*
cap *n.* boné *m*
capable *adj.* capaz *mf*
capital *n.* capital *m*
captain *n.* capitão *m*
car *n.* carro *m*
card *n.* cartão *m*
cardboard *n.* papelão *m,*
   cartão *m*
care *n.* cuidado *m; v.* cuidar
careful *adj.* cuidadoso(a)
   m(f)
carpet *n.* tapete *m*
carry *v.* carregar
carton *n.* caixa de papelão *f*
case *n.* caso *m,* caixa *f*
cash *n.* dinheiro *m;*
   v. receber
cashier *n.* caixa *mf*
casino *n.* cassino *m*
castle *n.* castelo *m*
casual *adj.* ocasional *mf*
cat *n.* gato *m*
catalog *n.* catálogo *m*
catch *v.* pegar
cathedral *n.* catedral *f*
Catholic *n; adj.* católico(a)
   m(f)
Catholicism *n.* Catolicismo
   m
caution *n.* cuidado *m*

cautious *adj.* cauteloso(a)
   m(f)
cave *n.* caverna *f*
CD *n.* CD *m*
CD player *n.* CD player *m*
CD-ROM *n.* CD-rom *m*
ceiling *n.* teto *m*
celebrate *v.* celebrar
cell *n.* célula *f,* cela *f*
cellar *n.* adega *f*
cemetery *n.* cemitério *m*
center *n.* centro *m;*
   v. centrar
centimeter *n.* centímetro *m*
central *adj.* central *mf*
century *n.* século *m*
ceremony *n.* cerimônia *f*
chain *n.* corrente *f*
chair *n.* cadeira *f*
chance *n.* chance *f*
change *n.* troco *m,*
   mudança *f; v.* mudar
chapter *n.* capítulo *m*
character *n.* caráter *m*
charge *n.* carga *f; v.* cobrar
chat *n.* bate-papo *m;*
   v. bater-papo
cheap *adj.* barato(a) *m(f)*
cheat *v.* fraudar
check *n.* cheque *m,*
   verificação *f; v.* conferir
checkbook *n.* cartão de
   cheques *m*
checkroom *n.* sala de
   inspeção *f*
cheek *n.* bochecha *f*
cheeky *adj.* insolente *mf*
cheerful *adj.* alegre *mf*
cheers! *interj.* saúde!
cheese *n.* queijo *m*
chef *n.* cozinheiro(a) chefe
   m(f)
chemical *n; adj.* produto
   químico *m*

chemist *n.* químico(a) *m(f)*, farmacêutico(a) *m(f)*
chemistry *n.* química *f*
chess *n.* xadrez *m*
chest *n.* peito *m*, cofre *m*
chew *v.* mastigar
child *n.* criança *f*
childhood *n.* infância *f*
chin *n.* queixo *m*
china *n.* porcelana *f*
choice *n.* escolha *f*
choke *v.* engasgar, sufocar
choose *v.* escolher
chop *v.* cortar
chore *n.* tarefa *f*
Christian *adj.* cristão *m*, cristã *f*
Christianity *n.* Cristianismo *m*
Christmas *n.* Natal *m*
church *n.* igreja *f*
cigar *n.* charuto *m*
cigarette *n.* cigarro *m*
circle *n.* círculo *m*
circumstance *n.* circunstância *f*
circus *n.* circo *m*
citizen *n.* cidadão *m*, cidadã *f*
city *n.* cidade *f*
civilization *n.* civilização *f*
classic *adj.* clássico(a) *m(f)*
clean *adj.* limpo(a) *m(f)*; *v.* limpar
clever *adj.* inteligente *mf*
client *n.* cliente *mf*
cliff *n.* penhasco *m*
climate *n.* clima *m*
climb *n.* subida *f*; *v.* escalar
clinic *n.* clínica *f*
clock *n.* relógio *m*
close *adv.* perto; *v.* fechar
closed *adj.* fechado(a) *m(f)*
cloth *n.* pano *m*

clothe *v.* vestir
clothes *n.* roupas *f.pl*
cloud *n.* nuvem *f*
coast *n.* orla *f*
coat *n.* revestimento *m*
cobbler *n.* sapateiro *m*
code *n.* código *m*
coffee *n.* café (drink) *m*
coffee shop *n.* café (coffee bar) *m*
coffin *n.* caixão *m*
coin *n.* moeda *f*
cold *n.* frio; *adj.* frio(a) *m(f)*
collect call *n.* chamada a cobrar *f*
collection *n.* coleção *f*
college *n.* colégio *m*, faculdade *f*
collide *v.* colidir
collision *n.* colisão *f*
color *n.* cor *f*
column *n.* coluna *f*
comb *n.* pente *m*; *v.* pentear
combination *n.* combinação *f*
come *v.* vir
comfortable *adj.* confortável *mf*
comforter *n.* acolchoado *m*
comma *n.* vírgula *f*
comment *n.* comentário *m*
commission *n.* comissão *f*
committee *n.* comitê *m*
common *adj.* comum *mf*
communicate *v.* comunicar
communication *n.* comunicação *f*
company *n.* companhia *f*
compare *v.* comparar
comparison *n.* comparação *f*

compartment *n.*
compartimento *m*

compass *n.* bússola *f*

compensate *v.* compensar

competence *n.*
competência *f*

competition *n.*
competição *f*

complain *v.* queixar

complaint *n.* queixa *f*

complete *adj.* completo(a)
m(f); v. completar

completion *n.* conclusão *f*

complicate *v.* complicar

compliment *n.* elogio *m;*
v. elogiar

comply *v.* cumprir

compose *v.* compor

composition *n.*
composição *f*

comprehensive *adj.*
detalhado(a) *m(f)*

computer *n.* computador *m*

concern *n.* interesse *m*

concert *n.* concerto *m*

concrete *n.* concreto *m;*
adj. concreto(a) *m(f)*

condemn *v.* condenar

condition *n.* condição *f*

condolences *n.*
condolências *f*

condom *n.* camisinha *f*

conductor *n.* condutor(~a)
m(f)

confess *v.* confessar

confession *n.* confissão *f*

confidence *n.* confiança *f*

confirm *v.* confirmar

conflict *n.* conflito *m;*
v. conflitar

confuse *v.* confundir

congratulate *v.* felicitar

congratulations *n.*
felicitações *f.pl*

connect *v.* conectar

connection *n.* conexão *f*

conscious *adj.* consciente
mf

consequence *n.*
conseqüência *f*

conserve *v.* conservar

consider *v.* considerar

consonant *n.* consoante *f*

constipation *n.* prisão de
ventre *f*

consul *n.* cônsul *m,*
consulesa *f*

consulate *n.* consulado *m*

contact *n.* contato *m;*
v. contatar

contact lenses *n.* lentes de
contato *f*

contagious *adj.*
contagioso(a) *m(f)*

contain *v.* conter

container *n.* recipiente *m*

contaminate *v.* contaminar

contempt *n.* desprezo *m*

content *adj.* contente *mf;*
n. conteúdo *m*

continent *n.* continente *m*

continue *v.* continuar

contraceptive *n.*
contraceptivo *m;*
adj. contraceptivo(a)
m(f)

contract *n.* contrato *m;*
v. contratar

contrary *n.* contrário *m;*
adj. contrário(a) *m(f)*

control *n.* controle *m;*
v. controlar

convent *n.* convento *m*

conversation *n.*
conversação *f*

convert *n.* convertido(a)
m(f); v. converter

convertible *adj.* conversível *mf*

convince *v.* convencer

cook *n.* cozinheiro(a) *m(f);* *v.* cozinhar

cooker *n.* fogão *m*

cool *adj.* fresco(a) *m(f);* *v.* esfriar

copy *n.* cópia *f; v.* copiar

cord *n.* fio *m,* cabo *m*

cordless *adj.* sem fio *m*

core *n.* núcleo *m*

cork *n.* rolha *f*

corner *n.* canto *m*

corpse *n.* cadáver *m*

correct *adj.* correto(a) *m(f);* *v.* corrigir

correction *n.* correção *f*

correspondence *n.* correspondência *f*

cost *n.* custo *m; v.* custar

cot *n.* cama de campanha *f*

cotton *n.* algodão *m*

couch *n.* sofá *m*

cough *n.* tosse *f; v.* tossir

count *n.* contagem *f;* *v.* contar

counter *n.* balcão *m*

country *n.* país *m*

couple *n.* casal *m,* par *m*

course *n.* curso *m*

court *n.* corte *m*

courtyard *n.* pátio *m*

cousin *n.* primo(a) *m(f)*

cover *n.* tampa *f*

cow *n.* vaca *f*

crack *n.* racho *m; v.* quebrar

cradle *n.* berço *m*

craft *n.* ofício *m*

craftsman *n.* artesão *m,* artesã *f*

crash *n.* estrondo *m;* *v.* colidir

crawl *v.* rastejar

crazy *adj.* louco(a) *m(f)*

cream *n.* creme *m*

create *v.* criar

credit card *n.* cartão de crédito *m*

crew *n.* tripulação *f*

crime *n.* crime *m*

criticism *n.* crítica *f*

criticize *v.* criticar

croft *n.* chácara *f*

crop *n.* safra *f*

cross *n.* cruz *f; v.* atravessar

crossing *n.* cruzamento *m*

crossword *n.* palavras cruzadas *f.pl*

crowd *n.* multidão *f*

cruise *n.* cruzeiro *m;* *v.* cruzar

crumb *n.* migalha *f*

crumble *v.* esmigalhar

crust *n.* crosta *f*

crutch *n.* muleta *f*

cry *n.* grito *m,* choro *m;* *v.* gritar, chorar

cuddle *v.* abraçar, acariciar

cuff *n.* punho *m*

culture *n.* cultura *f*

cup *n.* xícara *f*

cupboard *n.* armário *m*

cure *n.* cura *f; v.* curar

curious *adj.* curioso(a) *m(f)*

curl *n.* caracol *m; v.* enrolar

currency *n.* moeda corrente *f*

current *adj.* corrente *mf*

curtain *n.* cortina *f*

curve *n.* curva *f; v.* torcer

cushion *n.* almofada *f*

custom *n.* costume *m*

customer *n.* cliente *mf*

customs *n.* alfândega *f*

cut *n.* corte *m; v.* cortar

cute *adj.* bonitinho(a) *m(f),* gracinha *mf*

D

dad *n.* papai *m*

daily *adj.* diário(a) *m(f);*
adv. diariamente

dairy *n.* leiteria *f,*
lacticínios *m*

damage *n.* danos *m;*
v. danificar

damp *n.* umidade *f;*
adj. úmido(a) *m(f)*

dance *n.* dança *f; v.* dançar

dance club *n.* clube de
dança *m*

danger *n.* perigo *m*

dangerous *adj.* perigoso(a)
m(f)

dare *v.* ousar

dark *adj.* escuro(a) *m(f)*

darkness *n.* escuridão *f*

date[1] *n.* data *f,* tâmara *f*

date[2] *v.* datar, namorar

daughter *n.* filha *f*

daughter-in-law *n.* nora *f*

dawn *n.* alvorecer *m*

day *n.* dia *m*

daylight *n.* luz do dia *f*

dead *adj.* morto(a) *m(f)*

deadly *adj.* mortal *mf*

deaf *adj.* surdo(a) *m(f)*

deafness *n.* surdez *f*

deal *n.* negócio *m,* acordo *m*

dealer *n.* negociante *mf*

dean *n.* decano *m*

dear *adj.* caro(a) *m(f)*

death *n.* morte *f*

debt *n.* débito *m*

decade *n.* década *f*

decaffeinated *adj.*
descafeinado(a) *m(f)*

decay *n.* decadência *f*

decease *n.* falecimento *m*

deceit *n.* engano *m*

deceive *v.* enganar

December *n.* dezembro *m*

decency *n.* decência *f*

decentralization *n.*
descentralização *f*

deception *n.* engano *m,*
decepção *f*

decimal *adj.* decimal *m*

decimate *v.* dizimar

decision *n.* decisão *f*

deck *n.* plataforma *f*

declare *v.* declarar

decline *n.* declínio *m;*
v. recusar

decode *v.* decodificar

decorate *v.* decorar

decoration *n.* decoração *f*

decrease *n.* diminuição *f;*
v. diminuir

dedicate *v.* dedicar

dedication *n.* dedicação *f*

deed *n.* escritura *f,* feito *m*

deep *adj.* profundo(a) *m(f)*

default *v.* faltar, estar
ausente

defeat *n.* derrota *f*

defect *n.* defeito *m*

defend *v.* defender

defense *n.* defesa *f*

definition *n.* definição *f*

deflate *v.* esvaziar

defuse *v.* desarmar

degree *n.* grau *m*

dehydration *n.*
desidratação *f*

delay *n.* atraso *m; v.* atrasar

delete *v.* suprimir

delight *n.* prazer *m,*
deleite *m*

delicious *adj.* delicioso(a)
m(f)

deliver *v.* entregar

delivery *n.* entrega *f*

demand *n.* demanda *f;*
v. demandar

democracy *n.* democracia *f*

demonstration n. demonstração f

dent n. racho m; v. dentear

dentist n. dentista mf

deny v. negar

deodorant n. desodorante m

departure n. partida f

depend v. depender

depict v. retratar

depleted adj. depauperado(a) m(f)

deplore v. deplorar

deploy v. dispor, instalar

deport v. deportar

deposit n. depósito m; v. depositar

depression n. depressão f

depth n. profundidade f

deregulate v. liberar

descend v. descer

descent n. descida f

describe v. descrever

description n. descrição f

desert n. deserto m; v. desertar

deserve v. merecer

desire n. desejo m; v. desejar

desk n. mesa f

despise v. desprezar

despite prep. apesar de

dessert n. sobremesa f

destination n. destinação f, destino m

destine v. destinar

destroy v. destruir

detach v. separar

detail n. detalhe m; v. detalhar

detect v. detectar, descobrir

detective n. detetive mf

detour n. desvio m

develop v. desenvolver

devil n. diabo(a) m(f)

dew n. orvalho m

diabetes n. diabete f

diagnosis n. diagnóstico m

diagonal n. diagonal f

dial v. discar

dialect n. dialeto m

dialogue n. diálogo m

diamond n. diamante m

diaper n. fralda f

diary n. diário m

dictionary n. dicionário m

die n. dado m; v. morrer

diet n. dieta f

difference n. diferença f

different adj. diferente mf

difficult adj. difícil mf

difficulty n. dificuldade f

digest n. resumo m; v. digerir

digestion n. digestão f

digital adj. digital mf

dimension n. dimensão f

dining room n. sala de jantar f

dinner n. jantar m

diplomacy n. diplomacia f

direct adj. direto(a) m(f)

direction n. sentido m

director n. diretor(~a) m(f)

dirt n. sujeira f

dirty adj. sujo(a) m(f)

disable v. incapacitar

disadvantage n. desvantagem f

disagree v. discordar

disagreement n. desacordo m

disallow v. banir, anular

disappear v. desaparecer

disappointment n. decepção f

disarm v. desarmar

disarray n. desordem f

disaster *n.* desastre *m*

discharge *n.* descarga *f;* *v.* descarregar

discipline *n.* disciplina *f*

disconnect *v.* cortar, apagar

discount *n.* desconto *m*

discover *v.* descobrir

discreet *adj.* discreto(a) *m(f)*

discuss *v.* discutir

discussion *n.* discussão *f*

disease *n.* doença *f*

disembark *v.* desembarcar

disgust *n.* aversão *f*

dish *n.* prato *m*

dishwasher *n.* máquina de lavar *f*

disk *n.* disco *m*

dislike *n.* desagrado *m*

dislodge *v.* desalojar

dismiss *v.* despedir, descartar

disobey *v.* desobedecer

disown *v.* repudiar

dispatch *n.* remessa *f;* *v.* despachar

display *n.* exposição *f;* *v.* exibir

disposable *adj.* descartável *mf*

distance *n.* distância *f*

distinct *adj.* distinto(a) *m(f)*

distinguish *v.* distinguir

distract *v.* distrair

distribute *v.* distribuir

distribution *n.* distribuição *f*

disturb *v.* perturbar

ditch *n.* vala *f*

dive *n.* mergulho *m;* *v.* mergulhar

diver *n.* mergulhador(~a) *m(f)*

divide *v.* dividir

divorce *n.* divórcio *m;* *v.* divorciar

do *v.* fazer

doctor *n.* doutor(~a) *m(f)*

dodgy *adj.* arriscado(a) *m(f)*

dog *n.* cachorro *m*

doll *n.* boneca *f*

dollar *n.* dólar *m*

domain *n.* domínio *m*

donkey *n.* burro *m*

door *n.* porta *f*

dormitory *n.* dormitório *m*

dose *n.* dose *f*

dot *n.* ponto *m*

double *n.* sósia *mf,* dobro *m; v.* dobrar

doubt *n.* dúvida *f; v.* duvidar

dough *n.* massa de farinha *f*

down *prep.* por, abaixo; *adv.* abaixo, para baixo

dozen *n.* dúzia *f*

draft *n.* rascunho *m*

drama *n.* drama *m*

draw *v.* puxar, desenhar

drawing *n.* desenho *m*

dream *n.* sonho *m; v.* sonhar

dress *n.* vestido *m; v.* vestir

drink *n.* bebida *f; v.* beber

drip *n.* gota *f; v.* gotejar

drive¹ *n.* energia *f,* peça de computador *f*

drive² *v.* dirigir carro, mover

driver *n.* motorista *mf*

driver's license *n.* carteira de motorista *f*

drop *n.* gota *f,* queda *f; v.* cair

drown *v.* afogar

drug *n.* droga *f*

drunk *adj.* bêbado(a) *m(f)*

dry *adj.* seco(a) *m(f);*
  v. secar
dryer *n.* secador *m*
duck *n.* pato(a) *m(f)*
due *adj.* devido(a) *m(f)*
dull *adj.* aborrecido(a) *m(f);*
  enfadonho(a) *m(f)*
duly *adv.* devidamente
dumb *adj.* mudo(a) *m(f)*
dump *n.* depósito de lixo *m*
during *prep.* durante
dusk *n.* anoitecer *m*
dust *n.* poeira *f*
duty *n.* dever *m*, imposto *m*
dwarf *n.* anão *m*, anã *f*
dwell *v.* morar
dye *n.* tintura *f; v.* tingir

E

each *adj.* cada; *pron.* cada
  um(a) *m(f)*
eager *adj.* entusiasmado(a)
  m(f), desejoso *(a) m(f)*
ear *n.* orelha *f*
early *adv.* cedo
earn *v.* ganhar
earnings *n.* salário *m*
earring *n.* brinco *m*
earth *n.* terra *f*
earthquake *n.* terremoto *m*
ease *n.* sossego *m;*
  v. acalmar
easily *adv.* facilmente
east *n.* leste *m*
Easter *n.* Páscoa *f*
easy *adj.* fácil *mf*
eat *v.* comer
ebb tide *n.* maré baixa *f*
economy *n.* economia *f*
edge *n.* borda *f*
edition *n.* edição *f*
education *n.* educação *f*
effective *adj.* eficaz *mf*

effort *n.* esforço *m*
egg *n.* ovo *m*
eight *num.* oito
either *adj.* qualquer um(a)
  m(f)
elastic *n.* elástico *m;*
  adj. elástico(a) *m(f)*
elbow *n.* cotovelo *m*
elder *adj.* mais velho(a)
  m(f)
election *n.* eleição *f*
electric *adj.* elétrico(a) *m(f)*
electrician *n.* eletricista *m*
electricity *n.* eletricidade *f*
elegant *adj.* elegante *mf*
elevator *n.* elevador *m*
eleven *num.* onze
else *adv.* mais
E-mail *n.* E-mail *m*
embarrass *v.* constranger
embassy *n.* embaixada *f*
emergency *n.* emergência *f*
emigrate *v.* emigrar
employee *n.* empregado(a)
  m(f)
employer *n.*
  empregador(~a) *m(f)*
employment *n.* emprego *m*
empty *adj.* vazio(a) *m(f);*
  v. esvaziar
enclose *v.* incluir
enclosure *n.* anexo(a) *m(f),*
  terreno cercado *m*
encounter *n.* encontro *m;*
  v. encontrar
encyclopedia *n.*
  enciclopédia *f*
end *n.* fim *m; v.* acabar
endless *adj.* infinito(a) *m(f)*
endorse *v.* endossar
endow *v.* dotar
enemy *n.* inimigo(a) *m(f)*
energetic *adj.* energético(a)
  m(f)

energy *n.* energia *f*

engagement *n.* compromisso *m*

engine *n.* motor *m*

engineer *n.* engenheiro(a) *m(f)*

England *n.* Inglaterra *f*

English *n; adj.* inglês *m,* inglesa *f*

engrave *v.* gravar

engraving *n.* gravação *f*

enjoy *v.* gozar

enlarge *v.* aumentar

enormous *adj.* enorme *mf*

enough *adj.; pron; adv.* bastante

enter *v.* entrar

entertain *v.* entreter

enthusiasm *n.* entusiasmo *m*

entire *adj.* inteiro(a) *m(f)*

entrance *n.* entrada *f*

envelope *n.* envelope *m*

environment *n.* ambiente *m*

envoy *n.* enviado(a) *m(f)*

envy *n.* inveja *f; v.* invejar

epidemic *n.* epidemia *f*

equal *adj.* igual *mf; v.* igualar

equality *n.* igualdade *f*

equipment *n.* equipamento *m*

equivalent *n; adj.* equivalente *mf*

era *n.* era *f*

erase *v.* apagar

error *n.* erro *m*

escalator *n.* escada rolante *f*

escape *n.* fuga *f; v.* escapar

escort *n.* escolta *f; v.* escoltar

especially *adv.* especialmente

essential *adj.* essencial *mf*

essentially *adv.* essencialmente

establish *v.* estabelecer

establishment *n.* estabelecimento *m*

estate *n.* patrimônio *m*

estimate *n.* estimativa *f; v.* avaliar

eternal *adj.* eterno(a) *m(f)*

euro *n.* euro *m*

Europe *n.* Europa *f*

European *n.; adj.* europeu *m,* européia *f*

European Union *n.* União Européia *f*

evacuate *v.* evacuar

evade *v.* evadir

evaluate *v.* avaliar

eve *n.* véspera *f*

even *adj.* plano(a) *m(f),* igual *mf; adv.* até, mesmo

evening *n.* noite *f*

event *n.* evento *m*

ever *adv.* sempre

every *adj.* cada *mf*

everybody *pron.* todos(as) *m.pl(f.pl),* todo mundo (collective)

everyday *adj.* todo dia *m*

evidence *n.* evidência *f*

exact *adj.* exato(a) *m(f)*

exaggerate *v.* exagerar

examination *n.* exame *m*

examine *v.* examinar

example *n.* exemplo *m*

exceed *v.* exceder

excellent *adj.* excelente *mf*

except *prep.* exceto; *v.* excetuar

exception *n.* exceção *f*

excess *n.* excesso *m*

exchange *n.* troca *f,*
câmbio *m; v.* trocar

exchange rate *n.* taxa de
câmbio *f*

excite *v.* excitar

excitement *n.* excitação *f*

exclude *v.* excluir

excursion *n.* excursão *f*

excuse *n.* desculpa *f;*
v. desculpar

execute *v.* executar

exercise *n.* exercício *m;*
v. exercitar

exhaust *n.* exaustor *m;*
v. esgotar

exhausted *adj.* esgotado(a)
m(f), cansado(a) *m(f)*

exhibit *v.* exibir

exhibition *n.* exibição *f*

exile *n.* exílio *m;*
adj. exilado(a) *m(f);*
v. exilar

exist *v.* existir

existence *n.* existência *f*

exit *n.* saída *f; v.* sair

expect *v.* esperar

expectation *n.* expectativa *f*

expel *v.* expulsar

expense *n.* despesa *f*

expensive *adj.* caro(a) *m(f)*

experience *n.* experiência *f*

expert *n; adj.* perito(a) *m(f)*

expire *v.* expirar

explain *v.* explicar

explanation *n.* explicação *f*

explosion *n.* explosão *f*

export *n.* exportação *f;*
v. exportar

expose *v.* expor

express *adj.* expresso(a)
m(f)

expulsion *n.* expulsão *f*

exquisite *adj.*
requintado(a) *m(f)*

extend *v.* prolongar

extension *n.* extensão *f*

external *adj.* externo(a)
m(f)

extinguisher *n.* extintor *m*

extract *n.* extrato *m;*
v. extrair

extraordinary *adj.*
extraordinário(a) *m(f)*

extreme *adj.* extremo(a)
m(f)

eye *n.* olho *m*

eyebrow *n.* sobrancelha *f*

eyelash *n.* cílio *m*

eyelid *n.* pálpebra *f*

F

fabric *n.* tecido *m*

fabricate *v.* inventar

façade/facade *n.* fachada *f*

face *n.* face *f*

face-lift *n.* cirurgia plástica
da face *f*

facetious *adj.*
zombeteiro(a) *m(f),*
irônico(a) *m(f)*

facile *adj.* simplório(a) *m(f)*

fact *n.* fato *m*

factory *n.* fábrica *f*

fad *n.* moda passageira *f*

fade *v.* apagar, desbotar

fail *v.* falhar

failure *n.* falha *f*

faint *n.* desmaio *m;*
adj. fraco(a) m*(f);*
v. desmaiar

fair *n.* feira *(f); adj.* justo(a)
m(f), claro(a) *m(f)*

faith *n.* fé *f*

faithful *adj.* fiel *mf*

fake n. falsificação f;
   adj. falso(a) m(f);
   v. fingir
fall n. queda f; v. cair
false adj. falso(a) m(f)
family n. família f
famous adj. famoso(a) m(f)
fan n. ventilador m, fã mf
far adv; adj. distante
farce n. farsa f
farm n. fazenda f
farmer n. fazendeiro(a)
   m(f)
fashion n. moda f
fast¹ n. jejum m; v. jejuar
fast² adv. depressa;
   adj. rápido(a) m(f)
fasten v. prender
fat n. gordura f;
   adj. gordo(a) m(f)
fate n. destino m
father n. pai m
father-in-law n. sogro m
faucet n. torneira f
fault n. falta f
favor n. favor m
favorite n; adj. favorito(a)
   m(f)
fear n. medo m, temor m;
   v. temer
feather n. pena f
February n. fevereiro m
fee n. taxa f, honorários
   m.pl
feed n. ração f; v. alimentar
feel n. sensação f; v. sentir
feeling n. sentimento m
fellow n. companheiro(a)
   m(f)
female n. fêmea f;
   adj. feminino(a) m(f)
fence n. cerca f
fend v. defender
ferry n. balsa f

feud n. inimizade f, briga f
fever n. febre f
few pron.; adj. poucos(as)
   m.pl(f.pl)
fiancé (ée) n. noivo(a) m(f)
fib n. mentira f
fiber n. fibra f
fiddle n. violino m;
   v. trapacear
field n. campo m
fight n. luta f; v. lutar
figure n. figura f; v. supor,
   imaginar
file n. arquivo m
fill v. encher
film n. filme m
filter n. filtro m; v. filtrar
filthy adj. imundo(a) m(f)
final adj. final mf
financial adj. financeiro(a)
   m(f)
find v. achar
finding n. achados m.pl
fine n. multa f; adj. bom m,
   boa f; adv. muito bem
finger n. dedo m
fingerprint n. impressão
   digital f
finish v. terminar
fire n. fogo m; v. incendiar
fireman n. bombeiro m
fireplace n. lareira f
fireworks n. fogos de
   artifício m.pl
firm n. firma comercial f;
   adj. firme mf
first n.; adj. primeiro(a)
   m(f); adv. primeiro
fiscal adj. fiscal mf
fish n. peixe m; v. pescar
fisherman n. pescador m
fist n. punho m
fit adj. adequado(a) m(f);
   v. ajustar

five *num.* cinco
fix *v.* consertar, arrumar
fixed assets *n.* ativo fixo *m*
fizz *v.* borbulhar, efervescer
flag *n.* bandeira *f*
flake *n.* floco *m*, lasca *f*
flame *n.* chama *f*
flank *n.* flanco *m*, lado *m*
flare *n.* chama *f; v.* inflamar
flash *n.* flash *m*, lampejo *m;*
    v. brilhar
flashlight *n.* lanterna
    elétrica *f*
flat *adj.* liso(a) *m(f)*
flatter *v.* lisonjear
flavor *n.* sabor *m*
flea *n.* pulga *f*
flea market *n.* brechó *m*
flee *v.* fugir
flight *n.* vôo *m*, fuga *f*
flight attendant *n.*
    comissário(a) de bordo
    m(f)
flirt *n.* flerte *m; v.* flertar
float *v.* flutuar
flood *n.* inundação *f;*
    v. inundar
floor *n.* chão *m*
flop *n.* fracasso *m;*
    v. fracassar
florist *n.* florista *f*
flour *n.* farinha *f*
flow *n.* fluxo *m*
flower *n.* flor *f*
flu *n.* gripe *f*
fluent *adj.* fluente *mf*
fluffy *adj.* macio(a) *m(f)*,
    fofo(a) *m(f)*
fly *n.* mosca *f; v.* voar
fog *n.* névoa *f*
fold *n.* dobra *f; v.* dobrar
folk *n.* povo *m;*
    adj. popular *mf*
follow *v.* acompanhar

folly *n.* bobagem *f*,
    loucura *f*
food *n.* comida *f*
fool *n; adj.* bobo(a) *m(f)*,
    tolo(a) *m(f)*
foot *n.* pé *m*
football/soccer *n.* futebol *m*
for *prep; conj.* para
forbid *v.* proibir
force *n.* força *f; v.* forçar
fore *pref.* ante-, na frente
forearm *n.* antebraço *m*
forefinger *n.* dedo
    indicador *m*
forehead *n.* testa *f*
foreign *adj.* estrangeiro *m*
foreigner *n.* estrangeiro(a)
    m(f)
forest *n.* floresta *f*
forever *adv.* para sempre
forget *v.* esquecer
forgive *v.* perdoar
fork *n.* garfo *m*
form *n.* formulário *m;*
    v. formar
formal *adj.* formal *mf*
former *adj.* anterior *mf*
formula *n.* fórmula *f*
forward *adj.; adv.* para
    frente; *v.* encaminhar
foundation *n.* fundação *f*
fountain *n.* fonte *f*
four *num.* quatro
fragile *adj.* frágil *mf*
frail *adj.* fraco(a) *m(f)*
frame *n.* moldura *f*
France *n.* França *f*
franchise *n.* franquia *f*
fraud *n.* fraude *f*
free *adj.* livre *mf*, grátis *mf*
freedom *n.* liberdade *f*
freeze *v.* congelar
freezer *n.* congelador *m*

French *n.; adj.* francês *m,* francesa *f*
frequent *adj.* freqüente *mf*
fresh *adj.* fresco(a) *m(f)*
friction *n.* fricção *f*
Friday *n.* sexta-feira *f*
friend *n.* amigo(a) *m(f)*
friendly *adj.* amigável *mf*
friendship *n.* amizade *f*
fright *n.* susto *m; v.* assustar
frog *n.* rã *f*
from *prep.* de
front *n; adj.* parte dianteira *f*
frost *n.* geada *f*
frozen *adj.* congelado(a) *m(f)*
fruit *n.* fruta *f*
fry *v.* fritar
frying pan *n.* frigideira *f*
fuel *n.* combustível *m*
full *adj.* cheio(a) *m(f)*
full-time *adj.* tempo integral
fume *n.* fumaça *f; v.* fumegar
fun *n.* divertimento *m*
funeral *n.* funeral *m*
funnel *n.* funil *m*
funny *adj.* engraçado(a) *m(f)*
fur *n.* pele *f*
furniture *n.* móveis *m.pl,* mobília *f*
fuse *n.* fusível *m*
fussy *adj.* exigente *mf,* complicado(a) *m(f)*
future *n.* futuro *m; adj.* futuro(a) *m(f)*

G

gag[1] *n.* piada *f,* mordaça *f,* censura *f*
gag[2] *v.* censurar, calar

gain *n.* ganho *m; v.* ganhar
gait *n.* modo de andar *m*
gale *n.* ventania *f*
gallery *n.* galeria *f*
gallon *n.* galão *m*
gamble *v.* apostar
game *n.* jogo *m*
gang *n.* bando *m*
gap *n.* abertura *f*
garage *n.* garagem *f*
garbage *n.* lixo *m*
garden *n.* jardim *m*
gardener *n.* jardineiro(a) *m(f)*
garlic *n.* alho *m*
gas *n.* gás *m,* gasolina *f*
gasp *n.* falta de ar *f; v.* afogar
gate *n.* portão *m*
gather *v.* recolher, ajuntar
gauge *n.* medida *f,* tamanho *m*
gay *adj.* gay *m; alegre mf*
gaze *n.* olhar fixo *m; v.* fitar
gear *n.* equipamento *m,* marcha de carro *f*
general *n.* geral *m,* general *m*
gentle *adj.* suave *mf,* amável *mf*
geography *n.* geografia *f*
germ *n.* germe *m,* micróbio *m*
German *n; adj.* alemão *m,* alemã *f*
Germany *n.* Alemanha *f*
gesture *n.* gesto *m*
get *v.* receber, obter
ghost *n.* espírito *m,* fantasma *m*
giant *n.* gigante *mf*
gift *n.* presente *m*
girl *n.* menina *f,* moça *f*
girlfriend *n.* namorada *f*

give *v.* dar
glad *adj.* contente *mf*
glance *n.* relance *m;*
   v. olhar
glare *n.* brilho *m; v.* brilhar
glass *n.* vidro *m*, copo *m*
glasses *n.* óculos *m*
glaze *n.* vidro *m;*
   v. envidraçar
glove *n.* luva *f*
gloom *n.* tristeza *f*
glue *n.* cola *f; v.* colar
go *v.* ir
goal *n.* objetivo(a) *m(f)*
goat *n.* cabra *f*
God *n.* Deus *m*
goddaughter *n.* afilhada *f*
godfather *n.* padrinho *m*
godmother *n.* madrinha *f*
gods *n.* mercadoria *f*
godson *n.* afilhado *m*
gold *n.* ouro *m*
good *adj.* bom *m*, boa *f*
good-bye! *interj.* tchau!
   Adeus!
goose *n.* ganso *m*
gory *adj.* sangrento(a) *m(f)*
gossip *n.* boato *m;*
   v. fofocar
government *n.* governo *m*
gown *n.* roupão *m*
grab *v.* agarrar
grade *n.* grau *m; v.* graduar
graduate *n.* graduado(a)
   m(f); v. formar-se
graft *n.* enxerto *m;*
   v. enxertar
grain *n.* grão *m*, cereal *m*
gram *n.* grama *m* (peso)
grammar *n.* gramática *f*
grandchildren *n.* netos
   mf.pl
granddaughter *n.* neta *f*
grandfather *n.* avô *m*

grandmother *n.* avó *f*
grandparents *n.* avós *pl*
grandson *n.* neto *m*
grant[1] *n.* subsídio *m*, bolsa
   de estudo *f*
grant[2] *v.* conceder
grape *n.* uva *f*
grasp *n.* alcance *m;*
   v. entender
grass *n.* grama *f*
grave *n.* sepultura *f*
gravel *n.* pedregulho *m*
gravestone *n.* lápide *f*
graveyard *n.* cemitério *m*
gray *adj.* cinzento(a) *m(f)*
grease *n.* graxa *f*, gordura *f*
great *adj.* grande *mf*
Great Britain *n.* Grã
   Bretanha *f*
great-grandfather *n.*
   bisavô *m*
great-grandmother *n.*
   bisavó *f*
greed *n.* ganância *f*
green *adj.* verde *mf*
greet *v.* cumprimentar
grid *n.* grade *f*
grief *n.* pesar *m*, tristeza *f*
grill *n.* grelha *f*
grin *n.* riso sardônico *m*
grind *v.* triturar
grit *n.* grão de areia *m*
grocer *n.* dono(a) de
   mercearia *m(f)*
groceries *n.* mantimentos
   m.pl
grocery store *n.* mercearia *f*
groin *n.* virilha *f*
groom *n.* noivo *m*
gross *adj.* grosso(a) *m(f)*,
   bruto(a) *m(f)*
ground *n.* solo *m*, terra *f*
group *n.* grupo *m;*
   v. agrupar

grow *v.* crescer
grown-up *n.* adulto(a) *m(f)*
growth *n.* crescimento *m*
guarantee *n.* garantia *f;*
   v. garantir
guard *n.* protetor(~a) *m(f);*
   v. proteger
guess *n.* suposição *f;*
   v. supor
guest *n.* convidado(a) *m(f)*
guesthouse *n.* pensão *f,*
   albergue *m*
guide *n.* guia *mf; v.* orientar
guild *n.* grêmio *m*
guilt *n.* culpa *f*
guilty *adj.* culpado(a) *m(f)*
gum *n.* gengiva *f,* goma *f*
gun *n.* injetor *m,* arma de
   fogo *f*
gush *n.* jorro *m; v.* jorrar
gust *n.* rajada *f*
gut *n.* intestino *m*
gutter *n.* calha *f*
guy *n.* rapaz *m*
gynecologist *n.*
   ginecologista *mf*

H
habit *n.* costume *m,*
   hábito *m*
hack *n.* corte *m; v.* cortar
haggle *v.* pechinchar,
   regatear
hail *n.* granizo *m; v.* saudar
hair *n.* cabelo *m*
haircut *n.* corte de
   cabelo *m*
hairdresser *n.*
   cabelereiro(a) *m(f)*
hairspray *n.* fixador para
   cabelo *m*
half[1] *n.* metade *f;*
   adj. meio(a) *m(f)*

half[2] *v.* reduzir pela metade
hall *n.* salão *m*
ham *n.* presunto *m*
hammer *n.* martelo *m;*
   v. martelar
hand *n.* mão *f*
handful *n.* punhado *m*
handicap[1] *n.* incapacidade
   f, desvantagem *f*
handicap[2] *v.* prejudicar
handkerchief *n.* lenço *m*
handle *n.* alça *f,* maçaneta *f*
handout *n.* esmola *f,*
   doação *f*
handshake *n.* aperto de
   mão *m*
handy *adj.* prático(a) *m(f),*
   conveniente *mf*
hang *v.* pendurar
hanger *n.* cabide *m*
hangover *n.* ressaca *f*
hapless *adj.* azarado(a)
   m(f)
happen *v.* acontecer
happiness *n.* felicidade *f*
happy *adj.* feliz *mf*
harass *v.* perturbar,
   interferir
harassment *n.*
   perseguição *f*
harbor *n.* porto *m*
hard *adj.* duro(a) *m(f)*
harden *v.* endurecer
hardship *n.* sofrimento *m,*
   pobreza *f*
hardware *n.* maquinário m
harm *n.* dano *m;*
   v. machucar, prejudicar
harness *n.* arreio *m*
harsh *adj.* duro(a) *m(f),*
   severo(a) *m(f)*
harvest *n.* colheita *f,* safra *f*
hassle *n.* complicação *f;*
   v. complicar

hat *n.* chapéu *m*
hate *n.* ódio *m; v.* odiar
haunted *adj.* mal-
assombrado(a) *m(f)*
have *v.* ter
havoc *n.* destruição *f*
hawker *n.* camelô *mf,*
mascate *mf*
hawk *n.* falcão *m*
hay *n.* feno *m*
hay fever *n.* febre do feno *f*
hazard *n.* risco *m,* perigo
m, acaso *m*
hazy *adj.* nublado(a) *m(f)*
he *pron.* ele *m*
head *n.* cabeça *f*
headache *n.* dor de
cabeça *f*
headlight *n.* farol alto *m*
headline *n.* manchete *f*
headquarters *n.* matriz *f,*
quartel general *m*
heal *v.* curar, cicatrizar
health *n.* saúde *f*
healthy *adj.* saudável *mf*
heap *n.* monte *m,* pilha *f*
hear *v.* ouvir
hearing *n.* audição *f*
heart *n.* coração *m*
heat *n.* calor *m;*
v. esquentar
heater *n.* aquecedor *m*
heaven *n.* céu *m*
heavy *adj.* pesado(a) *m(f)*
hectic *adj.* confuso(a) *m(f),*
agitado(a) *m(f)*
heel *n.* calcanhar *m,*
salto *m*
height *n.* altura *f*
heir *n.* herdeiro(a) *m(f)*
helicopter *n.* helicóptero *m*
hell *n.* inferno *m*
hello! *interj.* olá!
helmet *n.* capacete *m*

help *n.* ajuda *f; v.* ajudar
hem *n.* bainha *f*
hen *n.* galinha *f*
hence *adv.* portanto, daí
henceforth *adv.* daqui prá
frente
her *pron.* ela *f,* dela *f*
herb *n.* erva *f*
here *adv.* aqui
herewith *adv.* em anexo,
junto
heroin *n.* heroína *f*
hers *pron.* a dela *f*
hesitate *v.* hesitar
heyday *n.* apogeu *m*
hi! *interj.* oi!
hiccough/hiccup *n.* soluço
m, problema *f;*
v. soluçar
hide *v.* esconder
hiding *n.* surra *f*
high *adj.* alto(a) *m(f),*
grande *mf,*
elevado(a) *m(f)*
highbrow *adj.* intelectual
mf
high school *n.* escola de
curso médio *f*
highway *n.* auto-estrada *f*
hijack *n.* seqüestro *m;*
v. seqüestrar
hike *n.* carona *m;*
v. caminhar
hill *n.* colina *f*
him *pron.* ele *m,* o *m*
hip *n.* quadril *m*
hire *n.* aluguel *m; v.* alugar
his *pron.* dele *m*
historic *adj.* histórico(a)
m(f)
history *n.* história *f*
hit *n.* batida *f,* sucesso *m;*
v. bater
hitchhike *v.* pegar carona

hive *n.* colméia *f*

hoarse *adj.* rouco(a) *m(f)*

hoax *n.* brincadeira *f*, trote *m*

hob *n.* boca de fogão *f*

hold *v.* segurar

hole *n.* buraco *m*

holiday *n.* feriado *m*

holy *adj.* santo(a) *m(f)*, sagrado(a) *m(f)*

home *n.* lar *m*

homeland *n.* pátria *f*

homesickness *n.* saudades *f.pl*

homework *n.* lição de casa *f*

honey *n.* mel *m*

hood *n.* capa *f*

hook *n.* gancho *m; v.* fisgar

hoop *n.* arco *m*

hop *n.* lúpulo *m; v.* saltar

hope *n.* esperança *f; v.* esperar

hopeless *adj.* desesperado(a) *m(f)*

horn *n.* chifre *m*

horse *n.* cavalo *m*

hose *n.* mangueira *f*

hospital *n.* hospital *m*

hospitality *n.* hospitalidade *f*

host *n.* anfitrião *m*

hostage *n.* refém *mf*

hostel *n.* albergue *m*, hospedaria *f*

hostess *n.* anfitriã *f*

hot *adj.* quente *mf*

hotel *n.* hotel *m*

hour *n.* hora *f*

house *n.* casa *f; v.* abrigar

how *adv.* como

however *adv.* de todo modo; *conj.* contudo

hug *n.* abraço *m; v.* abraçar

huge *adj.* enorme *mf*, imenso(a) *m(f)*

hum *v.* cantarolar

human *adj.* humano(a) *m(f)*

humble *adj.* humilde *mf*

humid *adj.* úmido(a) *m(f)*

humor *n.* humor *m*

hunchback *n.* corcunda *f*

hundred *num.* cem

hunger *n.* fome *f*

hungry *adj.* faminto(a) *m(f)*

hunt *n.* caça *f; v.* caçar

hunter *n.* caçador(~a) *m(f)*

hurricane *n.* furacão *m*

hurry *n.* pressa *f*

hurt *v.* machucar, doer, magoar

husband *n.* marido *m*

hut *n.* cabana *f*

hygiene *n.* higiene *f*

hyphen *n.* hífen. *m*

I

I *pron.* eu

ice *n.* gelo *m*

ice cream *n.* sorvete *m*

ice cube *n.* cubo de gelo *m*

ice hockey *n.* hóquei sobre o gelo *m*

ice skate *n.* patim sobre o gelo *m*

icy *adj.* gelado(a) *m(f)*

idea *n.* idéia *f*

ideal *adj.* ideal *mf*

identical *adj.* idêntico(a) *m(f)*

identify *v.* identificar

identity *n.* identidade *f*

identity card *n.* carteira de identidade *f*

idiom *n.* idioma *f*, expressão idiomática *f*

idiot *n; adj.* idiota *mf*
idle¹ *adj.* preguiçoso(a)
   m(f), ocioso(a) *m(f)*
idle² *v.* ficar parado
i.e. *(abbrev.)* isto é, ou seja
if *conj.* se
ignition *n.* ignição *f*
ignore *v.* ignorar
ill *adj.* doente *mf; adv.* mal
illegal *adj.* ilegal *mf*
illness *n.* doença *f*
illustration *n.* ilustração *f*
image *n.* imagem *f*
imagination *n.*
   imaginação *f*
imagine *v.* imaginar
imitate *v.* imitar
immature *adj.* imaturo(a)
   m(f)
immediately *adv.*
   imediatamente
immense *adj.* imenso(a)
   m(f)
impartial *adj.* imparcial *mf*
impeach *v.* impugnar
imperfect *adj.*
   imperfeito(a) *m(f)*
imperil *v.* pôr em perigo
imply *v.* implicar, sugerir
import *n.* importação *f;*
   v. importar
importance *n.*
   importância *f*
important *adj.* importante
   mf
impose *v.* impor
impossible *adj.* impossível
   mf
impound *v.* confiscar
impoverish *v.* empobrecer
imprecise *adj.* impreciso(a)
   m(f), vago(a) *m(f)*
in *prep.* em, dentro de
inability *n.* incapacidade *f*

inadequacy *n.*
   insuficiência *f*
inappropriate *adj.*
   impróprio(a) *m(f)*
in-between *n;*
   adj. intermediário(a)
   m(f)
inception *n.* começo *m,*
   início *m*
inch *n.* polegada *f*
incident *n.* incidente *m*
incline *n.* inclinação *f;*
   v. inclinar
include *v.* incluir
income *n.* renda *f*
inconvenient *adj.*
   inconveniente *mf*
increase *n.* aumento *m;*
   v. aumentar
incur *v.* incorrer em
indeed *adv.* de fato,
   realmente
indemnity *n.* seguro *m,*
   indenização *f*
index *n.* índice *m*
indicate *v.* indicar
indict *v.* acusar
indifferent *adj.* indiferente
   mf
indigestion *n.* indigestão *f*
indirect *adj.* indireto(a)
   m(f)
indoors *adv.* em lugar
   fechado
induce *v.* induzir, causar
inducement *n.* incentivo *m*
indulge *v.* satisfazer
industry *n.* indústria *f*
inedible *adj.* não
   comestível *mf*
infant *n.* bebê *m*
infect *v.* infectar
infection *n.* infecção *f*
inferior *adj.* inferior *mf*

inferno *n.* fogo *m*, incêndio *m*

inflow *n.* afluência *f*

influence *n.* influência *f*

information *n.* informação *f*

inhabitant *n.* habitante *mf*

initial *adj.* inicial *mf*

initiate *v.* iniciar

inject *v.* injetar

injection *n.* injeção *f*

injure *v.* ferir

injury *n.* ferimento *m*

ink *n.* tinta *f*

inland *n.* interior *m*

in-laws *n.* parentes por casamento *m.pl*

innermost *adj.* mais íntimo(a) *m(f)*

inn *n.* albergue *m*, bar *m*

innocent *adj.* inocente *mf*, ingênuo(a) *m(f)*

input *n.* entrada *f*

inquire *v.* perguntar

inquiry *n.* pergunta *f*, inquérito *m*

insane *adj.* louco(a) *m(f)*

insect *n.* inseto *m*

insert *n.* folha solta *f*; *v.* introduzir

inside *n.* interior *m*; *adv.* dentro; *prep.* dentro de

insist *v.* insistir

insomnia *n.* insônia *f*

inspect *v.* inspecionar

inspector *n.* inspetor(~a) *m(f)*

install *v.* instalar

installation *n.* instalação *f*

instead of *adv.* em vez de

instrument *n.* instrumento *m*

insulate *v.* isolar

insulation *n.* isolamento *m*

insult *n.* insulto *m*; *v.* insultar

insurance *n.* seguro *m*

insure *v.* assegurar

intelligence *n.* inteligência *f*

interest *n.* interesse *m*; *v.* interessar

interesting *adj.* interessante *mf*

interior *n.* interior *m*; *adj.* interno(a) *m(f)*

international *adj.* internacional *mf*

Internet *n.* Internet *f*

interpret *v.* interpretar

intersection *n.* intersecção *f*

intervene *v.* intervir

intervention *n.* intervenção *f*

interview *n.* entrevista *f*

intestine *n.* intestino *m*

into *prep.* em, dentro de

intoxicated *adj.* intoxicado(a) *m(f)*, bêbado(a) *m(f)*

introduce *v.* introduzir

introduction *n.* introdução *f*

invent *v.* inventar

invention *n.* invenção *f*

investigate *v.* investigar

invitation *n.* convite *m*

invite *v.* convidar

invoice *n.* fatura *f*

involve *v.* implicar

inward *adj.* interno(a) *m(f)*, íntimo(a) *m(f)*

iron *n.* ferro *m*; *v.* passar a ferro

ironing board *n.* tábua de passar roupa *f*

Islam *n.* Islã *m*

island *n.* ilha *f*

isolate *v.* isolar

issue *n.* edição *f*, questão *f*

it *pron.* ele *m*, ela *f*
Italy *n.* Itália *f*
Italian *n; adj.* italiano(a) *m(f)*
itch *n.* coceira *f*
item *n.* item *m*
its *pron.* dele *m*, dela *f*

J

jab *n.* vacina *f*, injeção *f*
jack *n.* macaco de carro *m*
jacket *n.* paletó *m*
jackpot *n.* grande prêmio *m*, loto *f*
jagged *adj.* denteado(a) *m(f)*
jail *n.* cadeia *f; v.* prender
jam *n.* geléia *f*, engarrafamento de trânsito *m*
janitor *n.* zelador(~a) *m(f)*
January *n.* janeiro *m*
jar *n.* jarro *m*, frasco *m*
jaundice *n.* icterícia *f*
jaw *n.* queixo *m*, mandíbula *f*
jealous *adj.* ciumento(a) *m(f)*
jealousy *n.* ciúme *m*
jeans *n.* calça de brim *f*, jeans *m*
jeer *v.* vaiar
jelly *n.* geléia *f*, gelatina *f*
jellyfish *n.* água-viva *f*
jeopardize *v.* ameaçar
jeopardy *n.* ameaço *m*
jerk *n.* solavanco *m*, babaca *mf; v.* sacudir
jest *n.* brincadeira *f*
jet *n.* jato *m*
Jew *n.* judeu *m*, judia *f*
jewel *n.* jóia *f*
jeweler *n.* joalheiro *m*

jewelry *n.* joalheria *f*
Jewish *adj.* judeu *m*, judia *f*, judaico(a) *m(f)*
job *n.* emprego *m*, trabalho *m*
jog *v.* movimentar, jogar objeto
join *v.* juntar, afiliar
joint *n.* junta *f*, união *f*, conjunto *m*; *adj.* comum *mf*
joke *n.* piada *f; v.* gracejar
jolly *adj.* alegre *mf*
jolt *n.* sacudida *f*
journal *n.* diário *m*, revista *f*
journalist *n.* jornalista *mf*
journey *n.* viagem *f*, jornada *f*
joy *n.* alegria *f*
judge *n.* juiz(~a) *m(f)*; *v.* julgar
judgment *n.* decisão *f*, opinião *f*
jug *n.* jarro *m*
juggle *v.* equilibrar, fazer malabarismo
juice *n.* suco *m*
juicy *adj.* suculento(a) *m(f)*
July *n.* julho *m*
jumble *n.* mistura *f*, confusão *f*
jump *n.* salto *m; v.* pular
jumper cables *n.* cabo de ligação *m* (*fazer chupeta*)
jumpy *adj.* nervoso(a) *m(f)*
junction *n.* cruzamento de estrada *m*
June *n.* junho *m*
junk *n.* tranqueira *f*, lixo *m*
just *adj.* justo(a) *m(f)*; *adv.* apenas
justice *n.* justiça *f*

justify *v.* justificar
juvenile *n.* jovem *mf;*
   adj. juvenil *mf*

K

keen *adj.* entusiasmado(a)
   m(f), desejoso(a) *m(f)*
keep *v.* guardar, manter
keeper *n.* guardião *m,*
   guardiã *f*
keg *n.* barrilinho *m*
kernel *n.* semente *f*
kettle *n.* chaleira *f*
key *n.* chave *f*
keyboard *n.* teclado *m*
keyhole *n.* buraco de
   fechadura *m*
kick *n.* ponta-pé *m;*
   v. chutar
kid *n.* criança *f,* cabrito *m*
kidnap *n.* seqüestro *m;*
   v. seqüestrar
kidney *n.* rim *m*
kill *v.* matar
killer *n.* assassino(a) *m(f)*
kilo *n.* quilo *m*
kilometer *n.* quilômetro *m*
kin *n.* parente(a) *m(f)*
kind *n.* tipo *m; adj.* gentil
   mf, generoso(a) *m(f)*
kindergarten *n.* jardim de
   infância *m*
kindness *n.* bondade *f*
king *n.* rei *m*
kingdom *n.* reino *m*
kinky *adj.* esquisito(a)
   m(f), pervertido(a) *m(f)*
kipper *n.* arenque
   defumado *m*
kiss *n.* beijo *m; v.* beijar
kitchen *n.* cozinha *f*
kit *n.* conjunto de objetos *m*

kite *n.* papagaio de
   empinar *m,* pipa *f*
kitty *n.* vaquinha *f,* fundo
   comum *m*
knack *n.* jeito *m*
knead *v.* amassar
knee *n.* joelho *m*
kneecap *n.* rótula *f*
knickers *n.* calcinhas *f.pl,*
   cuecas *f.pl*
knife *n.* faca *f*
knit *n.* tricô *m; v.* tricotar
knob *n.* maçaneta *f,*
   montinho *m*
knock *n.* batida *f; v.* bater
knot *n.* nó *m; v.* dar nó
know *v.* saber, conhecer
knowledge *n.*
   conhecimento *m*
knuckle *n.* nó *m*

L

label *n.* etiqueta *f*
labor *n.* trabalho *m*
laboratory *n.* laboratório *m*
lace *n.* renda *f,* cordão *m;*
   v. fazer coquetel
lack *n.* falta *f; v.* faltar
lad *n.* rapaz *m*
ladder *n.* escada *f*
lady *n.* fama *f,* senhora *f*
lag *v.* ficar para trás
lager *n.* cerveja clara *f*
lake *n.* lago *m*
lamb *n.* cordeiro *m*
lame *adj.* manco(a) *m(f)*
lamp *n.* abajur *m,*
   lâmpada *f*
land *n.* terra *f; v.* aterrissar
landlord *n.* proprietário *m*
landscape *n.* paisagem *f*
lane *n.* pista *f*
language *n.* língua *f*

lantern *n.* lanterna *f*
lap *n.* colo *m*
laptop (computer) *n.* laptop (computador) *m*
lard *n.* banha *f*
large *adj.* grande *mf*
lash *n.* chicote *m*; *v.* chicotear
lass *n.* moça *f*
last[1] *adj.* último(a) *m(f)*; *adv.* em último lugar
last[2] *v.* durar
late *adj.* atrasado(a) *m(f)*; *adv.* tarde
later *adv.* mais tarde
laugh *n.* riso *m*; *v.* rir
launch *n.* lançamento *m*; *v.* lançar
laundromat *n.* lavanderia automática *f*
laundry *n.* lavanderia *f*, lavagem *f*
laundry detergent *n.* sabão em pó *m*
lavender *n.* lavanda *f*
lavish *adj.* luxuoso(a) *m(f)*, gastador(~a) *m(f)*
law *n.* lei *f*
lawful *adj.* legal *mf*
lawn *n.* gramado *m*
lawsuit *n.* processo *m*
lawyer *n.* advogado(a) *m(f)*
lax *adj.* relaxado(a) *m(f)*, desmazelado(a) *m(f)*
laxative *n.* laxante *m*
lay[1] *n.; adj.* leigo(a) *m(f)*
lay[2] *v.* deitar, colocar
layer *n.* camada *f*
laze *v.* descansar, vadiar
lazy *adj.* preguiçoso(a) *m(f)*
lead[1] *n.* chumbo *m*, dianteira *f*
lead[2] *v.* levar, liderar
leadership *n.* liderança *f*

leaf *n.* folha *f*
league *n.* liga *f*
leak *n.* vazamento *m*; *v.* vazar
lean[1] *adj.* magro(a) *m(f)*
lean[2] *v.* encostar
leap year *n.* ano bissexto *m*
learn *v.* aprender
lease *n.* aluguel *m*, leasing *m*; *v.* arrendar
least *n.* menor *mf*; *adj.* mínimo(a) *m(f)*; *adv.* o(a) menos
leather *n.* couro *m*
leave *v.* sair, abandonar
lecture *n.* palestra *f*
leek *n.* alho-poró *m*
left *adj.* esquerdo(a) *m(f)*
leg *n.* perna *f*
legal *adj.* legal *mf*
legend *n.* lenda *f*
legitimate *adj.* legítimo(a) *m(f)*
leisure *n.* lazer *m*
lemon *n.* limão *m*
lend *v.* emprestar a alguém
length *n.* comprimento *m*
lenient *adj.* indulgente *mf*
lens *n.* lente *f*
Lent *n.* Quaresma *f*
less *adv.* menos
lesson *n.* lição *f*
let *v.* deixar, alugar
letter *n.* carta *f*, letra *f*
lettuce *n.* alface *f*
level *n.* nível *m*; *adj.* plano(a) *m(f)*
levy *n.* imposto *m*
liability *n.* responsabilidade *f*
liable *adj.* responsável *mf*
liaison *n.* ligação *f*
liar *n.* mentiroso(a) *m(f)*
liberty *n.* liberdade *f*

librarian *n.* bibliotecário(a) *m(f)*

library *n.* biblioteca *f*

license *n.* licença *f*

license plate *n.* placa de carro *f*

lick *n.* lambida *f*; *v.* lamber

lid *n.* tampa *f*

lie *n.* mentira *f*; *v.* mentir

life *n.* vida *f*

life jacket *n.* colete salva-vida *m*

lift *n.* elevador *m*; *v.* elevar

light *n.* luz *f*; *adj.* leve *mf*; *v.* iluminar

lighter *n.* isqueiro *m*

lightning *n.* relâmpago *m*

like¹ *prep.* como; *adj.* similar *mf*

like² *v.* gostar

limb *n.* membro *mf*

lime *n.* limão galego *m*

limit *n.* limite *m*; *v.* limitar

limp *n.* coxo(a) *m(f)*; *adj.* mole *mf*; *v.* mancar

line *n.* linha *f*, fila *f*

linen *n.* linho *m*

linger *v.* demorar, atrasar

link *n.* ligação *f*; *v.* ligar

lip *n.* lábio *m*

lipstick *n.* batom *m*

liquid *n.* líquido *m*; *adj.* líquido(a) *m(f)*

liqueur *n.* licor *m*

liquor *n.* bebida destilada *f*

list *n.* lista *f*; *v.* listar

listen *v.* escutar

liter *n.* litro *m*

literature *n.* literatura *f*

litter *n.* lixo *m*; *v.* sujar

little *adj.* pequeno(a) *m(f)*; *adv.* pouco

live *adj.* vivo(a) *m(f)*; *v.* viver

liver *n.* fígado *m*

living room *n.* sala de estar *f*

load *n.* carga *f*, peso *m*; *v.* carregar

loaf *n.* filão de pão *m*

loan *n.* empréstimo *m*

loathe *v.* odiar

lobby *n.* saguão *m*

lobster *n.* lagosta *f*

local *adj.* local *mf*

lock *n.* fechadura *f*; *v.* trancar

locker *n.* cadeado *m*

locksmith *n.* chaveiro *m*

lodge *n.* residência temporária *f*

loft *n.* sótão *m*

log *n.* lenha *f*, registro *m*; *v.* registrar

loin *n.* lombo de carne *m*

loiter *v.* vaguear, vagabundear

lone *adj.* solitário(a) *m(f)*

loneliness *n.* solidão *f*

long¹ *adj.* longo(a) *m(f)*

long² *v.* desejar, esperar, ansiar

look *n.* olhar *m*; *v.* olhar

loose¹ *adj.* solto(a) *m(f)*, frouxo(a) *m(f)*

loose² *v.* perder, afrouxar

loot *n.* saque *m*; *v.* saquear

lose *v.* perder

loser *n.* perdedor(~a) *m(f)*, fracasso *m*

loss *n.* perda *f*

lost *adj.* perdido(a) *m(f)*

lot *n.* lote *m*, sorte *f*

lotion *n.* loção *f*

loud *adj.* barulhento(a) *m(f)*

loudspeaker *n.* alto-falante *m*

lounge *n.* sala de estar *f*,
   salão *m*
lout *n.* desordeiro(a) *m(f)*
love *n.* amor *m*; *v.* amar
low *adj.* baixo(a) *m(f)*
lower *v.* abaixar, rebaixar
luck *n.* sorte *f*
luggage *n.* bagagem *f*
lump *n.* monte *m*,
   pedaço *m*
lunch *n.* almoço *m*
lung *n.* pulmão *m*
lust *n.* luxúria *f*, desejo *m*;
   v. cobiçar
luxurious *adj.* suntuoso(a)
   m(f)
luxury *n.* luxo *m*
lying *n.* mentira *f*;
   adj. mentiroso(a) *m(f)*

M

machine *n.* máquina *f*
mad *adj.* louco(a) *m(f)*
madam *n.* senhora *f*
made *v.* *(pp.=make)* feito(a)
   m(f), produzido(a) *m(f)*
magazine *n.* revista *f*
magic *n.* mágica *f*;
   adj. mágico(a) *m(f)*
magician *n.* mágico *m*
magnet *n.* ímã *f*
magnifying glass *n.* lupa *f*
maid *n.* solteira *f*,
   empregada doméstica *f*
maiden name *n.* nome de
   solteira *m*
mail *n.* correio *m*; *v.* postar
mailbox *n.* caixa postal *f*
maim *v.* aleijar
main *adj.* principal *mf*
maintain *v.* manter
maintenance *n.*
   manutenção *f*

maize *n.* milho *m*
majority *n.* maioria *f*
make *n.* marca *f*; *v.* fazer,
   fabricar
makeup *n.* maquiagem *f*
maladjusted *adj.*
   desajustado(a) *m(f)*
male *n.* macho *m*;
   adj. macho *m*,
   masculino(a) *m(f)*
malice *n.* má intenção *f*
malingerer *n.* doente
   fingido(a) *m(f)*
mall (shopping) *n.* saguão
   de shopping *m*
man *n.* homem *m*
manage *v.* dar um jeito,
   administrar
manager *n.* gerente *mf*
mandatory *adj.*
   obrigatório(a) *m(f)*
mangrove *n.* mangue *m*
manifold *adj.* múltiplo(a)
   m(f)
maniac *n.* maníaco(a)
   m(f), louco(a) *m(f)*
mankind *n.* humanidade *f*
manner *n.* maneira *f*
manual *n.*; *adj.* manual *m*
many *adj.*; *pron.* muitos(as)
   m.pl(f.pl)
map *n.* mapa *m*
March *n.* março *m*
margin *n.* margem *f*
mare *n.* égua *f*
marine *adj.* marinho(a)
   m(f)
mark *n.* marca *f*; *v.* marcar
market *n.* mercado *m*;
   v. comercializar
marmalade *n.* geléia de
   laranja *f*
marriage *n.* casamento *m*
marry *v.* casar

masculine *adj.*
masculino(a) *m(f)*
mash *n.* purê *m*; *v.* amassar
mask *n.* máscara *f*;
v. mascarar
mason *n.* pedreiro *m*,
maçom *m*
mass *n.* massa *f*, missa *f*;
v. juntar, unir-se
massive *adj.* enorme *mf*
master *n.* mestre *mf*;
v. dominar
mat *n.* tapete pequeno *m*
match *n.* fósforo *m*, jogo *m*;
v. igualar
matching *adj.*
combinado(a) *m(f)*
matchless *adj.*
incomparável *mf*
mate *n.* companheiro(a)
m(f); *v.* acasalar
material *n.*; *adj.* material *m*
maternity *n.* maternidade *f*
matron *n.* enfermeira
chefe *f*
matter *n.* assunto *m*,
matéria *f*;
v. ter importância
mattress *n.* colchão *m*
mature *adj.* maduro(a)
m(f); *v.* amadurecer
maturity *n.* maturidade *f*
maximum *n.*;
adj. máximo(a) *m(f)*
May *n.* maio *m*
may *v.* poder
maybe *adv.* pode ser, talvez
mayor *n.* prefeito(a) *m(f)*
maze *n.* labirinto *m*
me *pron.* me, mim, eu
meal *n.* refeição *f*
mean¹ *adj.* mesquinho(a)
m(f), médio(a) *m(f)*

mean² *v.* significar
meaning *n.* significado *m*
means *n.* meios *m.pl*
meantime *adv.*
entrementes
measure *n.* medida *f*;
v. medir
meat *n.* carne *f*
mechanic *n.* mecânico *m*
mechanical *adj.*
mecânico(a) *m(f)*
medal *n.* medalha *f*
meddle *v.* intrometer
medical *adj.* médico(a)
m(f)
medication *n.* medicação *f*
medicine *n.* medicina *f*
medieval *adj.* medieval *mf*
mediocre *adj.* mediocre *mf*
meet *v.* encontrar
meeting *n.* reunião *f*
melee *n.* briga *f*, barulho *m*
mellow¹ *adj.* amolecido(a)
m(f), suave *mf*
mellow² *v.* amadurecer,
amolecer
melt *v.* derreter
member *n.* membro *mf*
memento *n.* lembrança *f*
memorize *v.* memorizar
memory *n.* memória *f*
menace *n.* ameaça *f*;
v. ameaçar
mend *n.* remendo *m*;
v. consertar
menial *adj.* serviço inferior
m, manual *m*
menstruation *n.*
menstruação *f*
mention *n.* menção *f*;
v. mencionar
menu *n.* menu *m*,
cardápio *m*

merchandise *n.*
mercadoria *f*

mercy *n.* piedade *f*

mere *adj.* mero(a) *m(f)*,
simples *mf*

merge *v.* juntar, fundir

merger *n.* fusão *f*

Merry Christmas! *interj.*
Feliz Natal!

mess *n.* confusão *f*,
cantina *f*

message *n.* mensagem *f*

messenger *n.*
mensageiro(a) *m(f)*

metal *n.* metal *m*

meter *n.* metro *m*

metric *adj.* métrico(a) *m(f)*

microwave *n.* microondas *m*

middle *n.* meio *m*;
adj. médio(a) *m(f)*

midget *n.* anão *m*, anã *f*

midnight *n.* meia-noite *f*

midst *n.* meio *m*

might *n.* poder *m*,
potência *f*

migration *n.* migração *f*

mild *adj.* suave *mf*

mile *n.* milha *f*

milestone *n.* marco *m*

military *n.*; *adj.* militar *mf*

milk *n.* leite *m*

mill *n.* moinho *m*

million *n.* milhão *m*

mind *n.* mente *f*; *v.* cuidar

mine *pron.* o meu *m*,
a minha *f*

minimum *adj.* mínimo(a)
m(f)

minister *n.* ministro(a)
m(f)

minor *n.* menor de idade
mf

minority *n.* minoria *f*

mint *n.* hortelã *f*

minus *prep.* menos;
adj. negativo(a) *m(f)*

minute *n.* minuto *m*

mirror *n.* espelho *m*

miscarriage *n.* aborto
espontâneo *m*

miscellaneous *adj.*
vários(as) *m.pl(f.pl)*

misconception *n.*
concepção errada *f*

misconduct *n.* má
conduta *f*

mislay *v.* extraviar, perder

mislead *v.* enganar

miss[1] *n.* senhorita *f*, falta *f*

miss[2] *v.* sentir falta, errar,
falhar

mission *n.* missão *f*

mist *n.* neblina *f*

mistake *n.* erro *m*;
v. confundir

mister *n.* senhor *m*

mistress *n.* amante *f*, dona
de casa *f*, diretora *f*

misunderstanding *n.*
engano *m*

mix *v.* misturar

moan *n.* gemido *m*;
v. gemer

mob *n.* multidão *f*

mock *adj.* falso(a) *m(f)*;
v. zombar

model *n.* modelo *m*

modem *n.* modem *m*

moderate *adj.*
moderado(a) *m(f)*

modern *adj.* moderno(a)
m(f)

modest *adj.* modesto(a)
m(f)

modify *v.* modificar

moist *adj.* úmido(a) *m(f)*

moisture *n.* umidade *f*

mold *n.* molde *m*
molest *v.* molestar
mom *n.* mamãe *f*
moment *n.* momento *m*
monastery *n.* monastério *m*
Monday *n.* segunda-feira *f*
money *n.* dinheiro *m*
monk *n.* monge *m*
monkey *n.* macaco *m*
monster *n.* monstro *m*
month *n.* mês *m*
monument *n.* monumento *m*
mood *n.* estado de espírito *m*
moon *n.* lua *f*
mop *n.* vassoura de pano *f*; *v.* esfregar
more *adj.*; *adv.* mais
moreover *adv.* além do mais
morning *n.* manhã *f*
moron *n.* idiota *mf*
mortgage *n.* hipoteca *f*
mosque *n.* mesquita *f*
mosquito *n.* mosquito *m*
most *adj.*; *adv.* a maioria *mf*
mother *n.* mãe *f*
mother-in-law *n.* sogra *f*
motion *n.* movimento *m*
motivation *n.* motivação *f*
motive *n.* causa *f*
motorbike *n.* motocicleta *f*
mount *n.* monte *m*, montagem *f*; *v.* montar
mountain *n.* montanha *f*
mouse *n.* rato *m*
mouth *n.* boca *f*
move *n.* movimento *m*; *v.* mexer
movie *n.* filme *m*
movie theater *n.* cinema *m*
much *adv.* muito *mf*
muck *n.* sujeira *f*; *v.* fazer bobagem

mud *n.* lama *f*
muffle *v.* abafar
mug *n.* caneca *f*
mugger *n.* assaltante *mf*
multiply *v.* multiplicar
mumble *n.* resmungo *m*; *v.* balbuciar
mumps *n.* caxumba *f*
murder *n.* assassinato *m*; *v.* assassinar
murderer *n.* assassino(a) *m(f)*
murky *adj.* obscuro(a) *m(f)*
muscle *n.* músculo *m*
museum *n.* museu *m*
mushroom *n.* cogumelo *m*
music *n.* música *f*
musician *n.* músico *m*
must *n.* dever *m*; *v.* dever, precisar
mustard *n.* mostarda *f*
mute *adj.* mudo(a) *m(f)*

N
nag *v.* apoquentar
nagging *n.* queixas *f.pl*; *adj.* contínuo(a) *m(f)*, persistente *mf*
nail *n.* unha *f*, prego *m*; *v.* pregar
nail polish *n.* esmalte para unhas *m*
nail polish remover *n.* removedor de esmalte *m*
naked *adj.* nu *m*, nua *f*, despido(a) *m(f)*
name *n.* nome *m*; *v.* nomear, denominar
nap *n.* soneca *f*; *v.* cochilar
napkin *n.* guardanapo *m*
narrow *adj.* estreito(a) *m(f)*; *v.* reduzir

nasty *adj.* mau *m*, má *f*, desagradável *mf*, ruim *mf*

nation *n.* nação *f*

nationality *n.* nacionalidade *f*

native *n.*; *adj.* nativo(a) *m(f)*

natural *adj.* natural *mf*

nature *n.* natureza *f*

naughtiness *n.* travessura *f*

naughty *adj.* travesso(a) *m(f)*

nausea *n.* náusea *f*

navel *n.* umbigo *m*

navigate *v.* navegar

navy *n.* marinha *f*

near[1] *adv.* perto; *adj.* vizinho(a) *m(f)*; *prep.* perto de

near[2] *v.* aproximar-se

nearly *adv.* quase

neat *adj.* puro(a) *m(f)*, arrumado(a) *m(f)*

necessary *adj.* necessário(a) *m(f)*

necessity *n.* necessidade *f*

neck *n.* garganta *f*, pescoço *m*, decote *m*

necklace *n.* colar *m*

need *n.* necessidade *f*; *v.* precisar

needle *n.* agulha *f*

negative *adj.* negativo(a) *m(f)*

neglect *n.* descuido *m*; *v.* descuidar

negligence *n.* negligência *f*

negligible *n.* insignificante *mf*, ínfimo(a) *m(f)*

neighbor *n.* vizinho(a) *m(f)*

neighborhood *n.* vizinhança *f*, bairro *m*

neither *conj.* nem; *pron.* nenhum(~a) *m(f)*

nephew *n.* sobrinho(a) *m(f)*

nerve *n.* nervo *m*

nervous *adj.* nervoso(a) *m(f)*

nest *n.* ninho *m*; *v.* aninhar

net *n.* rede *f*; *adj.* líquido(a) *m(f)*

network *n.* rede de trabalho *f*

neutral *adj.* neutro(a) *m(f)*

never *adv.* nunca

new *adj.* novo(a) *m(f)*

news *n.* notícia *f*

newspaper *n.* jornal *m*

newsstand *n.* banca de jornal *f*

New Year *n.* Ano Novo *m*

New Year's Eve *n.* Véspera de Ano Novo *f*

next *adj.* próximo(a) *m(f)*; *adv.* depois

nibble *v.* petiscar

nice *adj.* bonito(a) *m(f)*, agradável *mf*

nickname *n.* apelido *m*

niece *n.* sobrinha *f*

night *n.* noite *f*

nightmare *n.* pesadelo *m*

nine *num.* nove

nipple *n.* bico *m*

no *adv.* não; *adj.* nenhum(~a) *m(f)*

nobility *n.* nobreza *f*

nobody *pron.* ninguém

nod[1] *n.* aceno de cabeça *m*

nod[2] *v.* acenar *sim* com a cabeça

noise *n.* barulho *m*

noisy *adj.* barulhento(a) *m(f)*

non- *pref.* não-, anti-, des. . . , in . . .

none *pron.* ninguém, nenhum(~a) *m(f)*
noon *n.* meio-dia *m*
normal *adj.* normal *mf*
north *n.* norte *m*
nor *conj.* nem
nose *n.* nariz *m*
nostril *n.* narina *f*
nosy *adj.* intrometido(a) *m(f)*
not *adv.* não
notary *n.* tabelião *m*, cartório *m*, tabelionato *m*
note *n.* nota *f; v.* notar, observar
notebook *n.* caderno *m*
nothing *n.* nada *m*
notice *n.* aviso *m; v.* observar
notify *v.* notificar
noun *n.* substantivo *m*
nourishing *adj.* nutritivo(a) *m(f)*
novel *n.* romance literário *m*
November *n.* novembro *m*
now *adv.* agora
nowadays *adv.* hoje em dia
nowhere *adv.* em nenhuma parte
nude *n.* nu *m; adj.* nu(~a) *m(f)*
null *adj.* nulo(a) *m(f)*
nullify *v.* anular
numb *adj.* insensível *mf; v.* anestesiar
number *n.* número *m*
numerous *adj.* inúmeros(as) *m.pl(f.pl)*
nun *n.* freira *f*
nurse *n.* enfermeiro(a) *m(f); v.* cuidar
nut *n.* noz *f*, porca de parafuso *f*

O

oak *n.* carvalho *m*
oath *n.* juramento *m; v.* jurar
oats *n.* aveia *f*
obey *v.* obedecer
object *n.* objeto *m*
objection *n.* objeção *f*
oblige *v.* fazer favor
obliged *adj.* obrigado(a) *m(f)*
oblivion *n.* esquecimento *m*
obscene *adj.* obsceno(a) *m(f)*
obscure *adj.* obscuro(a) *m(f); v.* escurecer
observation *n.* observação *f*
observe *v.* observar, cumprir
obsession *n.* obsessão *f*
obsolete *adj.* obsoleto(a) *m(f)*
obstacle *n.* obstáculo *m*
obstinate *adj.* obstinado(a) *m(f)*, teimoso(a) *m(f)*
obtain *v.* obter
obvious *adj.* óbvio(a) *m(f)*
occasion *n.* ocasião *f*
occasional *adj.* ocasional *mf*
occasionally *adv.* ocasionalmente
occult *adj.* oculto(a) *m(f)*
occupation *n.* ocupação *f*
occupy *v.* ocupar
occur *v.* ocorrer
ocean *n.* oceano *m*
October *n.* outubro *m*
odd *adj.* estranho(a) *m(f)*, ímpar *mf*
odds *n.* probabilidade *f*
odor *n.* odor *m*
of *prep.* de

of course *adv.*
naturalmente
off *adj.* desligado(a) *m(f)*;
adv. fora; *prep.* de
offend *v.* ofender
offensive *adj.* ofensivo(a)
m(f)
offer *n.* oferta *f; v.* oferecer
office *n.* escritório *m*
officer *n.* funcionário(a)
m(f), oficial *mf*
official *adj.* oficial *mf*
often *adv.* freqüentemente
oil *n.* óleo *m*
oily *adj.* gorduroso(a) *m(f)*
old *adj.* velho(a) *m(f)*
old-fashioned *adj.*
antiquado(a) *m(f)*
olive *n.* azeitona *f*
omelet *n.* omelete *f*
omen *n.* presságio *m*
omission *n.* omissão *f,*
descuido *m*
on[1] *prep.* sobre, em;
adv. em cima
on[2] [- **is on**] *v.* ligar, acender
once *adv.* uma vez;
conj. depois de
one *num.* um(~a) *m(f)*;
pron. alguém
oneself *pron.* si mesmo(a)
m(f)
onion *n.* cebola *f*
only *adv.* somente;
adj. único(a) *m(f)*;
conj. só que
onset *n.* começo *m*
onto *prep.* para diante
open *adj.* aberto(a) *m(f)*;
v. abrir
open-minded *adj.* pessoa
aberta a novas idéias *f*
operation *n.* operação *f*

operator *n.* operador(~a)
m(f)
opinion *n.* opinião *f*
opponent *n.* oponente *mf*
oppose *v.* opor
opposite[1] *n.* contrário *m;*
adj. oposto(a) *m(f)*
opposite[2] *adv.* em frente;
prep. em frente de
opt *v.* optar
optician *n.* oculista *mf*
option *n.* opção *f*
oral *n.; adj.* oral *mf*
orange *n.* laranja *f;*
adj. alaranjado(a) *m(f)*
orchestra *n.* orquestra *f*
ordeal *n.* provação *f*
order *n.* ordem *f,* pedido *m;*
v. encomendar
ordinal *adj.* ordinal *mf*
ordinary *adj.* ordinário(a)
m(f)
organ *n.* órgão *m*
organization *n.*
organização *f*
organize *v.* organizar
origin *n.* origem *f*
original *adj.* original *mf*
other *adj.* outro(a) *m(f)*
ought *v.* dever fazer
ounce *n.* onça = 28 gramas *f*
our *adj.* nosso(a) *m(f)*,
nossos(as) *m.pl(f.pl)*
ours *pron.* o(a) nosso(a)
m(f), os(as) nossos(as)
m.pl(f.pl)
ourselves *pron.* nós
mesmos
out *adv.* para fora de
outbreak *n.* surto *m,*
epidemia *f*
outburst *n.* explosão *f*
outcast *n.* pessoa excluída *f*
outcome *n.* resultado *m*

outcry *n.* protesto *m*

outdated *adj.* antiquado(a) *m(f)*

outdo *v.* ultrapassar

outdoor *adj.* ao ar livre

outer *adj.* externo(a) *m(f)*

outfit *n.* roupagens *f.pl*, equipamento *m*

outgoing *adj.* extrovertido(a) *m(f)*, espontâneo(a) *m(f)*

outing *n.* passeio *m*, excursão *f*

outlast *v.* sobreviver

outlaw *n.* criminoso(a) *m(f)*

outlet *n.* escoadouro *m*

outlook *n.* perspectiva *f*

outpost *n.* posto avançado *m*

output *n.* produção *f*, saída *f*

outset *n.* início *m*, começo *m*

outside[1] *n.* exterior *m*; *adj.* externo(a) *m(f)*

outside[2] *adv.* fora; *prep.* de fora

outsider *n.* forasteiro(a) *m(f)*

oven *n.* forno *m*

over *prep.* sobre; *adv.* por cima; *adj.* acabado(a) *m(f)*

overall *adj.* total *mf*; *adv.* totalmente

overalls *n.* casaco *m*, sobretudo *m*

overbearing *adj.* arrogante *mf*

overcast *adj.* nublado(a) *m(f)*

overcome *v.* superar

overdo *v.* exagerar

overdose *n.* dose excessiva *f*

overdraft *n.* saldo negativo *m*

overdue *adj.* atrasado(a) *m(f)*

overheat *v.* superaquecer

overjoyed *adj.* encantado(a) *m(f)*

overkill *n.* exagero *m*

overlap *n.* sobreposição *f*; *v.* sobrepor

overlook *v.* omitir, perdoar

overnight *adj.* da noite para o dia *f*

overrate *v.* supervalorizar, superestimar

overreach *v.* exceder

overreact *v.* reagir com exagero

override *v.* sobrepujar

overrule *v.* mudar a decisão

overrun *v.* ultrapassar

overseas *n.* ultra-mar *m*, exterior *m*

overseer *n.* supervisor(~a) *m(f)*

overshadow *v.* eclipsar

oversight *n.* descuido *m*

overspend *v.* gastar demais

overstep *v.* ultrapassar o limite

overstate *v.* exagerar

overtake *v.* ultrapassar

overtime *n.* hora extra *f*

overwork *n.* excesso de trabalho *m*

owe *v.* dever

own *adj.* próprio(a) *m(f)*; *v.* possuir

owner *n.* proprietário(a) *m(f)*

oxygen *n.* oxigênio *m*

oyster *n.* ostra *f*

P

pace *n.* passo *m*, ritmo *m*
pacemaker *n.* marca-passo *m*
pacify *v.* acalmar
pack[1] *n.* pacote *m*, embalagem *f*
pack[2] *v.* arrumar malas, embalar
package *n.* pacote *m*
pad *n.* bloco de papel *m*
padlock *n.* cadeado *m*
page[1] *n.* página *f*
page[2] *v.* chamar alguém
paid *adj.* pago(a) *m(f)*
pain *n.* dor *f*
painful *adj.* doloroso(a) *m(f)*
paint *n.* pintura *f*; *v.* pintar
painting *n.* pintura *f*
pair *n.* par *m*
pajamas *n.* pijama *m*
pal *n.* companheiro(a) *m(f)*
palace *n.* palácio *m*
pale *adj.* pálido(a) *m(f)*
palm *n.* palma *f*, palmeira *f*
pan *n.* panela *f*
panel *n.* painel *m*
pant *v.* ofegar
pants *n.* calças *f.pl*
panties *n.* calcinhas *f.pl*
paper *n.* papel *m*, artigo *m*, jornal *m*, exame *m*
paragon *n.* modelo *mf*
paralysis *n.* paralisia *f*
paralyze *v.* paralisar
parcel *n.* pacote *m*
pardon *n.* perdão *m*; *v.* perdoar
parents *n.* pais *m.pl*
park *n.* parque *m*; *v.* estacionar
parking lot *n.* estacionamento *m*

part *n.* parte *f*
part-time *adj.* meio expediente *m*
partner *n.* sócio(a) *m(f)*
party *n.* partido *m*, festa *f*
pass *n.* passagem *f*; *v.* passar, transmitir
passenger *n.* passageiro(a) *m(f)*
passport *n.* passaporte *m*
past *n.* passado *m*; *adj.* passado(a) *m(f)*
pasta *n.* massa *f*
paste *n.* pasta *f*; *v.* colar
pastry *n.* empadas *f.pl*, tortas *f.pl*
patch *n.* retalho *m*; *v.* remendar
path *n.* caminho *m*
patient *n.* paciente *mf*
patron *n.* freguês *m*, freguesa *f*, cliente *mf*
patronize *v.* subestimar
pattern *n.* padrão *m*, modelo *m*
pause *n.* pausa *f*; *v.* pausar
pave *v.* pavimentar
paw *n.* pata de animal *f*
pay *n.* salário *m*; *v.* pagar
payment *n.* pagamento *m*
peace *n.* paz *f*
peak *n.* pico *m*
pear *n.* pêra *f*
pearl *n.* pérola *f*
pebble *n.* pedrinha *f*
pedal *n.* pedal *m*; *v.* pedalar
peddler *n.* camelô *mf*
pedestrian *n.* pedestre *mf*
pee *n.* pipi *m*; *v.* urinar
peer *n.* colega *mf*, par *m*
peg *n.* pregador de roupa *m*
pen *n.* caneta *f*
pencil *n.* lápis *m*

people *n.* pessoas *f.pl,* povo *m*
pepper *n.* pimenta *f*
percent *n.* por cento *m*
perfect *adj.* perfeito(a) *m(f)*
perform *v.* executar
performance *n.* desempenho *m*
perfume *n.* perfume *m*
perhaps *adv.* talvez
peril *n.* perigo *m*
period *n.* período *m,* menstruação *f*
permit *n.* permissão *f; v.* permitir
person *n.* pessoa *f*
personal *adj.* pessoal *mf*
personnel *n.* recursos humanos *m.pl*
peruse *v.* examinar
pet *n.* animal de estimação *m*
petite *adj.* pequeno(a) *m(f)*
petty *adj.* mesquinho(a) *m(f)*
pharmacy *n.* farmácia *f*
phase *n.* fase *f*
phial/vial *n.* frasco *m*
phone *n.* telefone *m; v.* telefonar
phonebook *n.* lista telefônica *f*
phony/phoney *adj.* falso(a) *m(f); n.* impostor *m*
photo *n.* foto *f*
photocopy *n.* xerox *f,* fotocópia *f*
photograph *n.* fotografia *f*
phrase *n.* frase *f*
physical *adj.* físico(a) *m(f)*
physician *n.* médico(a) *m(f)*
pick *n.* picareta *f; v.* escolher

picnic *n.* piquenique *m*
picture *n.* imagem *f*
pie *n.* torta *f*
piece *n.* pedaço *m,* peça *f*
pig *n.* porco *m*
pile *n.* pilha *f; v.* empilhar
pill *n.* pílula *f*
pillow *n.* travesseiro *m*
pillowcase *n.* fronha *f*
pilot *n.* piloto(a) *m(f); v.* pilotar
pin *n.* alfinete *m*
pinch *n.* beliscão *m; v.* beliscar
pine *n.* pinheiro *m*
pink *adj.* cor-de-rosa *f*
pint *n.* pinta = 568ml *f*
pipe *n.* cano *m,* cachimbo *m*
pit *n.* fossa *f*
pity *n.* pena *f,* compaixão *f*
place *n.* lugar *m; v.* colocar
plain *adj.* simples *mf; adv.* claramente; *n.* planície *f*
plan *n.* plano *m; v.* planejar
plane *n.* avião *m,* plano *m; adj.* plano(a) *m(f)*
planet *n.* planeta *m*
plant *n.* planta *f*
plastic *n.* plástico(a) *m(f)*
plate *n.* placa *f,* prato *m*
play *n.* jogo *m; v.* jogar, brincar
please *interj.* por favor
pleasure *n.* prazer *m*
plenty *n.* abundância *f*
plug *n.* tomada *f; v.* tapar
plum *n.* ameixa *f*
plumber *n.* encanador *m*
plural *n.; adj.* plural *m*
plus *prep.* mais
pocket *n.* bolso *m*
pocketknife *n.* canivete *m*

poetry *n.* poesia *f*
point *n.* ponto *m*;
   v. apontar
poison *n.* veneno *m*;
   v. envenenar
poisonous *adj.*
   venenoso(a) *m(f)*
pole *n.* pólo *m*, poste *m*
police *n.* polícia *f*
police officer *n.* policial *mf*
police station *n.* delegacia
   de polícia *f*
policy *n.* política *f*
polite *adj.* educado(a) *m(f)*,
   cortês *mf*
political *adj.* político(a)
   m(f)
politics *n.* política *f*
poll *n.* votação *f*
pond *n.* lago *m*
pony *n.* pônei *m*
pool *n.* piscina *f*, conjunto
   m; *v.* juntar
poor *adj.* pobre *mf*
pope *n.* papa *m*
population *n.* população *f*
pork *n.* carne de porco *f*
portrait *n.* retrato *m*
porter *n.* carregador *m*,
   porteiro *m*
position *n.* posição *f*;
   v. posicionar
positive *adj.* positivo(a)
   m(f)
possible *adj.* possível *mf*
post *n.* correio *m*
postcard *n.* cartão postal *m*
post office *n.* agência de
   correio *f*
pot *n.* pote *m*, maconha *f*
pottery *n.* cerâmica *f*
poultry *n.* aves comestíveis
   f.pl
pound *n.* libra *f*

pour *v.* despejar
powder *n.* pó *m*
power *n.* poder *m*, energia *f*
practical *adj.* prático(a)
   m(f)
practice *n.* prática *f*;
   v. praticar
praise *n.* elogio *m*;
   v. elogiar
prawn/shrimp *n.*
   camarão *m*
pray *v.* rezar
prayer *n.* reza *f*, aquele que
   reza *m*
preach *v.* fazer sermões
precaution *n.* precaução *f*
precede *v.* preceder
precedent *n.* precedente *m*
precinct *n.* distrito *m*
precious *adj.* precioso(a)
   m(f)
predict *v.* predizer
precise *adj.* exato(a) *m(f)*
prefer *v.* preferir
pregnant *adj.* grávida *f*,
   prenha *f*
prepaid *adj.* pago
   antecipadamente *m*
prepare *v.* preparar
prescription *n.* receita
   médica *f*
present *n.*; *adj.* presente *m*;
   v. apresentar
president *n.* presidente *m*
press *n.* imprensa *f*;
   v. apertar
pressure *n.* pressão *f*
pretty *adj.* bonito(a) *m(f)*;
   adv. consideravelmente
prevent *v.* impedir
previous *adj.* precedente
   m, anterior *mf*
price *n.* preço *m*

prick *n.* picada *f*, alfinete *m*; *v.* picar

pride *n.* orgulho *m*; *v.* orgulhar

priest *n.* padre *m*

prime minister *n.* primeiro ministro *m*

principal *adj.* principal *mf*

principle *n.* princípio *m*

print *n.* impressão *f*; *v.* imprimir

prior *adj.* anterior *mf*

prison *n.* prisão *f*

prisoner *n.* presidiário(a) *m(f)*

privacy *n.* privacidade *f*

private *adj.* particular *mf*

privilege *n.* privilégio *m*

prize *n.* prêmio *m*

probable *adj.* provável *mf*

problem *n.* problema *m*

produce *n.* produção *f*; *v.* produzir

product *n.* produto *m*

profession *n.* profissão *f*

profile *n.* perfil *m*

profit *n.* lucro *m*; *v.* lucrar

program *n.* programa *m*

progress *n.* progresso *m*; *v.* progredir

project *n.* projeto *m*; *v.* projetar

promenade *n.* passeio *m*, caminhada *f*

promise *n.* promessa *f*; *v.* prometer

proof *n.* prova *f*

property *n.* propriedade *f*

proposal *n.* proposta *f*

propose *v.* propor

protect *v.* proteger

protection *n.* proteção *f*

protest *n.* protesto *m*; *v.* protestar

Protestant *n.*; *adj.* Protestante *mf*

proud *adj.* orgulhoso(a) *m(f)*

prove *v.* provar

proverb *n.* provérbio *m*

provide *v.* fornecer

province *n.* província *f*, distrito *m*

prudent *adj.* prudente *mf*

pub *n.* bar inglês *m*

public *n.* público *m*; *adj.* público(a) *m(f)*

public transport *n.* transporte público *m*

publicity *n.* publicidade *f*

publish *v.* publicar

pull *v.* puxar

pulse *n.* pulso *m*

pump *n.* bomba *f*; *v.* bombear

purchase *n.* compra *f*; *v.* comprar

pure *adj.* puro(a) *m(f)*

purple *adj.* roxo(a) *m(f)*

purpose *n.* finalidade *f*

purse *n.* bolsa *f*

push *v.* empurrar

put *v.* por, colocar

Q

qualify *v.* qualificar

quality *n.* qualidade *f*

quantity *n.* quantidade *f*

quarantine *n.* quarentena *f*

quarrel *n.* discussão *f*, briga *f*

quash *v.* anular

quasi- *pref.* quase

quarter *n.* quarto *m*, trimestre *m*

queasy *adj.* enjoado(a) *m(f)*

queen *n.* rainha *f*

query *n.* dúvida *f*
quest *n.* busca *f*
question *n.* pergunta *f*
quick *adj.* rápido(a) *m(f)*
quiet *adj.* quieto(a) *m(f)*,
calmo(a) *m(f)*
quilt *n.* coberta *f*, colcha *f*
quit *v.* deixar, sair, parar de
quite *adv.* muito, bastante,
completamente
quote *n.* citação *f*; *v.* citar

R

rabbi *n.* rabino *m*
rabbit *n.* coelho *m*
rabies *n.* raiva *f*
race *n.* corrida *f*, raça *f*;
v. correr
racism *n.* racismo *m*
rack *n.* bagageiro *m*
racket *n.* raquete de tênis *f*,
negócio ilegal *m*
racketeer *n.* chantagista *mf*
radio *n.* rádio *m*
rag *n.* trapo *m*
rage *n.* raiva *f*
railroad *n.* estrada de
ferro *f*
rain *n.* chuva *f*; *v.* chover
rainbow *n.* arco-íris *m*
raincoat *n.* capa de chuva *f*
rainy *adj.* chuvoso(a) *m(f)*
raise *n.* aumento *m*;
v. elevar, educar
RAM (computer) *n.*
memória RAM *f*
ramp *n.* rampa *f*
rampage *n.* disparato *m*,
loucura *f*
rancid *adj.* rançoso(a) *m(f)*
random *adj.* aleatório(a)
m(f)

range *n.* extensão *f*;
v. percorrer
rank *n.* fila *f*, posto na
carreira militar *m*
rape *n.* violação *f*, estupro
m; *v.* estuprar
rare *adj.* raro(a) *m(f)*
rash *n.* brotoeja na pele *f*
rate *n.* taxa *f*, proporção *f*,
preço *m*
rather *adv.* um tanto, meio
rave *v.* enfurecer
raw *adj.* cru(~a) *m(f)*
ray *n.* raio *m*
raze *v.* destruir, arrasar
razor *n.* navalha *f*,
barbeador *m*
razorblade *n.* lâmina de
barbeador *f*
reach *n.* alcance *m*;
v. atingir
react *v.* reagir
reaction *n.* reação *f*
read *v.* ler
reader *n.* leitor(~a) *m(f)*
ready *adj.* pronto(a) *m(f)*
real *adj.* real *mf*
real estate *n.* imóveis *m.pl*
reality *n.* realidade *f*
realize *v.* perceber
rear *n.* parte traseira *f*;
v. criar
reason *n.* razão *f*;
v. argumentar
recall *n.* lembrança *f*;
v. lembrar
receipt *n.* recibo *m*
receive *v.* receber
receiver *n.* receptor(~a)
m(f)
recent *adj.* recente *mf*
reception *n.* recepção *f*
recipe *n.* receita *f*

reckless *adj.* descuidado(a)
   m(f)
reckon *v.* calcular
recognize *v.* reconhecer
recommend *v.* recomendar
record[1] *n.* registro *m*,
   gravação *f*
record[2] *v.* registrar, gravar
recover *v.* recuperar
red *adj.* vermelho(a) *m(f)*
red tape *n.* burocracia *f*
redeem *v.* resgatar
reduce *v.* reduzir
reduction *n.* redução *f*
refer *v.* consultar, referir
referee *n.* árbitro *m*
refresh *v.* refrescar, lavar,
   descansar
refreshment *n.* comidas *f*;
   e refrescos *m*
refrigerator *n.* geladeira *f*
refund *n.* reembolso *m*;
   v. reembolsar
refuse *n.* lixo *m*; *v.* recusar
regard *n.* consideração *f*;
   v. respeitar
regarding *prep.* com
   respeito a
region *n.* região *f*
register *n.* registro *m*;
   v. registrar
regret *n.* pesar *m*;
   v. lamentar, arrepender
regular *adj.* regular *mf*
regulation *n.* regulamento
   m
relationship *n.*
   relacionamento *m*
relative *n.* parente *mf*;
   adj. relativo(a) *m(f)*
relax *v.* descansar,
   descontrair
reliable *adj.* confiável *mf*
relief *n.* alívio *m*, relevo *m*

relieve *v.* aliviar
religion *n.* religião *f*
religious *adj.* religioso(a)
   m(f)
rely *v.* confiar
remain *v.* ficar, sobrar
remark *n.* observação *f*;
   v. observar
remember *v.* lembrar
remote *adj.* remoto(a) *m(f)*
removal *n.* mudança *f*
remove *v.* remover
renew *v.* renovar
renovation *n.* renovação *f*
renown *n.* reputação *f*,
   fama *f*
rent *n.* aluguel *m*; *v.* alugar
repair *n.* conserto *m*;
   v. consertar
repeat *n.* repetição *f*;
   v. repetir
repellent *n.* repelente *mf*
repetition *n.* repetição *f*
replace *v.* substituir
reply *n.* resposta *f*;
   v. responder
report *n.* relatório *m*;
   v. relatar
represent *v.* representar
representative *n.*
   representante *mf*
republic *n.* república *f*
reputation *n.* reputação *f*
request *n.* pedido *m*;
   v. pedir
require *v.* requerer, exigir
requirement *n.* exigência *f*
rescue *n.* salvamento *m*;
   v. salvar
research *n.* pesquisa *m*;
   v. pesquisar
reservation *n.* reserva *f*
reserve *v.* reservar
reset *v.* reajustar

residence *n.* residência *f*
resist *v.* resistir
resolve *n.* resolução *f*;
    v. resolver
resort *n.* estação de férias *f*;
    v. recorrer
respect *n.* respeito *m*;
    v. respeitar
respond *v.* responder,
    reagir
response *n.* resposta *f*,
    reação *f*
responsibility *n.*
    responsabilidade *f*
responsible *adj.*
    responsável *mf*
rest *n.* descanso *m*;
    v. descansar
restaurant *n.* restaurante *m*
restore *v.* restaurar
restrict *v.* restringir, limitar
rest room *n.* banheiro
    público *m*, toalete *f*
result *n.* resultado *m*;
    v. resultar
retire *v.* aposentar
return *v.* retornar
reverse *n.* reverso *m*
review *n.* revisão *f*, sumário
    m; *v.* examinar
reward *n.* recompensa *f*;
    v. recompensar
rhythm *n.* ritmo *m*
rib *n.* costela *f*
ribbon *n.* fita *f*
rice *n.* arroz *m*
rich *adj.* rico(a) *m(f)*
ride *n.* passeio *m*;
    v. passear
right *n.* direito *m*;
    adj. certo(a) *m(f)*,
    correto(a) *m(f)*
ring *n.* anel *m*; *v.* telefonar
rinse *v.* enxaguar

riot *n.* motim *m*, baderna *f*
ripe *adj.* maduro(a) *m(f)*
rise *v.* ascender, subir
risk *n.* risco *m*; *v.* arriscar
river *n.* rio *m*
road *n.* estrada *f*
rob *v.* roubar
robbery *n.* roubo *m*,
    saque *m*
robe *n.* roupão *m*, beca *f*
rock *n.* rocha *f*; *v.* balançar
rod *n.* vara *f*
role *n.* papel *m*
roll *n.* rolo *m*; *v.* rolar
romance *n.* romance *m*
roof *n.* telhado *m*
room *n.* quarto *m*
roommate *n.* companheiro
    de quarto *m*
root *n.* raiz *f*
rope *n.* corda *f*
rotten *adj.* podre *mf*
rough *adj.* áspero(a) *m(f)*,
    grosseiro(a) *m(f)*
round *adj.* redondo(a)
    m(f); *n.* giro *m*
route *n.* caminho *m*
row *n.* fileira *f*, discussão *f*
royal *adj.* real *mf*
rub *n.* fricção *f*; *v.* esfregar
rubber band *n.* elástico *m*
rude *adj.* rude *mf*
rug *n.* tapete *m*
ruin *n.* ruína *f*; *v.* estragar
rule *n.* régua *f*, regra *f*;
    v. governar
run[1] *n.* funcionamento *m*,
    corrida *f*
run[2] *v.* funcionar, correr
rush[1] *n.* precipitação *f*,
    pânico *m*, corrida *f*
rush[2] *v.* correr, apressar
rust *n.* ferrugem *f*;
    v. enferrujar

S

sabbatical *n.* ano sabático *m*, período de estudos *m*

sack *n.* saco *m*; *v.* despedir do emprego

sad *adj.* triste *mf*

s.a.e. *n. (abbrev.)* envelope selado para retorno *m*

saddle *n.* sela *f*

safe *n.* cofre *m*; *adj.* seguro(a) *m(f)*

safety *n.* segurança *f*

safety pin *n.* colchete *m*

sag *v.* afrouxar

sail *n.* vela de barco *f*; *v.* velejar

sailboat *n.* barco a vela *m*

sailor *n.* marinheiro *m*

sake *n.* causa *f*, motivo *m*

salad *n.* salada *f*

salary *n.* salário *m*

sale *n.* venda *f*, liquidação *f*

saliva *n.* saliva *f*

salt *n.* sal *m*; *v.* salgar

same *adj.* mesmo(a) *m(f)*

sample *n.* amostra *f*; *v.* experimentar

sand *n.* areia *f*; *v.* lixar

sandal *n.* sandália *f*

sandwich *n.* sanduíche *m*

sanitary pad *n.* toalha sanitária *f*

Santa Claus *n.* Papai Noel *m*

satisfy *v.* satisfazer

Saturday *n.* sábado *m*

sauce *n.* molho *m*

sausage *n.* lingüiça *f*, salsicha *f*

save *v.* salvar; *prep.* salvo, exceto

savory *adj.* saboroso(a) *m(f)*

say *v.* dizer

scale *n.* escala *f*

scales *n.* escalas *f.pl*

scampi *n.* lagostinha *f*

scar *n.* cicatriz *f*

scare *n.* susto *m*; *v.* assustar

scarf *n.* cachecol *m*

scenery *n.* paisagem *f*, cenário *m*

scent *n.* aroma *m*, perfume *m*

schedule *n.* programação *f*

scholarship *n.* bolsa de estudos *f*

school *n.* escola *f*

science *n.* ciência *f*

scientific *adj.* científico(a) *m(f)*

scissors *n.* tesoura *f*

score *n.* contagem *f*; *v.* marcar

scrap *n.* sucata *f*; *v.* jogar fora, sucatar

scratch *n.* arranhão *m*; *v.* riscar, arranhar

scream *n.* grito *m*; *v.* gritar

screen *n.* tela *f*

screw *n.* parafuso *m*

screwdriver *n.* chave de fenda *f*

script *n.* roteiro de cinema *m*

sculptor *n.* escultor(~a) *m(f)*

sculpture *n.* escultura *f*

sea *n.* mar *m*

seam *n.* costura *f*

search *n.* busca *f*; *v.* procurar

seasickness *n.* enjôo de mar *m*

season *n.* estação *f*; *v.* temperar

seat *n.* assento *m*

seat belt *n.* cinto de
segurança *m*
seaweed *n.* alga marinha *f*
second *n.* segundo *m*;
adv. em segundo
secret *n.* segredo *m*;
adj. secreto(a) *m(f)*
secretary *n.* secretária *f*
section *n.* seção *f*
security *n.* segurança *f*
see *v.* ver
seed *n.* semente *f*
seem *v.* parecer
seize *v.* agarrar
seizure *n.* ataque *m*,
acesso *m*
select *adj.* seleto(a) *m(f)*;
v. selecionar
selection *n.* seleção *f*
self *pron. reflex.* auto-, se
self-service *n.* auto-
serviço *m*
sell *v.* vender
semester *n.* semestre *m*
send *v.* enviar
sender *n.* remetente *mf*
senior *adj.* mais velho *m*
sense *n.* sentido *m*
sentence *n.* sentença *f*
separate *adj.* separado(a)
m(f); *v.* separar
separation *n.* separação *f*
September *n.* setembro *m*
series *n.* série *f*
serious *adj.* sério(a) *m(f)*
service *n.* serviço *m*
set *n.* conjunto *m*;
adj. fixo(a) *m(f)*; *v.* fixar
settle *v.* arrumar
settlement *n.* colônia *f*,
pagamento *m*
settler *n.* colonizador(~a)
m(f)
seven *num.* sete

several *adj.* diversos(as)
m.pl(f.pl)
sew *v.* costurar
sex *n.* sexo *m*
shade *n.* sombra *f*
shake *v.* agitar
shallow *adj.* raso(a) *m(f)*
shame *n.* vergonha *f*
shampoo *n.* xampu *m*
shape *n.* forma *f*; *v.* formar
share[1] *n.* parte *f*, ação da
bolsa *f*
share[2] *v.* partilhar
shark *n.* tubarão *m*
sharp *adj.* afiado(a) *m(f)*;
adv. em ponto
shatter *v.* destruir
shave *v.* barbear
she *pron.* ela *f*
sheer *adj.* puro(a) *m(f)*
sheet *n.* folha *f*, lençol *m*
shelf *n.* prateleira *f*
shell *n.* concha *f*
shellfish *n.* crustáceo *m*
shelter *n.* abrigo *m*
shepherd *n.* pastor *m*
shift *n.* mudança *f*;
v. mudar
shine *n.* brilho *m*; *v.* brilhar
ship *n.* navio *m*
shirt *n.* camisa *f*
shock *n.* choque *m*;
v. chocar
shoe *n.* sapato *m*
shoelace *n.* cordão de
sapato *m*
shoemaker *n.* sapataria *f*
shoe polish *n.* graxa de
sapato *f*
shoot *v.* atirar
shop *n.* loja *f*; *v.* fazer
compras
shore *n.* litoral *m*
short *adj.* curto(a) *m(f)*

shorten *v.* encurtar
shorts *n.* shorts *m*, calção *m*
shot *n.* tiro *m*
shoulder *n.* ombro *m*
shout *n.* grito *m*; *v.* gritar
show *n.* show *m*; *v.* mostrar
shower¹ *n.* chuva *f*,
    chuveiro *m*
shower² *v.* chover, banhar
shrimp *n.* camarão *m*
shrink *v.* encolher
shut *v.* fechar
shutter *n.* obturador *m*,
    veneziana *f*
shuttle *n.* ponte aérea *f*
shy *n.* tímido
sick *adj.* doente *mf*,
    enjoado(a) *m(f)*
side *n.* lado *m*
sidewalk *n.* calçada de rua *f*
sight *n.* vista *f*
sightseeing *n.* turismo *m*
sign *n.* sinal *m*; *v.* assinar
signal *n.* aviso *m*;
    v. sinalizar
signature *n.* assinatura *f*
sign language *n.*
    linguagem de sinais *f*
silence *n.* silêncio *m*
silent *adj.* silencioso(a) *m(f)*
silk *n.* seda *f*
silly *adj.* bobo(a) *m(f)*
silver *n.* prata *f*
similar *adj.* similar *mf*
simple *adj.* simples *mf*
since *prep.* desde;
    adv. depois;
    conj. desde que
sincere *adj.* sincero(a) *m(f)*
sing *v.* cantar
singer *n.* cantor(~a) *m(f)*
single *adj.* único(a) *m(f)*
sink *n.* pia *f*; *v.* afundar
sip *v.* beber devagar

Sir *n.* Senhor *m*
sister *n.* irmã *f*
sister-in-law *n.* cunhada *f*
sit *v.* sentar
site *n.* local *m*
six *num.* seis
size *n.* tamanho *m*
skate *n.* patim *m*; *v.* patinar
ski *n.* esqui *m*; *v.* esquiar
skin *n.* pele *f*; *v.* descascar
skip *n.* salto *m*; *v.* pular
skirt *n.* saia *f*
skull *n.* crânio *m*
sky *n.* céu *m*
slang *n.* gíria *f*
slap *n.* tapa *m*;
    v. esbofetear
sleep *n.* sono *m*; *v.* dormir
sleeping pill *n.* sonorífero *m*
sleeve *n.* manga *f*
slice *n.* fatia *f*; *v.* fatiar
slide *n.* escorregador *m*;
    v. escorregar
slim *adj.* magro(a) *m(f)*;
    v. emagrecer
slip *n.* tropeço *m*;
    v. deslizar
slipper *n.* chinelo *m*
slope *n.* rampa *f*
slow *adj.* lento(a) *m(f)*
small *adj.* pequeno(a) *m(f)*
smart *adj.* elegante *mf*,
    esperto(a) *m(f)*
smash *v.* quebrar
smashing *adj.* excelente *mf*
smell *n.* cheiro *m*; *v.* cheirar
smile *n.* sorriso *m*; *v.* sorrir
smoke *n.* fumaça *f*;
    v. fumar
smooth *adj.* macio(a) *m(f)*;
    v. alisar
smuggle *v.* contrabandear
snack *n.* petisco *m*;
    v. petiscar

snake *n.* cobra *f*

sneeze *n.* espirro *m*;
v. espirrar

snore *n.* ronco *m*; *v.* roncar

snow *n.* neve *f*; *v.* nevar

so *adv.* tão, assim

soak *v.* ensopar

soap *n.* sabão *m*

soccer *n.* futebol *m*

sock *n.* meia de calçar *f*;
v. socar

sofa *n.* sofá *m*

soft *adj.* macio(a) *m(f)*

soil *n.* solo *m*

sole *n.* sola *f*; *adj.* único(a)
m(f)

solid *adj.* sólido(a) *m(f)*

some *adj.; pron.* alguns
m.pl, algumas *f.pl*

somebody *pron.* alguém

something *pron.* algo

sometimes *adv.* às vezes

son *n.* filho *m*

song *n.* canção *f*

son-in-law *n.* genro *m*

soon *adv.* logo

sore *adj.* dolorido(a) *m(f)*

sorrow *n.* tristeza *f*

sorry *interj.* desculpe!;
adj. triste *mf*

sort *n.* tipo *m*

sound *adj.* sólido(a) *m(f)*;
n. som *m*

soup *n.* sopa *f*

sour *adj.* azedo(a) *m(f)*

south *n.* sul *m*

souvenir *n.* embrança *f*

soy *n.* soja *f*

spa *n.* estância *f*

space *n.* espaço *m*

Spain *n.* Espanha *f*

Spanish *n.;*
adj. espanhol(~a) *m(f)*

spare part *n.* peça de
reposição *f*

spark *n.* faísca *f*

speak *v.* falar

special *adj.* especial *mf*

specialty *n.* especialidade *f*

spectator *n.* espectador(~a)
m(f)

speech *n.* discurso *m*

speed *n.* velocidade *f*

spell *n.* feitiço *m*, período
m; *v.* soletrar

spend *v.* gastar

spider *n.* aranha *f*

spine *n.* espinha dorsal *f*

spit *n.* espeto *m*; *v.* cuspir

split *v.* dividir

spoil *v.* estragar

sponge *n.* esponja *f*

sponsor *n.*
patrocinador(~a) *m(f)*

spontaneous *adj.*
espontâneo(a) *m(f)*

spoon *n.* colher *f*

sport *n.* esporte *m*

spring *n.* mola *f*; *v.* pular

square *n.* quadrado *m*

squeeze *n.* aperto *m*;
v. apertar

stadium *n.* estádio *m*

stage *n.* palco *m*, estágio *m*

stain *n.* mancha *f*;
v. manchar

stainless steel *n.* aço
inoxidável *m*

stair *n.* escada *f*

stale *adj.* estragado(a) *m(f)*

stamp *n.* selo *m*; *v.* selar

staple[1] *n.* grampo *m*,
comida trivial *f*

staple[2] *v.* grampear

star *n.* estrela *f*; *v.* estrelar

start *n.* começo *m*;
v. começar

starter *n.* porção de comida *f*, entrada *f*

starve *v.* passar fome

state *n.* estado *m*

station *n.* estação *f*

statue *n.* estátua *f*

stay *n.* estadia *f*; *v.* ficar

steady *adj.* firme *mf*

steak *n.* bife *m*

steal *v.* roubar

steam *n.* vapor *m*

step *n.* passo *m*, degrau *m*

stepbrother *n.* meio-irmão *m*

stepdaughter *n.* enteada *f*

stepmother *n.* madrasta *f*

stepsister *n.* meio-irmã *f*

stepson *n.* enteado *m*

stick[1] *n.* pau *m*

stick[2] *v.* colar, aderir

still *adj.* quieto(a) *m(f)*; *adv.* ainda

sting *n.* picada *f*; *v.* picar

stink *n.* fedor *m*; *v.* feder

stitch *n.* ponto *m*; *v.* costurar

stocking *n.* meia *f*, meia-calça *f*

stomach *n.* estômago *m*, barriga *f*

stone *n.* pedra *f*

stool *n.* banquinho *m*, fezes *f*

stop *n.* parada *f*; *v.* parar

storage *n.* armazenamento *m*

store *n.* loja *f*

storm *n.* tempestade *f*

story *n.* história *f*

stove *n.* fogão *m*

straight *n.* reta *f*; *adj.* direto(a) *m(f)*; *adv.* em linha reta

strain *n.* força *f*, tensão *f*; *v.* extenuar

strange *adj.* estranho(a) *m(f)*

stranger *n.* desconhecido(a) *m(f)*

straw *n.* palha *f*

stream *n.* riacho *m*

street *n.* rua *f*

strength *n.* força *f*

stress *n.* estresse *m*

stretch *n.* trecho *m*; *v.* esticar

string *n.* barbante *m*

strip *n.* faixa *f*; *v.* despir

stroke[1] *n.* golpe *m*, derrame cerebral *m*

stroke[2] *v.* acariciar

strong *adj.* forte *mf*

student *n.* estudante *mf*

study *n.* estudo *m*; *v.* estudar

stuff *n.* material *m*; *v.* rechear

stupid *adj.* idiota *mf*

stylish *adj.* elegante *mf*

subject *n.* assunto *m*

subtitle *n.* subtítulo *m*

subtract *v.* subtrair

suburbs *n.* subúrbio *m*

subway *n.* passagem subterrânea *f*

success *n.* sucesso *m*

such *adj.* tal *mf*; *adv.* tão

suck *v.* chupar

sue *v.* processar

suffer *v.* sofrer

sugar *n.* açúcar *m*

suicide *n.* suicídio *m*

suit *n.* terno *m*; *v.* convir

suitcase *n.* mala *f*

sum *n.* soma *f*

summary *n.* sumário *m*

sun *n.* sol *m*

Sunday *n.* domingo *m*
sunflower *n.* girassol *m*
sunglasses *n.* óculos de
sol *m*
sunny *adj.* ensolarado(a)
m(f)
sunrise *n.* nascer do sol *m*
sunset *n.* pôr do sol *m*
sunstroke *n.* insolação *f*
super *adj.* ótimo(a) *m(f)*
supermarket *n.*
supermercado *m*
supper *n.* ceia *f*
supple *adj.* flexível *mf*
supply *n.* fornecimento *m*;
v. fornecer
sure *adj.* certo(a) *m(f)*
surgeon *n.* cirurgião *m*,
cirurgiã *f*
surgery *n.* cirurgia *f*
surroundings *n.* arredores
m.pl
suspect *n; adj.* suspeito(a)
m(f); *v.* suspeitar
swamp *n.* pântano *m*
swap *v.* permutar
swear *v.* jurar, falar
palavrão
sweat *n.* suor *m*; *v.* suar
sweater *n.* suéter *m*
sweep *v.* limpeza *f*; *v.* varrer
sweet *adj.* doce *mf*
swell *v.* inchar
swelling *n.* inchaço *m*
swim *v.* nadar
swimming pool *n.* piscina *f*
swimsuit *n.* roupa de
banho *f*
swing *n.* balanço *m*;
v. balançar
Swiss *n.; adj.* suíço(a) *m(f)*
switch *n.* interruptor *m*;
v. trocar
Switzerland *n.* Suíça *f*

symptom *n.* sintoma *m*
synagogue *n.* sinagoga *f*
syringe *n.* seringa *f*

T
table *n.* mesa *f*, tabela *f*
tablecloth *n.* toalha de
mesa *f*
tablespoon *n.* colher de
sopa *f*
tablet *n.* comprimido *m*,
tabuleta *f*
tackle *n.* apetrechos *m.pl*;
v. atacar
tag *n.* etiqueta *f*
tail *n.* rabo *m*
tailor *n.* alfaiate *m*
take *v.* tomar, levar
tale *n.* conto *m*, história *f*
talk *n.* conversa *f*;
v. conversar
tall *adj.* alto(a) *m(f)*
tamper *v.* mexer, misturar
tampon *n.* tampão *m*
tan[1] *n.* bronzeado *m*;
adj. bronzeado(a) *m(f)*
tan[2] *v.* bronzear
tap *n.* torneira *f*, palmada *f*,
tapa *m*
tape *n.* fita *f*; *v.* gravar
tap water *n.* água da
torneira *f*
tar *n.* piche *m*
target *n.* alvo *m*
taste *n.* gosto *m*;
v. experimentar
tasteful *adj.* gostoso(a) *m(f)*
tasty *adj.* saboroso(a) *m(f)*
tattoo *n.* tatuagem *f*
tax *n.* imposto *m*;
v. tributar
taxi *n.* táxi *m*
tea *n.* chá *m*

teach *v.* ensinar

teacher *n.* professor(~a) *m(f)*

team *n.* equipe *f*

teapot *n.* bule de chá *m*

tear *n.* lágrima *f*, rasgo *m*; *v.* rasgar

tease *v.* provocar

teaspoon *n.* colher de chá *f*

teenager *n.* adolescente *mf*

teleconferencing *n.* teleconferência *f*

telephone *n.* telefone *m*; *v.* telefonar

telephone book *n.* lista telefônica *f*

telephone number *n.* número de telefone *m*

television *n.* televisão *f*

tell *v.* contar

telltale *adj.* revelador(~a) *m(f)*

temper *n.* temperamento *m*

temperature *n.* temperatura *f*

temple *n.* templo *m*

temporary *adj.* temporário(a) *m(f)*

tempt *v.* tentar

ten *num.* dez

tenant *n.* inquilino(a) *m(f)*

tend *v.* inclinar, cuidar, tratar, cultivar

tender¹ *adj.* macio(a) *m(f)*, dolorido(a) *m(f)*

tender² *n.* moeda corrente *f*

tennis *n.* tênis *m*

tense *adj.* tenso(a) *m(f)*

tent *n.* tenda *f*

term *n.* termo *m*, prazo *m*

terrace *n.* terraço *m*, fila de casas *f*

terrible *adj.* terrível *mf*

text *n.* texto *m*

textbook *n.* livro didático *m*

textile *n.* têxtil *mf*

than *conj.* do que

thank *v.* agradecer

thankful *n.* agradecido(a) *m(f)*

thank you! *interj.* obrigado!(a) *m(f)*

that *adj.* aquele(a) *m(f)*; *pron.* que

the *art.* o(a) *m(f)*, os(as) *m.pl(f.pl)*

theater *n.* teatro *m*

theft *n.* roubo *m*

their *adj.* deles *m.pl*, delas *f.pl*

theirs *pron.* o(a) dele(a) *m(f)*,os(as) deles(as) *m.pl(f.pl)*

them *pron. pl* os, as, a eles, a elas

then *adv.* então

there *adv.* lá, ali

thermometer *n.* termômetro *m*

these *pron. pl* estes, estas

they *pron. pl* eles

thick *adj.* grosso(a) *m(f)*, burro(a) *m(f)*

thickness *n.* espessura *f*

thief *n.* ladrão *m*, ladra *f*

thigh *n.* coxa *f*

thin *adj.* fino(a) *m(f)*

thing *n.* coisa *f*

think *v.* pensar

third *adj.* terceiro(a) *m(f)*

thirst *n.* sede *f*

thirsty *adj.* com sede, sedento(a) *m(f)*

this *adj.* este *m*, esta *f*; *pron.* este *m*, esta *f*, isto (neutral)

though *conj.* embora; *adv.* no entanto

thought *n.* pensamento *m*

thousand *num.* mil

threat *n.* ameaça *f*

threaten *v.* ameaçar

three *num.* três

thrill *n.* emoção *f*

thrive *v.* crescer, progredir

throat *n.* garganta *f*

through *prep;*
adv. através de

throw *v.* jogar, lançar

thumb *n.* polegar *m*

thunder *n.* trovão *m*

thunderstorm *n.*
tempestade *f*

Thursday *n.* quinta-feira *f*

ticket *n.* bilhete *m*

tickle *v.* fazer cócegas

tide *n.* maré *f*

tie *n.* laço *m; v.* amarrar,
empatar

tight *adj.* apertado(a) *m(f)*

time *n.* tempo *m*

tip *n.* ponta *f,* gorjeta *f,*
dica *f*

tire[1] *v.* cansar

tire[2] *n.* pneu *m*

tired *adj.* cansado(a) *m(f)*

tissue *n.* tecido *m*

title *n.* título *m*

to *prep.* a, para

tobacco *n.* tabaco *m*

today *n.* hoje *m*

toe *n.* dedo do pé *m*

together *adv.* junto

toilet *n.* toalete *m,*
banheiro *m*

toilet paper *n.* papel
higiênico *m*

token *n.* símbolo *m*

toll *n.* pedágio *m*

tomb *n.* túmulo *m*

tombstone *n.* lápide *f*

tomorrow *adv.* amanhã

tongue *n.* língua *f*

tonight *adv.* hoje à noite

too *adv.* demais, também

tool *n.* ferramenta *f*

tooth *n.* dente *m*

toothache *n.* dor de dente *f*

toothbrush *n.* escova de
dente *f*

toothpaste *n.* pasta de
dente *f*

toothpick *n.* palito *m*

top *n.* topo *m,* alto *m;*
adj. alto(a) *m(f)*

topple *v.* derrubar

torch *n.* lanterna *f*

toss *v.* jogar para cima,
virar

total *n.; adj.* total *mf;*
v. totalizar

touch *n.* toque *m; v.* tocar

touched *adj.* tocado(a) *m(f)*

tough *adj.* duro(a) *m(f),*
resistente *mf*

tour *n.* excursão *f*

tourism *n.* turismo *m*

tourist *n.* turista *mf*

tournament *n.* torneio *m*

tow *v.* rebocar

toward *prep.* para

towel *n.* toalha *f*

tower *n.* torre *f*

town *n.* cidade *f*

toy *n.* brinquedo *m;*
v. brincar

track *n.* caminho *m;*
v. caminhar

trade *n.* comércio *m;*
v. comerciar

tradition *n.* tradição *f*

traffic *n.* tráfego *m*

trail *n.* rastro *m; v.* rastrear

trailer *n.* reboque *m*

train *n.* trem *m; v.* treinar

tramp *n.* mendigo(a) *m(f)*

transfer *n.* transferência *f*
translate *v.* traduzir
translation *n.* tradução *f*
translator *n.* tradutor(~a) *m(f)*
transport *n.* transporte *m;* *v.* transportar
trap *n.* armadilha *f*
trash *n.* lixo *m*
trash can *n.* lata de lixo *f*
travel *n.* viagem *f; v.* viajar
traveler *n.* viajante *mf*
traveler's check *n.* cheque de viagem *m*
tray *n.* bandeja *f*
tread *n.* pisada *f; v.* pisar
treasure *n.* tesouro *m*
treat *n.* bom presente *m;* *v.* tratar
tree *n.* árvore *f*
trend *n.* tendência *f,* moda *f*
trial *n.* teste *m,* julgamento *m*
tribe *n.* tribo *f*
tribute *n.* tributo *m*
trick *n.* truque *m;* *v.* enganar
trim *v.* aparar
trimmings *n.* acompanhamento nas comidas *m*
trip *n.* viagem *f; v.* tropeçar
trouble *n.* problema *m;* *v.* incomodar
truck *n.* caminhão *m*
true *adj.* verdadeiro(a) *m(f)*
trunk *n.* tronco *m*
trust *n.* confiança *f;* *v.* confiar
truth *n.* verdade *f*
try *n.* tentativa *f; v.* tentar
tub *n.* banheira *f*
tube *n.* tubo *m,* metrô *m*

Tuesday *n.* terça-feira *f*
tuition *n.* ensino *m,* custo do ensino *m*
tumor *n.* tumor *m*
tuna *n.* atum *m*
tune *n.* melodia *f; v.* afinar, sintonizar
tunnel *n.* túnel *m*
turn *n.* volta *f; v.* virar
turnover *n.* volume de negócios *m*
tuxedo *n.* traje smoking *m*
tweezers *n.* pinça *f*
twice *adv.* duas vezes, duplamente
twin *adj.* gêmeo(a) *m(f)*
twins *n.* gêmeos *m.pl*
twist *n.* virada *f; v.* torcer
two *adj.* dois *m,* duas *f; num.* dois
type *n.* tipo *m; v.* teclar
typical *adj.* típico(a) *m(f)*

U

ugly *adj.* feio(a) *m(f)*
ulcer *n.* úlcera *f*
umbrella *n.* guarda-chuva *m*
unable *adj.* incapaz *mf*
unauthorized *adj.* desautorizado(a) *m(f)*
unaware *adj.* inconsciente *mf*
unbearable *adj.* insuportável *mf*
unbelievable *adj.* inacreditável *mf*
uncalled-for *adj.* desnecessário(a) *m(f)*
uncle *n.* tio *m*
uncomfortable *adj.* incômodo(a) *m(f)*

unconscious *adj.* inconsciente *mf*

under *prep.* sob, embaixo de; *adv.* embaixo

underground *adj.* subterrâneo(a) *m(f)*

understand *v.* compreender

undertake *v.* empreender

underwear *n.* roupa de baixo *f*

undo *v.* desfazer

undress *v.* despir

undue *adj.* indevido(a) *m(f)*

uneasy *adj.* inquieto(a) *m(f)*

uneven *adj.* desigual *mf*

unfamiliar *adj.* estranho(a) *m(f)*

unfair *adj.* injusto(a) *m(f)*

unfold *v.* desdobrar

unforgettable *adj.* inesquecível *mf*

unhappy *adj.* descontente *mf*

unhealthy *adj.* insalubre *mf*

uniform *n.* uniforme *m*; *adj.* uniforme *mf*

union *n.* união *f*

unique *adj.* original *mf*

unit *n.* unidade *f*

United States *n.* Estados Unidos *m*

universal *adj.* universal *mf*

universe *n.* universo *m*

university *n.* universidade *f*

unkempt *adj.* desleixado(a) *m(f)*

unknown *adj.* desconhecido(a) *m(f)*

unlawful *adj.* ilegal *mf*

unless *conj.* a menos que

unlike *adj.* diferente *mf*; *prep.* ao contrário de

unlikely *adj.* improvável *mf*

unlimited *adj.* ilimitado(a) *m(f)*

unload *v.* descarregar

unpack *v.* desempacotar

unplug *v.* desligar

unsafe *adj.* perigoso(a) *m(f)*

until *prep.* até

untoward *adj.* desfavorável *mf*

unusual *adj.* incomum *mf*

up *adv.* acima de, para cima

up-and-coming *adj.* prometedor(~a) *m(f)*

update *v.* atualizar

upgrade *v.* aperfeiçoar

upkeep *n.* manutenção *f*

upper *adj.* superior *mf*

uppermost *adj.* mais elevado(a) *m(f)*

upright *adj.* vertical *mf*

ups-and-downs *n.* altos e baixos *m.pl*

upset *n.* estrago *m*; *v.* estragar

upside-down *adv.* de cabeça para baixo

upstairs *adv.* piso superior

uptight *adj.* nervoso(a) *m(f)*, acanhado(a) *m(f)*

up-to-date *adj.* moderno(a) *m(f)*

urban *adj.* urbano(a) *m(f)*

urge *n.* vontade *f*

urgent *adj.* urgente *mf*

urinal *n.* urinol *m*

urine *n.* urina *f*

urn *n.* urna *f*

us *pron.* nos, nós

use *n.* uso *m*; *v.* usar

used *adj.* usado(a) *m(f)*

useful *adj.* útil *mf*

useless *adj.* inútil *mf*

user *n.* usuário(a) *m(f)*

usual *adj.* usual *mf*
usually *adv.* geralmente
utensil *n.* utensílio *m*
utter *adj.* completo(a) *m(f)*
U-turn *n.* virada 180° *f*

V

vacancy *n.* vaga *f*
vacant *adj.* desocupado(a) *m(f)*
vacation *n.* férias *f.pl*
vaccinate *v.* vacinar
vaccine *n.* vacina *f*
vacuum cleaner *n.* aspirador de pó *m*
vague *adj.* vago(a) *m(f)*
valid *adj.* válido(a) *m(f)*
validate *v.* validar
validity *n.* validade *f*
valley *n.* vale *m*
valuables *n.* artigos de valor *m.pl*
value *n.* valor *m*
van *n.* caminhonete *f*
vanilla *n.* baunilha *f*
vapor *n.* vapor *m*
various *adj.* vários(as) *m(f)*
vary *v.* variar
vast *adj.* vasto(a) *m(f)*
VCR *n.* gravador de vídeo *m*
VDU *n.* monitor *m*
vegetable *n.* vegetal *m*
vegetarian *n.*; *adj.* vegetariano(a) *m(f)*
veil *n.* véu *m*; *v.* velar
vein *n.* veia *f*
velvet *n.* veludo *m*
venereal disease *n.* doença venérea *f*
vengeance *n.* vingança *f*
venison *n.* carne de caça *f*
venom *n.* veneno *m*
vent¹ *n.* respiradouro *m*

vent² *v.* falar
venture *n.* empreendimento *m*; *v.* aventurar
verb *n.* verbo *m*
verdict *n.* veredicto *m*
verge *n.* beira *f*
verify *v.* verificar
versatile *adj.* versátil *mf*
versus *prep.* contra
vertebra *n.* vértebra *f*
vertigo *n.* vertigem *f*
very *adv.* muito
vessel *n.* vaso *m*, navio *m*
veterinarian *n.* veterinário(a) *m(f)*
veto *n.* veto *m*; *v.* vetar
vex *v.* irritar
vexed *adj.* polêmico, aborrecido, irritado(a) *m(f)*
via *prep.* por, via
viable *adj.* viável *mf*
vicious *adj.* violento(a) *m(f)*
victim *n.* vítima *mf*
view *n.* vista *f*, opinião *f*; *v.* examinar
vile *adj.* vil *mf*, repugnante *mf*
villa *n.* vila *f*
village *n.* aldeia *f*
vine *n.* videira *f*
vinegar *n.* vinagre *m*
vineyard *n.* vinhedo *m*
violent *adj.* violento(a) *m(f)*
virgin *n.* virgem *f*; *adj.* virgem *mf*
virtual *adj.* virtual *mf*
virtue *n.* virtude *f*
visa *n.* visto *m*
visibility *n.* visibilidade *f*
visit *n.* visita *f*; *v.* visitar
visitor *n.* visitante *mf*

vital *adj.* vital *mf,*
   essencial *mf*
vitamin *n.* vitamina *f*
vocabulary *n.* vocabulário *m*
voice *n.* voz *f*
void *adj.* vazio(a) *m(f)*
voltage *n.* voltagem *f,*
   tensão *f*
volunteer *n.* voluntário(a)
   m(f); v. oferecer
volume *n.* volume *m*
vomit *n.* vômito *m;*
   v. vomitar
vote *n.* voto *m; v.* votar
voucher *n.* vale m, bilhete *m*
vow *n.* voto *m*
vowel *n.* vogal *f*

W

wage *n.* salário *m*
waist *n.* cintura *f*
wait *n.* espera *f; v.* esperar
waiter *n.* garçom *m*
waiting *n.* espera *f*
waitress *n.* garçonete *f*
wake *v.* acordar
walk *n.* caminhada *f;*
   v. andar
wall *n.* parede *f*
wallet *n.* carteira *f*
wander *v.* perambular
want *n.* falta *f; v.* querer
war *n.* guerra *f*
ward *n.* ala *f,* bairro *m*
warm *adj.* morno(a) *m(f)*
warn *v.* prevenir
warning *n.* aviso *m*
warranty *n.* garantia *f*
wary *adj.* cauteloso(a) *m(f)*
wash *n.* lavagem *f; v.* lavar
wasp *n.* vespa *f*
waste[1] *n.* desperdício *m,*
   lixo *m*

waste[2] *v.* esbanjar,
   desperdiçar
watch[1] *n.* relógio *m*
watch[2] *v.* ver, assistir
water *n.* água *f; v.* regar
waterproof *adj.*
   impermeável *mf*
watt *n.* watt *m*
wave *n.* onda *f,* aceno *m;*
   v. acenar
wax *n.* cera *f; v.* encerar
way *n.* modo *m,* caminho *m*
weak *adj.* fraco(a) *m(f)*
weakness *n.* fraqueza *f*
wealth *n.* riqueza *f*
wealthy *adj.* rico(a) *m(f)*
weapon *n.* arma *f*
wear *n.* uso *m; v.* usar,
   vestir
weary *adj.* cansado(a) *m(f)*
weather *n.* tempo *m*
web *n.* teia *f*
website *n.* website *m*
wed *v.* casar
wedding *n.* bodas *f,*
   casamento *m*
wedding ring *n.* aliança *f*
Wednesday *n.* quarta-feira *f*
week *n.* semana *f*
weekday *n.* dia de
   semana *m*
weekend *n.* fim de
   semana *m*
weep *v.* chorar
weigh *v.* pesar
weight *n.* peso *m*
weird *adj.* estranho(a) *m(f)*
welcome[1] *n.* boas vindas *f.pl;*
   adj. bem-vindo(a) *m(f)*
welcome[2] *v.* acolher
well[1] *n.* poço *m*
well[2] *adv.* bem
west *n.* oeste *m,* ocidente *m*

wet *adj.* molhado(a) *m(f)*; *v.* molhar

what *pron.* que

whatever *adj.* qualquer *mf*

wheat *n.* trigo *m*

wheel *n.* roda *f*

when *adv.*; *conj.* quando

where *adv.*; *conj.* onde

wherever *adv.* onde quer que

whether *conj.* se

which *pron.* que; *adj. interrog.* qual?

while *n.* certo tempo *m*; *conj.* enquanto

white *adj.* branco(a) *m(f)*

who *pron.* que, qual, quem; *interrog.* que? qual? quem?

whoever *pron.* quem quer que

whole *adj.* inteiro(a) *m(f)*, todo(a) *m(f)*

why *n.* porquê; *adv.* por que

wide *adj.* largo(a) *m(f)*

widow *n.* viúva *f*

widower *n.* viúvo *m*

wife *n.* esposa *f*

wig *n.* peruca *f*

wild *adj.* selvagem *mf*

win *v.* vencer

wind[1] *n.* vento *m*

wind[2] *v.* dar corda em relógio

window *n.* janela *f*

windshield *n.* pára-brisa *m*

wine *n.* vinho *m*

wing *n.* asa *f*, ala *f*

winner *n.*; *adj.* vencedor(~a) *m(f)*

winter *n.* inverno *m*

wipe *v.* limpar

wire *n.* arame *m*, fio *m*

wise *adj.* sábio(a) *m(f)*

wish *n.* desejo *m*; *v.* desejar

wit *n.* presença de espírito *f*

with *prep.* com

withdraw *v.* retirar

within *prep.* dentro de; *adv.* dentro

without *prep.* sem

witness *n.* testemunha *f*; *v.* presenciar

woman *n.* mulher *f*

womanizer *n.* mulherengo *m*

wonderful *adj.* maravilhoso(a) *m(f)*

wolf *n.* lobo *m*

wood *n.* madeira *f*

wool *n.* lã *f*

word *n.* palavra *f*

work *n.* trabalho *m*; *v.* trabalhar

world *n.* mundo *m*

worldwide *adj.* global *mf*, mundial *mf*

worry *n.* preocupação *f*; *v.* preocupar

worse *adj.* pior *mf*; *adv.* pior; *n.* o pior *m*

worsen *v.* piorar

worship *n.* culto *m*, adoração *f*; *v.* adorar

worst *adj.* pior *mf*

worth *n.* valor *m*

worthy *adj.* merecedor(~a) *m(f)*

wound *n.* ferida *f*; *v.* ferir

wrap *v.* embrulhar pacote

wreck *n.* naufrágio *m*; *v.* destruir

wrinkle *n.* ruga *f*; *v.* enrugar

wrist *n.* pulso *m*

write *v.* escrever

writer *n.* escritor(~a) *m(f)*

wrong[1] *n.* injustiça *f*;
   adj. errado(a) *m(f)*
wrong[2] *v.* injustiçar

X
xenophobia *n.* xenofobia *f*
X-ray *n.* raio-X *m*

Y
yacht *n.* iate *m*
yard *n.* jarda *f*, quintal *m*
yawn *n.* bocejo *m*;
   v. bocejar
year *n.* ano *m*
yell *n.* berro *m*; *v.* berrar
yellow *adj.* amarelo(a) *m(f)*
yes *adv.* sim
yesterday *adv.* ontem
yet *adv.* ainda; *conj.* porém
yield *n.* produção *f*, renda *f*;
   v. render
YMCA *n.* ACM *f*

you *pron.* você, vocês
young *adj.* novo(a) *m(f)*,
   jovem *mf*
yours *pron.* teu *m*, tua *f*, de
   vocês *mf.pl*
yourself *pron.* você
   mesmo(a) *m(f)*
youth *n.* juventude *f*
youth hostel *n.* albergue da
   juventude *m*

Z
zeal *n.* zelo *m*
zero *num.* zero
zest *n.* entusiasmo *m*
zigzag *n.* ziguezague *m*
zip code *n.* código postal *m*
zipper *n.* zíper *m*
zone *n.* zona *f*
zoo *n.* jardim zoológico *m*
zoom *n.* zumbido *m*;
   v. enfocar
zucchini *n.* abobrinha *f*

PHRASEBOOK CONTENTS

BASICS

Yes	**Sim** (normally followed by **faz favor**)
No	**Não, obrigado.**
Maybe	**Pode ser, talvez, quem sabe**

Attention! — Portuguese has a strange idiom:

Pois sim > means "**certainly NOT**" or "in no circumstances whatsoever!"
Pois não > means "**YES**, with pleasure" or "How can I help you?"

Greetings and Niceties

Hello	**Oi, olá**
Please	**Favor** (normally **faz favor** or **por favor**, but when spoken, "**faz**" and "**por**" are almost inaudible)
OK? Are you alright?	**OK? Tudo bem?**
How are you?	**Como vai?**
Good	**Bom**
Not good	**Não 'tá bom, não é bom**
OK	**OK, está bem**
Nice to meet you	**Prazer**, or **prazer em conhecer**
Good morning	**Bom dia**
Good afternoon	**Boa tarde** (until 6 P.M.)
Good evening	**Boa noite** (on meeting)
Good night	**Boa noite** (on departing)
Good-bye!	**Tchau! Até logo!**
I am sorry; pardon.	**Desculpe**
Sorry for bothering you	**Desculpe incomodar**

Excuse me	**Com licença** (asking to make way or take something)
Don't mention it	**De nada**
Thank you very much	**Muito obrigado (a)**
Thank you	**Obrigado (a)**
Welcome	**Bem-vindo (a)**
What is your name?	**Qual é seu nome?**
My name is ...	**Meu nome é ...**
I like ...	**Eu gosto de ...**
I don't like ...	**Não gosto de ...**
I need ...	**Preciso ...**
I would like ...	**Queria ...**
I want ...	**Quero ...**
I don't want ...	**Não quero ...**

Being Understood

Do you speak English?	**Fala inglês?**
Do you understand?	**Entendeu?**
I do not understand	**Não entendo**
I understand	**Entendí**
I want ...	**Eu queria ...**
Please repeat that	**Quer repetir por favor**
Please write it down	**Favor escrever**

Common Questions

How far?	**É longe?**
How many?	**Quantos?**
How much?	**Quanto?**
How?	**Como?**
What?	**Que?**
Where is?	**Onde fica? Onde está?**
Where?	**Onde?**
Which?	**Qual?**
Who?	**Quem?**
Why?	**Porque?**

Hand Gestures

In Brazil

1. Raised palm of the hand = Hello! Alright? How are you? Thank you. And **STOP** (by traffic officials). Repeated raised palm of the hand = slow down and stop.
2. Horizontal palm of the hands moving forwards = After you! Go!
3. Crossed fingers = Friends (they are, we are)
4. Raised thumb in a fist = OK! Thank you! Alright!
5. A fig (the thumb between the index and middle fingers in a fist) = Good luck!

DO NOT, In Brazil

1. Make the American signal for **OK.** The thumb and index finger in a circle is equivalent to showing the back of the raised middle finger in America.
2. Wave the back of the hands towards another person as it shows disdain.

THINGS TO KNOW BEFORE TRAVELING

People

Brazil is a mixed race society. Half of the 170 million people originally came from European countries such as Portugal, Italy, Spain, Germany, Poland, and the Ukraine. The other half of the population is a mixture of former African slaves, indigenous peoples, and some Asian and Middle Eastern minorities. According to studies, there are 49 shades of skin complexion in Brazil from black to white. Thanks to mixed raced marriages Brazil has developed a race of its own, dominated by a very friendly tropical culture.

Dress Codes

Over the last fifty years the formal habit of wearing a suit, jacket and a tie has virtually disappeared. Nowadays, the work attire is more properly adapted to the tropical climate. Casual shirts, T-shirts, trousers and light suits are common and more comfortable in the tropical heat. In cases of first encounters and business engagements over-dressing is recommended for men; women generally have more freedom when choosing their attire. Only at very formal banquets and balls are dinner jackets and long dresses advisable.

Air-conditioning

You will find air-conditioning in the majority of first-class hotels, cinemas, theaters, offices, shopping malls, and some long distance coaches. In many places, however, the new trend of elegant ceiling fans is the fashion.

Tipping

This is less practiced than in the United States. "Keep the change" is a nice gesture (but not mandatory) for cab drivers, and other personnel (from a few *centavos* to 1 real). Normally, 10% is included in the check, so waiters, in most restaurants, don't expect tips. Tipping is only practical in most cases due to the shortage of small change. Barbers and porters might expect to receive something. Over-tipping is not recommended; R$1 (one real), in most cases, is considered OK.

Language

Most Brazilians like to think that they speak a little English. So, talk to them in simple phrases in both English and Portuguese, if you can. Whatever you do, avoid using Spanish without warning them first. An apology is ideal in these situations, "Sorry, I don't speak Portuguese. Do you understand Spanish?" *Desculpe, não falo Português. Você entende Espanhol?* A great deal of face-to-face communication is made through gestures and facial expressions. Shouting is of no help. Speak slowly and in a simplified manner.

Asking For Help to Solve a Problem

When faced with a difficult problem, the magic phrase is *faz favor, dá um jeitinho*—said in a humble, almost begging tone. "*Jeitinho*" is a "knack" or an unorthodox way of doing something. So, the nearest English translation for this would be something like "please, I am sure you can help me" or "please, I am sure you know another way to fix this." A tip for solving a problem is not necessary and sometimes insulting. Whatever you do never mention or offer a bribe to an official!

Physical Contact and Etiquette

With authorities keep a cool and distant attitude. Ask to speak with your consulate if a problem arises. With everybody else physical contact is very much appreciated. Handshakes with everyone from porters to business partners are expected. A pat on the shoulder is sometimes worth more than a tip. Embracing is not typical on a first encounter unless you have been communicating with the person for long time. Later on, a handshake and/or a pat on the shoulder are enough. When meeting socially, the etiquette with women includes handshakes and kisses on the cheek.

Invitations

If invited to someone's house for a dinner party, don't bring a bottle of wine, but a bottle of whisky! For the lady of the house flowers are a good choice. Small gifts from your country of origin are also very much appreciated. Another nice gesture is to treat your hosts to a meal at a restaurant of their choosing.

ACCOMMODATION

Hotels

The international hotels in Brazil have the same standards of accommodations as anywhere else in the world. For a more local flavor there are numerous hotels with the same—if not higher—standards. These are the nostalgic *Grand Hotels* from the *Belle Époque* that have managed to keep an ambiance of yesteryear as well as a taste of Brazilian culture intact. As a rule of thumb, any hotel that charges less than US$40 per person/night might not offer a reasonable standard.

Reservations

It is quite difficult to judge and reserve a hotel room from abroad. It is also usually unnecessary. Most hotels are not full and checking-in formalities are minimal. During the *Carnaval* season, however, you are advised to book in advance.

Prices

Everything is open to negotiation in Brazil. If you arrive without a firm booking in a hotel not belonging to an international chain, ask to speak with the manager, who, in many cases, is also the owner. State the duration of your stay and ask for the best possible price. You may be surprised at what you are offered.

Standards

In larger cities most rooms are double occupancy with satellite TV (American and European channels) and a private bathroom. Most hotel rooms are usually only furnished with twin beds. Therefore, depending on your needs, a double bed must be specifically requested. A rich and plentiful breakfast (normally self-service) is often included in the price. Room service is usually provided, but not always available. In many hotels fax machines are available.

Electricity

This is a nightmare. In cities, neighborhoods, and even within buildings some sockets are 110v and others are 220v. You must always read the notices above the sockets or ask Reception. Likewise, the Brazilian electrical sockets may differ from the European and American plugs. It is advisable that you buy a *universal* adaptor to suit your equipment before traveling to Brazil. If you have any problems ask the hotel for help. Brazilian sockets do not have a third hole to ground the connection, however, to prevent damage from lightening, etc, Brazilian buildings are normally protected. Still, for delicate and/or expensive equipment, it is not advisable to use them during severe thunderstorms.

Tipping

Porters, maids and room service staff will be happy with R$1.00. Waiters and bar staff do not normally expect tips because the service is included in the check. However, they will not refuse small change.

Hotel Cab Drivers

Receptionists and porters will promptly call *their* cabs, which are usually outside the hotel ready to go. This is more convenient and safer than looking for taxi stations or stopping cabs in the street. To be sure, always ask the hotel cab "how much?" They should also obey the price on the taximeter.

Other Accommodations

Less Expensive Hotels

You will have fewer services, probably be farther from the city center, and be generally less safe. These are also called *Outsides*.

Youth Hostels

The tourist offices (at airports, bus stations, offices in town) will indicate the nearest hostels.

Camping

It is only advisable on predetermined sites indicated and managed by established "camping associations." To go camping at will, by one's own initiative, is not common in Brazil and should be avoided for safety reasons.

Motels

In Brazil, motels are usually paid by the hour and designed for brief love encounters. Outside the big cities, however, motels might serve as hotels. First class hotels in Brazil will not book rooms by the hour!

adaptor	**adaptador**
air conditioning	**ar condicionado**
ambulance	**resgate, ambulância** (*See also "Medical Help"*)
balcony	**balcão, sacada**
bar with show	**boite, nightclube**
bath foam/bubbles	**espuma de banho**
bathroom	**banheiro**
bathtub	**banheira**
bed	**cama**

beer	**cerveja**
bill	**conta**
blow dryer	**secador de cabelo**
breakfast	**café da manhã**
broken	**quebrado**
champagne	**champanhe**
check	**conta**
cleaners/ dry-cleaners	**tintureiro, lavagem a seco**
cleaning lady	**faxineira (o)**
cleaning person	**faxineira**
comb	**pente**
dance	**danceteria**
deodorant	**desodorante**
dirty	**sujo**
discount	**desconto**
double bed	**cama de casal**
elevator	**elevador**
error	**erro**
foreign	**estrangeiro**
fork	**garfo**
glass	**copo**
gym	**sala de ginástica**
hairbrush	**escova de cabelos**
hairdresser	**cabelereira**
help	**ajuda**
hot water	**água quente**
housekeeper	**arrumadeira**
hygienic towel	**absorvente**
ice	**gelo**
keys	**chaves**
knife	**faca**
laundry services	**lavanderia**
light bulb	**lâmpada**
local food	**comida típica**
magazine	**revista**
maid	**arrumadeira**
manager	**gerente**
manicure	**manicure**
mini-fridge	**frigobar**

mistake	**erro**
music	**música**
newspaper	**jornal**
painkiller	**analgésico**
pillow	**travesseiro**
pillowcase	**fronha**
plate	**prato**
police	**polícia**
porter	**carregador, porteiro**
price	**preço**
radio	**rádio**
reception	**recepção, portaria**
remote control	**controle remoto**
restaurant	**restaurante**
room	**quarto**
room number	**número do quarto**
room service	**serviço de quarto (comida/bebida)**
safe	**cofre**
shampoo	**xampu**
shaver	**barbeador**
shaving cream	**creme de barbear**
sheets	**lençol**
shoe shiner	**engraxate**
shower	**chuveiro**
soap	**sabonete**
socket (electrical)	**soquete, plug**
soft drink	**refrigerante**
spoon	**colher**
swimming pool	**piscina**
switchboard	**telefonista**
telephone	**telefone**
toothbrush	**escova de dentes**
toothpaste	**pasta de dente**
towel	**toalha**
travel agency	**agência de turismo**
TV, television	**televisão**

view	**vista**
voltage	**voltagem**
warm covers	**cobertor**
water	**água**
window	**janela**
wine	**vinho**

Where is the nearest/cheapest/good hotel?
Onde tem um hotel perto/barato/bom?

What is the address?
Onde fica?

Could you write it down please?
Escreve, por favor?

I have a reservation.
Fiz uma reserva.

I have no reservation.
Não tenho reserva.

I need a room for . . .	**Preciso de um quarto para . . .**
. . . the night.	**. . . uma noite**
. . . three days	**. . . três dias**
. . . one week	**. . . uma semana**

What is your name?
Qual é o seu nome?

My name is . . .
Meu nome é . . .

Do you give a discount for more days?
Tem desconto para mais dias?

I would like a room with ... **Queria um quarto ...**
   ... a single bed   **... de solteiro**
   ... two twin beds   **... de duas camas**
   ... a double bed   **... cama de casal**
   ... a cot   **... com um berço**
   ... cable/satellite   **... televisão a cabo/**
      television   **satélite**

How much does it cost per night?
Qual é o preço por noite?

Does that include breakfast?
O café da manhã está incluído?

Do you accept credit card?
Aceita cartão de crédito?

Do you have room service?
Tem serviço de quarto?

I lost my key (card).
Perdi a chave (cartão) do quarto.

I need to send ... **Preciso mandar ...**
   ... a fax   **... um fax**
   ... an E-mail   **... um E-mail**
   ... a letter   **... uma carta**

I need to make a phone call.
Preciso de um telefone.

Do you have a safe?
Vocês têm um cofre?

I need to wash my clothes.
Preciso lavar minhas roupas.

The room is missing ... **No quarto não tem ...**
   ... fresh towels   **... toalhas limpas**
   ... clean sheets   **... lençóis limpos**
   ... soap, shampoo   **... sabonete, xampu**

It is not working.
Não está funcionando.

It is broken.
Está quebrado.

I want . . .	**Quero . . .**
. . . to eat something	**. . . comer algo**
. . . a doctor	**. . . um médico** (*See also "Medical Help"*)

Where is. . . ?	**Onde fica. . . ?**
. . . the laundry	**. . . a lavanderia**
. . . breakfast	**. . . o café da manhã**
. . . the conference room	**. . . a sala de conferências**
. . . the drugstore	**. . . a farmácia**
. . . the safe	**. . . o cofre**
. . . the sauna	**. . . a sauna**
. . . the swimming pool	**. . . a piscina**
. . . the beauty saloon	**. . . o salão de beleza**

I need to buy . . .	**Preciso comprar . . .**
. . . cigarettes	**. . . cigarros**
. . . flowers	**. . . flores**
. . . batteries	**. . . pilhas, baterias**
. . . an adapter	**. . . um adaptador**

What is the price?
Qual é o preço?

A cab please.
Um taxi por favor.

Go to this address.
Quero ir neste endereço.

MEANS OF COMMUNICATION

Hotel Room Telephones

You can ask the switchboard to help with your connections, but most hotels provide you with a direct line.

Public Phones

Each State has its official provider, but you are allowed to use any provider listed in the phone booths. (*See "Making A Phone Call" in the following section.*)

Phone Cards/Calling Cards

To use a public phone you need a phone card, which are available everywhere: newsstands, bars, and cigarette kiosks, etc. Buy a few cards as soon as you arrive to avoid future searches.

Public Phone Booths

These are a feature of the national folklore and humor. They are bright in color and are the shape of a big ear, thus, they are called *orelhão* (big ear).

Emergency Services

Police, Fire, and Rescue service (ambulance) can be called at no charge. Emergency numbers may vary according to the State. For most States the following is used:

Police ... **190** or **147**
— say *Polícia*

Ambulance/First Aid   ... 192
  — say *Ambulância*, *Resgate* (*see* Fire Department *below*)

Fire Department   ... 193
  — say *Fogo* (fire) or *Resgate* (rescue)[1]

Traffic accidents   ... 194
  — say *Acidente*

Civil defense   ... 199
  — say *Disastre* (disaster), *Desabamento* (collapse), *Enchente* (flood)

Phone Directory Help   ... 0800 77 15 102
  — say *Preciso o número de ...* (add the name of the person or place)

Faxes

Most hotels will be able to send and receive faxes for you. The post office will also have fax services. In addition, a number of shops can send faxes and make photocopies for you.

E-mail and Internet

Very few hotels will allow you to use their computers. However, some have TVnets in their rooms. Big cities also have Cybercafes.

International Delivery Companies

Most private international delivery services operate in Brazil and will come to collect your package at your hotel. Pre-payment is necessary.

---

1. Brazilian Fire Departments double as ambulances/first aid for populations where no ambulances are available. The key word is *Resgate* (rescue).

Tele- and Video Conferences

These are available at large hotels and conference centers. You must book in advance.

air mail	**via aérea**
authenticated photocopy[2]	**xerox autenticada**
cable TV[3]	**tv a cabo**
collect call (reverse the charge)	**chamada a cobrar**
delivery (private international) companies	**companhias de entrega particulares**
dial tone[4]	**sinal de chamando**
E-mail	**e-mail**
engaged	**ocupado**
engaged/ busy tone[5]	**sinal de ocupado**
express service	**sedex**
extension	**ramal**
fax	**fax**
foreign country	**país estrangeiro**
help	**ajuda**
intercity	**interurbano**
international phone calls	**telefonema internacional**
interstate	**entre estados**
mark	**selo, carimbo**
mobile (cellular) phones	**telefone celular**
no hurry	**sem pressa**
phone	**telefone**

---

2. *Xerox autenticada por um Tabelião* (Notary). These are to be found in city centers—they photocopy only originals and stamp them as to confirm its veracity.
3. Brazil has a variety of TV services: cable, satellite networks (DirectTV, Sky, Net, InternetTV), the receptionist/porter will tell you what is available in your room and how to operate it.
4. The dial tone is a continuous, low-pitch sound.
5. The busy tone is a very short, high-pitch, repetitive sound.

phone call	**telefonema**
phone card	**cartão de telefone**
phone line	**linha telefônica**
photocopy	**xerox**, **fotocópia**
post office	**correio**
receipt	**recibo**
receipt of delivery	**recibo de entrega**
satellite tv	**tv satélite**, **tv por assinatura**
stamp	**selo**, **carimbo**
telephone company	**operadora**
telephone operator	**telefonista**
urgent	**urgente**

Making a phone call

Follow the instructions below.

1. **To make a local phone call:**
    * listen to the dial tone (a single, continuous, low-pitch sound)
    * dial the desired local number

2. **To make a national call:**
    * dial 0 + XX (this is the number of the provider of your choice, for example 015, 021, 023, etc) + the city/area code (called DDD in Brazil) + the desired phone number

3. **To make an international call:**
    * dial 00 + XX (for example, 0015, 0021, 0023, etc) + the Country code + the city/area code (without the initial zero) + the desired phone number

4. **To make a collect call, both domestically and internationally:**
    * dial 9 before dialing the desired number sequence. You will hear a recorded message

that will ask you to give your name and where you are calling from. The person you are calling will have to accept the charges.

If you are still having trouble call the phone company, where an English-speaking operator will help you.

International calls:	**0800 70 32 111**
National calls:	**0800 70 32 110**

Do you speak English?
Fala inglês?

Can you help me, please?
Pode me ajudar por favor?

Could you please tell me the code for . . .	**Você pode me informar o código . . .**
. . . (country)	**. . . do país** (*name of country*)
. . . (city)	**. . . da cidade** (*name of city*)

Do you speak English?
Fala inglês?

Operator, I need help.
Telefonista, preciso de ajuda.

I am having problems making a telephone call.
Tenho dificuldades com um telefonema.

Please, I need to make . . .
Por favor, preciso fazer uma ligação para . . .
. . . an international call for country X.
. . . para o país X.
. . . a call to X (*city name, State*).
. . . para cidade X, estado X.

I want to make a collect call, please.
Quero fazer uma chamada a cobrar, por favor.

I am . . .	Estou . . .
. . . in another bedroom	. . . em outro quarto
. . . in the breakfast room	. . . na sala do café da manhã
. . . in the conference room	. . . na sala de conferência
. . . in the gym	. . . na sala de ginástica
. . . in the hall	. . . no saguão
. . . at the swimming pool	. . . na piscina
. . . outside	. . . lá fora

I want to talk to . . .
Quero falar com . . .

I would like to leave a message for . . .
Gostaria de deixar um recado para . . .

Sorry, wrong number.
Desculpe foi engano.

Are there any messages for me?
Tem algum recado para mim?

Tell the person that . . .	**Diga à pessoa que . . .**
. . . I am not here	. . . não estou aqui
. . . I am busy	. . . estou ocupado
. . . you could not find me	. . . você não me encontrou
. . . I went out	. . . saí, estou fora
. . . I am at this phone number	. . . estou neste telefone
. . . I am at this address (write it down)	. . . estou neste endereço (anote)
. . . Mr. / Mrs. . . . has called	. . . o Senhor/ a senhora . . . telefonou

Where is the nearest post office?
Onde é a agência do Correio mais perto?

What is the quickest way?
Como seria mais rápido?

Where can I send an E-mail?
Onde posso passar um e-mail?

How long does it take?
Quanto tempo leva?

I want to send this, please.
Quero mandar isto, por favor.

Can the hotel send this for me?[6]
Alguém do hotel poderia enviar isto?

Send the page for me . . .
Mande o boy me chamar . . .

How much is it?
Quanto é?

---

6. In this case, a "goodwill tip" is in order to anyone at the hotel, including the receptionist/manager. This guarantees quick service. Do not over tip. Something above R$1.00 is sufficient.

AIRPORT

Brazil has numerous international airports, but you are likely to arrive in São Paulo (Guarulhos Airport) or Rio de Janeiro (Galeão). In all of the international airports there are English-speaking personnel supplied by the airlines. Officials (Federal Police, Customs) usually do not speak English. Signs are likely to be displayed both in English and Portuguese.

Regional Air Travel

Practically every city with a population over 500,000 has an airport. Regional air travel is safe and affordable. Between large cities such as São Paulo and Rio there are shuttles (*Ponte Aérea*), where booking is not necessary and a plane departs every half-hour. Of course, the primary advantage of shuttle service is speed. The price of a ticket will vary. Normally you depart from and arrive at smaller airports in the city centers (e.g. Congonhas in São Paulo to Santos Dumont in Rio).

International Brazilian airports also have Duty-Free shops *on arrival*. They sell imported drinks, and electronics equipment. The shopping allowance is $500.00 per traveler. The prices are usually 25% cheaper than in the local shops.

Notes:
- if you carry medicines, it is advisable to have a medical doctor's prescription to legitimize its use;
- it is useful to ask the price and distance to the place you want to go; taxis have taximeters, but some drivers may ignore this;
- tipping cab drivers: R$1.00 plus small change (coins), in most cases, is sufficient.

airplane	**avião**
airport	**aeroporto**
arrival	**chegada**
baby changing room	**fraudário**
bus	**ônibus**
cab	**táxi**
carry-on bag	**sacola**
cash machine	**caixa automática**
check-in	**check-in**
control	**controle**
cost	**preço**
credit card	**cartão de crédito**
customs	**alfândega**
debit card	**cartão de débito**
departure	**partida**
destination	**destino**
drugstore	**farmácia**
exchange	**câmbio**
exit	**saída**
fine	**multa**
judge's office	**juizado, juiz**
luggage	**bagagem**
medical doctor	**médico**
minibus (*shared by several people*)	**lotação**
passport	**passaporte**
penalty	**multa**
pharmacy	**farmácia**
pilot	**piloto**
porter (*to carry luggage*)	**carregador**
price	**preço**
stewardess	**aeromoça**
suitcase	**mala**
taxi	**táxi**
terminal	**terminal**
there	**lá**
tip	**gorjeta**
to pay	**pagar**
tote bag	**sacola**

tourism	**turismo**
travel agency	**agência de viagem**
traveler	**viajante**
traveler's check	**cheque de viagem**
trip	**viagem**
trolley	**carrinho**
visa	**visto**
voyage	**viagem**
way out	**saída**
where?	**onde?**

I would like a . . .	**Quero . . .**
. . . one-way ticket	**. . . passagem só de ida**
. . . return trip ticket	**. . . passagem de ida e volta**

I would like to leave at . . . o'clock.
Desejo sair a . . . hora.
(*See "Quick Reference" for numbers and telling time*)

What are the departure times?
Quais os horários das partidas?

Where is. . . ?
Onde fica. . . ?

The plane is delayed.
O avião está atrasado.

The plane is cancelled.
O vôo foi cancelado.

Which airport?
Qual aeroporto?

How long? (*the trip/ the wait*)
Quanto tempo leva?

What is the price?
Qual é o preço?

What is this?
O que é isso?

I need . . .
Preciso . . .

Is it far?
É longe?

What do I need to do?
Que preciso fazer?

Nothing to declare.
Nada a declarar.

Open this case.
Abra esta mala.

Show me.
Me mostre.

Please!
Por favor!

Thank you!
Obrigado(a)!

TRANSPORTATION

In-town Transportation

Buses

The most widely used system of transportation is bus travel. In larger cities it is possible to go just about anywhere by bus. The difficulty, of course, is deciding which bus to take! Most buses have a description of their route posted on the front or side of the bus. The easiest solution is to ask someone in the hotel or wherever you are staying. In some larger cities, attendants at the bus stop will provide information and will even sell you tickets. If you climb on a bus without a ticket you can still buy one from the driver at no extra cost. Drivers can also give you information and will likely tell you when and where you should get off. Fellow passengers are also glad to help with directions.

Subway

São Paulo's subway is one of the most modern in the world. It is clean, efficient and cheap. Other large cities also have subways of good quality. Unfortunately they do not cover the entire span of the city. Still, many do have connections with buses. Unified tickets and transfers are also available for travelers switching from bus to subway and vice versa.

Cabs/Taxis

This is the most practical form of transportation for those unfamiliar with Brazilian cities. All have taximeters that will tell you the fare. When traveling longer distances, one should agree on a fee with the taxi driver first. Taximeters do not take effect outside the limits of the city, so always ask the price.

Cab Stations/Stands

Taxi stations are widespread throughout the big cities and you must go to the first cab in line. All cabs have an illuminated sign on top that says, "TAXI." If lit, the cab is free. Do not stand for a long time at a city corner waiting for a cab. It's much simpler to ask someone in uniform or to inquire at a nearby bar where the next taxi station is.

Lotação *or Minibuses*

This is a very convenient way to travel inside the big cities, however, it takes some practice getting use to them. These minibuses (10 to 12 passengers) follow the exact route of the buses with the advantage of being faster and sometimes less expensive. The attendant at the bus stop can help you. Inside the *lotação* there is also an attendant, you only need to say the place you want to go and the attendant will nod "yes" (climb in), or wave "no," (and depart).

Sightseeing Excursion Buses

These are the best, safest and most convenient way to see the sights. The guides always speak English.

Regional and National Travel

Coach/Bus Travel

You can go anywhere in Brazil by long-distance bus. The Brazilian national bussing system is the second best option to domestic air travel. There are several central bus stations in many towns, *Estação Rodoviária* (intercity bus centrals). You can, however, ask the driver to drop you anywhere you want along the route. You may call for information but they do not book seats over the phone. However, you may ask the hotel to buy the ticket for you. Prepaid tickets are necessary and can be purchased at cashiers that display the main destinations of that particular bus company. From other cities connections are probably necessary. A ticket costs approximately a third of the price of an airplane ticket. The buses are comfortable and equipped with toilets. Some have air-conditioning and reclining chairs. Beware: some trips can last up to 72 hours! Stops for meals are frequent. By-the-road restaurants, bars and cafés are safe, clean and usually offer a variety of local food and drink.

Rent-a-car

There are car rental agencies in Brazil. However, they are usually local and do not offer the same facilities as in other countries—for example, you usually must return your car to the pick up point. If you go off the main highways (*auto-estradas*) the road signals are poor and might not be in good condition.

Long Distance Cabs

In an emergency you can also book a taxi for long distance travel. You must always agree on the price first, considering all the details: stops, waiting time, return time, etc.

Plane

(*See "Airport" for information on plane travel*)

Journey by Train or Boat

Railways and boat trips are used mostly for leisure, but not regularly to get from point A to point B. Modern trains are used mostly within larger city limits. For long distances they are slow and largely inconvenient. The old Brazilian railways are romantic trips to the past and are worthwhile for those who have the time. Boat trips are also available and make for romantic getaways. Some meander alongside the beautiful Brazilian coast and stop at major cities and points of interest along the way. These boats are very comfortable and quite affordable. Others are designed as river cruises and are located in some of the most exciting natural settings in the world. Trips through the forests of Pantanal and the Amazon River Basin are often geared for comfort and sightseeing.

arrival	**chegada**
avenue	**avenida**
baggage	**bagagem**
boarding pass	**cartão de embarque**
boat	**navio, barco**
bus	**ônibus**
bus stop	**ponto de ônibus**
cab	**taxi**
cab stop	**parada de taxis**
city center	**centro da cidade**
coach	**ônibus**
departure	**partida**
driver	**motorista**
hand luggage	**bagagem de mão**
intercity bus station	**estação rodoviária**
intersection	**cruzamento**
minibus	**lotação**
number	**número**
passenger	**passageiro**
port	**porto**

porter	**carregador**
price	**preço**
ship, large boat	**navio**
station	**estação**
street	**rua**
subway	**metrô**
suitcases	**malas**
taxi	**taxi**
taxi station	**ponto de táxi**
terminal (bus)	**Rodoviária**
ticket	**passsagem**
train	**trem**
travel agency	**agência de viagem**

<u>Taxi</u>

Do I pay by the taximeter?
É por taximetro?

Take the quickest route.
Vá pelo caminho mais rápido.

Is it far?
É longe?

Is it a fixed price?
É preço fixo?

How much is it?
Quanto é?

Where is the next taxi stand?
Onde fica o ponto de táxi mais perto?

How do I get there?
Como chegar lá?

Take me to this address, please.
Me leve neste endereço por favor.

I am in a hurry.
Estou com pressa.

This is close enough.
Aqui está bom.

Is this. . . ?
Isso é. . . ?

Stop, please!
Pára, por favor!

BUSES/ COACHES AND MINIBUSES

How often does the bus come?
O ônibus tem toda hora?

Which one goes to. . . ?
Qual deles vai para. . . ?

Could you write it down, please?
Pode escrever para mim, por favor?

Can I reserve a space?
Posso reservar lugar?

Is this seat taken?
Está ocupado? (*pointing to the seat*)

That is my seat.
Esse é meu lugar.

That is my bag.
Essa é minha sacola.

Do I have to change buses?
Preciso trocar de ônibus?

I would like to go . . . (*polite way*)
Queria ir . . .

How much time will it take?
Quanto tempo demora?

How much longer?
Falta muito ainda?

Tell me when.
Me avise por favor. (*asking the driver of a bus where to get out*)

What is the arrival time?
Qual é a hora da chegada?

Is this the stop for. . . ?
Essa é a parada para. . . ?

Where can I use a telephone?
Onde posso telefonar?

MONEY

The Brazilian currency is the **Reais** (**Real**) represented by **R$**. One *Real* has 100 *centavos* (cents). The exchange rate is, of course, variable. The best rates can be obtained at banks, the worst at exchange bureaus. Most hotels accept traveler's checks and sometimes exchange banknotes, but the rate is uncertain.

Note:
Sometimes cab drivers and porters accept US dollars. This practice is **not** advisable as travelers are likely to receive poor exchange rates. Also, if at all possible, it is advisable to arrive in Brazil with some *Real* from the country of origin.

Banknotes and Coins

Coins

1, 5, 10, 25, 50 *centavos* and 1 *real*.

Banknotes

1, 2, 5, 10, 20, 50 and 100 *reais*. The 10 *reais* notes come in two forms–the old one is paper, and the new one is synthetic.

Exchanging Money

Banks

If you have the time and patience banks are the best places for rates and security. Ask or look for the section *Câmbio* (Foreign Exchange). The main banks in Brazil are: *Banco do Brasil, Banco Itaú, Banco Real, HSBC, Bank Boston, Bradesco, Unibanco.*

Hotels

They will cash your traveler's check, accept some debit cards and credit cards, but most of them will pay you the lower "tourist" rate.

Cash Machines (ATMs)

This is one of the best ways to take out some *reais.* American debit cards are accepted at most ATMs. Some will limit your withdrawal to 600 *reais,* others will deliver up to 1,000 *reais.* If possible, choose a cash machine inside a bank. *Banco 24 horas* is a cash machine that operates at practically all banks.

Security Tip

Always carry some 50 *reais* on you just in case you are mugged. This will likely satisfy the mugger and allow you to escape unscathed. Do not resist an assault. Avoid deserted places at night and try to keep a low profile. Also, in restaurants and stores, try not to let your debit card or credit card out of your sight. Duplication of cards, although very rare, has been known to happen.

account	**conta bancária**
bank	**banco**
banknote	**nota**
bill, check (*hotels, restaurants*)	**conta**
branch	**agência bancária**
cash machine	**caixa eletrônica**

cashier	**caixa**
change	**troco**
cheap	**barato**
check	**cheques**
checkbook	**talão de cheques**
clerk	**funcionário(a)**
coin	**moeda**
counter	**balcão**
credit card	**cartão de crédito**
currency	**moeda corrente**
debit card	**cartão de débito**
deposit	**depósito**
exchange	**câmbio**
exchange bureau	**casa de câmbio**
exchange rate	**taxa de câmbio**
expenses	**despesas**
expensive	**caro**
foreign currency	**moeda estrangeira**
help	**ajuda**
information	**informação**
line/ queue	**fila**
manager	**gerente**
money	**dinheiro**
money order	**ordem de pagamento, vale postal**
official rate	**dólar comercial**
parallel dollar (*at exchange bureaus*)	**dólar paralelo**
(to) pay	**pagar**
payment	**pagamento**
payment transfer	**transferência de fundos**
price	**preço**
receive	**receber**
safe box	**cofre**
security	**segurança**
tipping	**gorjeta**
tourist dollar	**dólar turismo**

transfer	**transferência**
traveler's check	**cheque de viagem**
withdrawal	**retirada**, **saque**

Where is the nearest bank?
Onde fica o banco mais próximo?

Could you change this to smaller notes?
Pode trocar em notas miúdas?

I would like to exchange these traveler's checks.
Queria trocar estes cheques de viagens.

Could you explain it to me?
O que é isso?

How much money can I withdraw with this card?
Quanto posso tirar com este cartão?

Show me . . .
Me mostra . . .

You gave me the wrong change.
Você me deu troco errado.

Call the manager.
Me chama o gerente.

Please!
Por favor!

I need . . .
Preciso . . .

I want . . .
Queria . . .

I would like . . .
Quero . . .

Keep the change for yourself.
Fica com o troco.

Keep the change.
Está certo.

Thank you!
Obrigado(a)!

DRINKS

Water

Tap water in Brazil is safe to drink. The water is treated and periodically tested. Public health is taken seriously in Brazil, and news of waterborne illnesses travel quickly. In most cases, locals will know what to do if there is an outbreak. If you are still unsure, boiling the water for approximately twenty minutes will greatly reduce your chances of getting sick. Water purifying tablets can also be bought in most major cities. Even in small villages you will find clean bars and other vendors where bottled water and soft drinks are sold.

There is also an abundance of natural springs in the mountain towns of Brazil. Locals use these fountains in their day-to-day lives; these natural springs are regularly checked by public health authorities. Never take the risk of drinking water from unknown brooks or rivers without the advice of locals.

Bottled Water

Some water in Brazil is naturally gasified, but others are carbonated. You must specify with (*com gás*) or without gas (*sem gás*).

Juices

It is worth trying some of the natural and exotic juices of Brazil. Water is rarely added, and they are usually made on the spot. You can specify your taste: pure, with sugar, ice, or milk.

Milk Shakes

If some milk, sugar, or ice is added, the juice becomes a *batida*. They are a quite thick and may constitute a meal in themselves. In some places a *batida* is an alcoholic drink since they add spirits. Make sure to specify.

Bottled Soft Drinks

You will find soft drinks everywhere including the usual international brands. However, try the local *Guaraná*, a bottled fizzy soft drink with several brand names, but nationally known by the generic name of *Guaraná*, an Amazonian fruit juice used for centuries by the local Indians. It is a mild stimulant, but less so than a cup of coffee. Bottled carbonated lemonades and orange juices are also common.

Beers

Brazil is the fourth largest beer producer in the world, in the same league as the United States and Germany. Brazilian beer is always of low fermentation. It is slightly more flavored than American beers, but lighter in taste than European beers. The alcoholic concentration is pretty standard, around 5%. If available, ask for a *chope*—draft beer on tap—instead of bottles or cans.

Spirits

The national spirit is made from sugarcane. It is a kind of white rum that has many nicknames: *pinga, cachaça*, etc. It is used in an excellent cocktail—*caipirinha*—mostly made from lime, sugar and ice and very similar to a daiquiri. It is possible to ask for *caipirinhas* made with other fruits such as *macarujá* (passion fruit).

Pure Brazilian Rums

Although they are not expensive to begin with, avoid the very cheap ones. They might have a

slightly yellow or blue tint to them. Prices vary from
$0.50 a liter to $25.00 a liter.

Wines

Brazilian wines vary widely in price and quality.
They come as dry, medium sweet, and sweet. The
colors are of the standard red, white and rosé.
Brazilian sparkling wines are not bad and are still
called *champanhas*, or *frisantes* (sparkling). You
may pay anything from US$1.00 to US$10.00 for a
bottle of Brazilian wine. Price is not a criterion of
good wine, but the well-known ones are usually
more expensive. There are also very drinkable
wines made from peaches, strawberries, and
pineapples.

NON-ALCOHOLIC DRINKS

apple	**maçã**
avocado	**abacate**
bottled water	**água mineral**
carrot	**cenoura**
cashew	**cajú**
cold	**gelado**
ice	**gelo**
juice	**suco**
lime	**limão**
mango	**manga**
melon	**melão**
milk	**leite**
milkshake	**vitamina**
mineral water	**água mineral**
orange	**laranja**
passion fruit	**maracujá**
peach	**pêssego**
pineapple	**abacaxi**
soft drink	**refrigerante, suco**
strawberry	**morango**
tea	**chá**

DRINKS

tomato	**tomate**
water	**água**
watermelon	**melancia**

ALCOHOLIC DRINKS

aperitif	**aperitivo**
beer on tap	**chope, chopp**
bottle	**garrafa**
bottle of beer	**cerveja em garrafa**
bubbling	**frisante**
can of beer	**cerveja em lata**
daiquiri	**caipirinha**
dark beer	**cerveja preta**
draft beer	**chope, chopp**
drink	**bebida, aperitivo**
dry	**seco**
fruit cocktail	**batida de fruta**
half bottle	**meia garrafa**
ice	**gelo**
imported	**importado**
liqueur	**licor**
liquor	**bebida destilada**
liter	**litro**
medium	**suave**
national	**nacional**
red wine	**vinho tinto**
sweet	**doce**
whisky	**whisky or uísque**
white rum	**pinga, cachaça**
white wine	**vinho branco**
wine	**vinho**

HOT DRINKS

black coffee (*without milk*)	**café preto** (***sem leite***)
cappuccino coffee	**cappuccino**
cocoa	**chocolate quente**
coffee	**café**

coffee (*with steamed milk*)	**café com leite**
espresso coffee	**café expresso**
milk	**leite**
skimmed milk	**leite desnatado**
sugar	**açúcar**
sweetener	**adoçante**
tea	**chá**

I would like some . . .	**Eu queria . . .**
. . . beer/ wine/ a soft drink/ juice	**. . . cerveja/ vinho/ refrigerante/ suco**

Ice, please.
Gelado, por favor.

How big is the bottle?
Qual o tamanho da garrafa?

What would you recommend?
O que você recomenda?

I want it with . . .	**Quero com . . .**
. . . ice/ sugar/ sweetener/ milk	**. . . gelo/ açúcar/ adoçante/ leite**

I want it without . . .	**Quero sem . . .**
. . . ice/ sugar/ milk	**. . . gelo, açúcar, leite**

EATING OUT

Making a reservation is not usually necessary. At popular restaurants, on special days, (like Sundays), and at certain hours you may have to wait before being seated.

1. Restaurants per kilo (*Restaurante por kilo*). These are self-service restaurants where you choose from the available items and place the desired quantity you want on your plate. Every food item costs the same amount per kilo. At the end of the line your plate is weighed and the cost is added to the bill, which you keep in your hands for a second helping. Order drinks from a waiter.

2. Snacks (*Porções*).
Usually located outdoors with tables and umbrellas, these places are meant for relaxing. Ask for "portions"—*porções* from your waiter or waitress. These plates are to be shared by all guests as appetizers, but you rarely need a full meal after the appetizers. The portions are usually prawns, diced beef, fried cheeses, meats, french fries, etc.

3. Special ethnic restaurants.
In many cities, you will find diverse cuisine from all parts of the world. These include exotic foods from other parts of Brazil that are uncommon to local Brazilians.

4. Rotation restaurants.
They are called *Rodízios* in Brazil. They serve you non-stop meat, chicken or fish. This is a "must" as they have a unique ambience to them. Like restaurants per kilo, you choose the trimmings (sides): french fries, rice, salads, vegetables, etc. Then you choose a table where a little ball or card awaits you; one side is green, the other side is red. If your card

is left green, the wait staff will continue placing all sorts of food on your plate: filet steaks, pork, sausages of all types, chicken, and more exotic birds, etc. You can always refuse whatever they put in front of you. If you want to stop, simply flip the card to the red side. Most *Rodízios* are of mixed meats, but you can find some that specialize only in chicken, game birds, or fish. The price is fixed, but it excludes drinks. Tipping is not needed as it is already added into the check. Just round the total up to the nearest *real*. A kind word to the cashier is appreciated—*Muito bom!* (Very good!).

5. Vegetarian restaurants and dishes.

You can ask for a vegetarian menu in any restaurant. There are also some very specialized vegetarian restaurants in many cities.

Food Poisoning

This is relatively rare in Brazil. Due to the quantity of fresh food and the safety precautions taken in the tropical climate, extra care goes into the preparation and preservation of food.

Staple foods

Throughout Brazil the most common foods are kidney beans, rice, steak, french fries, fried eggs, vegetables, greens and rich salads. Bread, butter and olives are common accompaniments.

Ethnic influences

Italian cuisine (pastas, pizzas, etc) is part of a normal Brazilian's diet. Arab nibbles (esfihas, kibes) are found together with Italian and Japanese snacks. You don't need to look for them, although there are specialized Japanese, Arabic, Italian, Chinese, French, Spanish, and Portuguese restaurants as well.

Notes:
- Ask for a full description of a dish before ordering, ask to try a spoonful in case of doubt; some regional foods are very hot (*apimentado*).
- Do not hesitate sending a dish back if you don't like it. Brazilians are very accommodating and are not likely to get annoyed by this. They take great pride in their food and aim to please.
- In Brazil, *couverts*, cover charges (bread, butter, olives, water, linen napkins) are never charged.

Tipping/Gratuity

If you are very pleased with the service, you may add an extra tip above the (10%) service tax already included. Ask to make sure the tip is already included.

SERVICE

bill	**conta**
cashier	**caixa**
check	**conta**
chef	**cozinheiro chefe**
cook	**cozinheiro**
dish	**prato (tipo de comida)**
maître d'	**maitre**
menu	**menu, cardápio**
napkin	**guardanapo**
table	**mesa**
tip	**gorjeta**
towel	**toalha**
waiter	**garção**
waitress	**garçonete**

DINNERWARE

cup	**xícara**
cutlery	**talheres**
dish	**prato**
fine glass	**taça**
fork	**garfo**
glass	**copo**
ice bucket	**balde de gelo**
knife	**faca**
mug	**caneca**
plate	**prato**
spoon	**colher**

FOOD PREPARATION

boiled	**cozido**
buttered	**à milanesa**
fried	**frito**
grilled	**grelhado, na chapa**
mash	**purê**
minced	**picadinho**
raw	**mal passado**
roasted	**assado**
sauce	**molho**
sautéed	**refogado**
sliced	**fatiado**
stewed	**ensopado**
thin slice	**fatias finas**
well done	**bem passado**

MEALS

breakfast	**café da manhã**
dinner	**jantar**
lunch	**almoço**
snack	**lanche**
supper	**ceia**

BREAKFAST FOODS

bread	**pão**
butter	**manteiga**
cereals	**cereais**
cheese	**queijo**
cold meats	**frios**
egg and bacon	**ovos com bacon**
fruits	**frutas**
jam	**geléia**
margarine spread	**margarina**
orange juice	**suco de laranja**
pancake	**panqueca**
porridge	**mingau**
sliced bread	**pão de forma**
toast	**torradas**
wholegrain bread	**pão integral**
yogurt	**iogurte**

CHEESES

cheddar	**cheder**
cottage cheese	**ricota**
curd cheese	**requeijão, catupiry**
fresh cheese	**queijo fresco**
gorgonzola	**gorgonzola**
grated cheese	**queijo ralado**
mozzarella	**mussarela**
parmesan	**parmesão**
Swiss cheese	**queijo suíço**

EGG DISHES

egg	**ovo**
fried egg	**ovo frito**
hard-boiled egg	**ovo cozido duro**
omelet	**omelete** (*you can have chives, cheese, tomatoes, etc*)

poached egg	**ovo pochê**
scrambled egg	**ovo mexido**
soft-boiled egg	**ovo cozido mole**
well-fried egg	**ovo bem frito**

STARTERS

bread	**pão**
butter	**manteiga**
cheese	**queijo**
cold plates	**frios**
frankfurter sausage	**salsicha**
hors d'ouvres	**canapés, salgadinhos**
hot dog	**cachorro quente**
mayonnaise	**maionese**
nibble	**belisco, salgados**
nuts	**amendoins**
olives	**azeitonas**
pate	**patê**
pickles	**picles**
quail eggs	**ovos de codorna**
salami	**salame**
sausage	**lingüiças**
savory snacks	**salgadinhos**
side-dishes	**porções**
starters	**salgadinhos, entrada**
toast	**torradas**

SPICES AND SAUCES

basil	**manjericão**
bay leaf	**folhas de louro**
chili	**pimenta malagueta**
garlic	**alho**
ketchup	**catchup, ketchup**
madeira sauce	**molho madeira**
marinade	**vinha d'alho**
mustard	**mostarda**
oil	**óleo**
olive oil	**azeite**

onion	cebola
oregano	orêgano
parsley	salsa
pepper	pimenta do reino
salt	sal
soy sauce	molho de soja, shoyu
spring onion, chive	cebolinha verde
tomato sauce	molho de tomate
vinaigrette	vinagrete
vinegar	vinagre
white sauce	molho branco
Worcestershire sauce	molho inglês

SALADS

cucumber	pepino
green salad (*raw*)	salada de folhas
lettuce	alface
radish	rabanete
watercress	agrião

ROOTS AND VEGETABLES

beetroot	beterraba
broccoli	brócoli
brussels sprout	couve-de-bruxelas
cabbage	repolho
carrot	cenoura
cauliflower	couve-flor
eggplant	berinjela
green beans	feijão verde
heart of palm	palmito
jersey potatoes	batatinha inglesa
manioc	mandioca
mash	purê
mushroom	cogumelo
onion	cebola

peas	**ervilha**
peas in a pod	**ervilha com casca**
potato	**batata**
spinach	**espinafre**
spring greens	**couve**
sweet corn	**milho verde**
sweet manioc	**mandioquinha**
sweet pepper	**pimentão**
sweet potato	**batata doce**
tomato	**tomate**
turnip	**nabo**
zucchini	**abobrinha**

FISH AND SEAFOOD

It is impossible to list all the fish and seafood available in the different regions of Brazil. Below are the most common fish and seafood you'll find. Some restaurants offer a *rodízio* (i.e. try a little of everything) as explained previously.

cod	**bacalhau**
crab	**carangueijo, siri**
little shark	**cação**
lobster	**lagosta**
mussel	**marisco**
octopus	**polvo**
oyster	**ostra**
pescada	**pescada** (*a small white fish with no bones*)
prawn	**camarão grande**
salmon	**salmão**
sardines	**sardinhas**
scampi	**lagostinha**
shrimps	**camarãozinho**
squid	**lula**
trout	**truta**
tuna	**atum**

<u>M</u>EATS

bacon	**bacon, toucinho**
barbecue	**churrasco**
beef	**vaca**
breast	**peito**
bull	**boi**
chicken	**galinha, frango**
duck	**pato**
frog	**rã**
goose	**ganso**
jerked/dried beef	**carne seca**
kid (*young goat*)	**cabrito**
lamb	**carneiro**
leg	**pernil**
meat	**carne**
minced	**moída**
pork	**porco**
quail	**codorna**
rabbit	**coelho**
rib	**costeleta**
sausage	**lingüiça**
skewer	**no espeto**
steak	**bife**
thigh	**coxa**
turkey	**peru**
veal	**vitela**

<u>S</u>OUPS

broth	**caldo**
soup	**sopa**
stew	**ensopado** (*vegetables, meat or fish, with little liquid*)

BRAZILIAN CUISINE

barbecue	**churrasco**
black beans with meats (*beef, pork, sausages*)	**feijoada**
boneless	**sem osso**
fried manioc flour with many ingredients	**farofa**
fried potatoes/chips	**batatas fritas**
grilled	**grelhado**
kidney beans	**feijão**
meat	**carne**
rice	**arroz**
steak	**bife**
with the bone	**com osso**

COMMON INTERNATIONAL DISHES

cheese and tomato sauce pizza	**pizza de mussarela**
chocolate pizza	**pizza doce de chocolate**
esfiha	**esfiha, mini pizzas** (*with minced meat toppings*)
garlic and oil	**alho e óleo**
gnocchi	**inhoque** (*pasta made from potato flour*)
kibe	**quibe, croquettes** (*minced meat cakes*)
lasagna	**lazanha**
pasta	**macarrão**
pizza	**pizza**
risotto	**risoto**
rucula and parma ham pizza	**pizza de rúcula e presunto**
spring rolls	**pastel** (*meat, shrimp, hearts of palm, cheese fillings*)
wood oven pizza	**pizza à lenha**

<u>FRUITS</u>

apple	**maçã**
banana	**banana**
grape	**uva**
guava	**goiaba**
kiwi	**kiwi**
lime	**limão**
mango	**manga**
melon	**melão**
orange	**laranja**
papaya	**papaya, mamão**
passion fruit	**maracujá**
pineapple	**abacaxi**
tangerine	**mexerica**
watermelon	**melancia**

<u>SWEETS, CAKES AND DESSERTS</u>

biscuits	**biscoitos**
cakes	**bolos**
candy/sweet	**doce**
caramel	**caramelados**
cookies	**bolachas**
dried fruits	**frutas secas**
fruit in syrup	**frutas em calda**
honey	**mel**
ice cream	**sorvetes**
jam	**geléia**
jelly	**gelatina**
mousse	**mousse**
popcorn	**pipoca**
pudding	**pudim**
tart, pie	**torta**

We would like to eat something.
Queremos comer algo.

We would like breakfast/ lunch/ dinner.
Queremos café da manhã/ almoçar/ jantar.

Do you have. . . ?
Tem. . . ?

I would like. . . , please.
Quero. . . , por favor.

Explain this to me!
Me diz o que é isso!

How big is the portion?
Porção para quantas pessoas?

I want something light and quick.
Quero algo ligeiro.

Is it very hot (*spicy*)?
É muito apimentado?

Sorry, I don't like this.
Desculpa, não gostei.

May I change it for something else?
Posso trocar por outra coisa?

May I try a little?
Posso provar?

Please bring some more of this.
Por favor traga mais disto.

What do you recommend. . . ?	**O que você recomenda. . . ?**
. . . for a starter?	**. . . para começar?**
. . . for a main course?	**. . . como prato principal?**
. . . for dessert?	**. . . como sobremesa?**

Please bring the bill.
Por favor, a conta.

The . . . is missing . . .
Está faltando o . . .

This is a tip for you.
Isso é para você.

(*In case no gratuity was added, or if you were especially happy with the service, give the tip directly to the waiter/ waitress*)

SHOPPING

Duty-free Shops in Brazilian Airports

Brazilian and imported goods are available on departure and on arrival. The imported goods are approximately 25% cheaper than you'll find in Brazilian shops. Brazilian duty-free goods are genuine and of good quality, but if you have time to shop around, you might find the same products elsewhere in a larger variety for a similar price. Thus, it's recommended that you buy imported products on arrival and Brazilian goods on departure. Standard Brazilian exports such as coffee, chocolates, liqueurs and some clothing make good purchases. There is a limit of US$500 per person for purchases on arrival.

Shopping Malls

In Brazil these are called shopping centers. In larger cities you will find shopping centers that offer a large variety of shops including supermarkets, boutiques, shoe shops, and exclusive women's clothing stores. The prices are competitive.

Best Buys

Precious Stones and Jewelry

As souvenirs, the geodes (stones with a cavity of crystals inside) come in all shapes and sizes and contain crystals of many different types of semi-precious stones. You can buy them rough (without polishing), or you can have them mounted (with matching polished stones). You can also ask the shopkeeper for certificates of authenticity. Buying the stones in a downtown area will give you the assurance of a reputable jeweler. Visiting an open-air market, where you will find interesting art objects as well as stones for low prices is always a viable option.

Wool Clothes

Wool products are everywhere in Brazil. However, in colder places (i.e. the south, southeast, and in mountain towns) you can buy good quality wool directly from the manufacturer at a more reasonable price.

Popular Arts and Crafts

These items are a matter of personal taste. Whatever you're interested in Brazil has much to offer. For instance, primitive and modern paintings, tapestries, sculptures (made of wood, clay, metal and stone); agate and onyx ashtrays and statues, soapstone boxes, as well as small polished agate and onyx stones sold by the kilo.

Shoes

Brazil is a large producer of shoes and leather products (handbags, clothes, art objects). (*See also* "*Shoes*")

Electronics

If you insist on an imported product you may have to pay international prices, however, many Brazilian products are of the same quality as their international competitors. If purchasing a Brazilian product please be aware that the specifications for use, such as the voltage requirements, may differ.

agate	**ágata**
amethyst	**ametista**
aquamarine	**água marinha**[7]
beryl	**berílio**
blue citrine	**citrina azul**
bracelet	**pulseira**
Brazilian stones	**pedras brasileiras**
brooch	**broche**
buy	**comprar**
citrine quartz	**quartzo citrina**
crystal	**cristal, quartzo**
earring	**brincos**
emerald	**esmeralda**
imperial topaz (authentic)	**topázio imperial**
gem	**gema**
geode	**geodo**
gold	**ouro**
jewel	**jóia**
jeweler	**joalheiro**
jewelry store	**joalheria**
karat	**quilate**
necklace	**gargantilha, corrente, colar**
onyx	**ônix**
pendant	**pingente**
platinum	**platina**
precious	**preciosa**
ring	**anel**
ruby	**rubi**
sapphire	**safira**
sell	**vender**
semi-precious	**semi-preciosa**
shop	**loja**
silver	**prata**
soapstone	**pedra sabão**

---

7. Blue citrine is identical to aquamarine, only an expert can tell the difference. Acquamarine is far more expensive.

stones	**pedras**
store	**loja**
topaz	**topázio**[8]
tourmaline	**turmalina**
white gold	**ouro branco**
yellow citrine	**citrina amarela**
	(*false topaz*)

Will you give me. . . ?	**O(a) senhor(~a) me dá. . . ?**
. . . a written warranty	**. . . certificado de garantia por escrito**
. . . an extra gift	**. . . um chorinho, um brinde**

What is the discount for all of it/everything?
Por tudo, quanto é o desconto?

How much?
Quanto custa?

I want something . . .	**Quero algo . . .**
. . . less expensive	**. . . não caro**
. . . of good quality	**. . . de boa qualidade**
. . . different	**. . . diferente**
. . . typical/ regional	**. . . típico da região/ regional**

Can I exchange this?
Posso trocar isto?

I want to return this.
Quero devolver isto.

You did not give me the correct change.
Você me deu o troco errado.

---

8. Yellow citrine is commonly called *topázio* in Brazil. The only real topaz is the *Topázio Imperial* that is also yellow. Always ask.

Can I pay by credit card?
Posso pagar com cartão de crédito?

Where can I find. . . ?
Onde poderia encontrar. . . ?

Can you help me?
Você pode me ajudar?

I'm just looking.
Estou só olhando.

That[9]	**aquele, aquela**
This	**este, esta**
These	**estes, estas**
Those	**aqueles, aquelas**

Can I look at it?
Posso olhar?

Do you have anything. . . ?	**Você tem algo. . . ?**
. . . bigger	**. . . maior**
. . . smaller	**. . . menor**
. . . cheaper	**. . . mais barato**

Can you write down the price?
Pode escrever o preço?

Do you have anything else?
Vocês tem algo mais?

I'll take it.
Eu vou levar isto.

---

9. See also *A Brief Grammar* for more information on gender and plural of demonstratives.

CLOTHING

Material

Wool and cotton are of good quality in Brazil. Colder areas such as the highlands and the southern states where there is a massive wool industry offer the best deals, but sweaters are a good buy anywhere in Brazil.

Returns

Brazilian shops are very accommodating and if you keep your receipt they will allow an exchange of any article kept in good condition.

Measurements

(These are only approximate sizes; you should try all articles before purchasing). Brazilian sizes are very similar to the Continental European ones.

Repairs and Adjustments

Most shops make their own adjustments or can recommend someone nearby to adjust the size.

Colors

See "Quick Reference."

<u>Women's Clothing</u>

Women's dresses and suits

<u>UK</u>	<u>USA</u>	<u>Europe</u> (approx. Brazil)
10	8	36
12	10	38
14	12	40
16	14	42
18	16	44
20	18	46 48 50

Women's chest and waist

Inches	28	30	32	34	36	38	40	42	44	46
CM		71	76	80	87	91	97	102	107	112	117

Women's sweaters

UK/USA 32 34 36 38 40
Europe   36 38 40 42 44 46 48 50
BRAZIL — approximate to European sizes

<u>Men's Clothing</u>

Sizes

UK/USA 36 38 40 42 44 46
Europe   46 48 50 52 54 56

Note:
There are shops specialized for Large and Extra
Large sizes

CLOTHING

baseball hat	**chapéu de praia**
bathing suit	**maiô**
bathrobe	**saída de banho**
beret	**boina**
bermuda shorts	**bermuda**
bikini	**biquíni**
blazer	**bleiser**
blouse	**blusa**
bowtie	**gravata borboleta**
bra	**sutiã**
brand	**marca (etiqueta)**
button	**botão**
cap	**boné, gorro**
cardigan	**agasalho, jaqueta, meia capa**
cashmere	**casimira**
clothes shop	**loja de roupas**
coat	**casaco**
collar	**colarinho**
cotton	**algodão**
denim	**brim**
dress	**vestido**
dressing gown	**penhoar, roupão**
elastic	**elástico**
fabric	**tecido, pano**
hat	**chapéu**
hood	**capuz**
jacket	**jaqueta**
jeans	**jeans**
label	**etiqueta**
leather	**couro**
leotard	**malha**
linen	**linho**
long	**longo**
low-neckline	**decote**
nightgown	**camisola**
pajamas	**pijama**
panties	**calcinha**
panty hose	**meia calça**
pullover	**pulôver**

robe	**roupão**
satin	**cetim**
shirt	**camisa**
shoe	**sapato**
shoelace	**cordão de sapato**
shoe shop	**loja de sapatos**
short	**curto**
shorts	**shorts**
silk	**seda**
silk tights	**meia de seda**
size	**tamanho**
skirt	**saia**
sleeve (*short, long*)	**manga (*curta, comprida*)**
socks	**meias soquete, meias ¾**
sport shoes	**tenis, chuteira**
suit	**terno**
sweater	**suéter**
swimming trunks	**calção de banho**
team jerseys (*soccer*)	**camisa de time de futebol**
tie	**gravata**
tissue	**tecido, pano**
trousers	**calças compridas**
t-shirt	**camiseta manga curta**
undershirt	**camiseta sem manga**
underwear (*female*) (*male*)	**roupas íntimas, lingerie cueca**
Velcro®	**velcro**
velvet	**veludo**
warm long-sleeved shirt	**moleton, malha**
wool	**lã**
zipper	**zipper**

May I try it on?
Posso experimentar?

Do you have all sizes?
Tem todos os tamanhos?

I would like to change it for . . .
Eu queria trocar por . . .

. . . a bigger (*smaller*) size.
. . . um tamanho maior (*menor*).

. . . something else.
. . . outra mercadoria.

I need to buy a gift for a woman.
Preciso comprar um presente para mulher.

What is the fabric?
Qual o tecido?

How much?
Quanto custa?

Would you give me a discount?
Me dá um desconto?

Give me a receipt.
Me dá a nota fiscal.

SHOES

Brazil produces quality shoes, from sandals to fashionable women's wear, which are exported to America and Europe.

The prices in Brazil make shoes a very good buy.

Below are some examples of the size numbers used in Europe, America and its rough correspondence to Brazilian sizes. In general, Brazilian sizes are 1 or 2 sizes smaller than European sizes. In Europe, the numbers also vary for children and adults. Thus a size 7 in Europe must be specified if it is a children's 7, or an adult's 7.

WOMEN'S SHOES

UK	USA	Europe	Brazil
4	5½	37	35 to 36
5	6½	38	36 to 37
6	7½	39	37
7	8½	41	39
8	9½	42	39 to 40

MEN'S SHOES

UK	USA	Europe	Brazil
7	7	41	39 to 40
8	8	42	40
9	9	43	41 to 42
10	10	44	42 to 43
11	45	45	44

Colors

See "Quick Reference."

SHOES

boot	**bota**
comfortable	**confortável**
formal shoe	**sapato social**
heel	**salto**
high heel	**salto alto**
large	**grande, largo**
larger	**maior**
leather	**couro**
low shoes	**salto baixo**
manmade, synthetic	**sintético**
moccasin	**mocassim**
sandals	**sandálias**
shoe	**sapato**
shoelace	**cordão de sapato**
slippers	**chinelos**
small	**pequeno**
smaller	**menor**
sole	**sola**
sports shoe (*sneaker*)	**sapato esporte**
suede	**camurça**
trainers/tennis shoes	**sapato tênis**
Velcro®	**velcro**
wider	**mais largo**
zip	**ziper, fecho ecler**

I would like to try
    that one . . .
       . . . in the window
       . . . over there
       . . . the blue one

Gostaria de experimentar
    aquele . . .
       . . . na vitrine
       . . . ali
       . . . o azul

Can I try it?
Posso experimentar?

May I walk a bit?
Posso andar um pouco aqui?

I need a bigger size.
Preciso de um tamanho maior.

I need a smaller size.
Preciso de um tamanho menor.

Which colors do you have?
Quais as cores que tem?

How much?
Quanto?

With discount?
Com desconto?

I will pay . . .	**Vou pagar . . .**
. . . cash	**. . . a vista**
. . . by credit/ debit card	**. . . com cartão de crédito/débito**

HAIRDRESSER AND BARBER

Some hotels have beauty salons. If not, the receptionists will direct you to the nearest one. Normally they are unisex. Many offer a wide range of services like manicures, pedicures and hairdressing. Prices are usually displayed. Tipping of 10% is normal.

barber	**barbeiro**
beard	**barba**
beauty salon	**salão de beleza**
blond	**loiro**
brown	**castanho**
brush	**escova**
cap	**touca**
comb	**pente, pentear**
curly	**encaracolado**
depilation	**depilação**
dry	**secar**
dryer	**secador**
dye	**tingir**
dye color	**cor da tintura** (*See "Quick Reference" for colors.*)
foot	**pé**
hair	**cabelo**
haircut	**cortar o cabelo**
hairdresser	**cabeleireira**
hand	**mão**
hydration	**hidratação**
long	**comprido**
longer	**mais comprido**
manicure	**manicure**
moustache	**bigode**
nail	**unha**
nail polish	**esmalte**
nail polish remover	**acetona**
pedicure	**pedicure**

perm	**permanente**
shave	**barbear**
shaver	**barbeador**
short	**curto**
shorter	**mais curto**
straighten	**alisar**
trim	**aparar, cortar as pontas**
wash	**lavar**
washing	**lavagem**
white hair	**cabelos brancos**

Where can I find a beauty salon?
Onde tem um salão de beleza?

Do I need an appointment?
Precisa marcar hora?

I would like . . .
Gostaria de . . .

   . . . a perm — **. . . uma permanente**
   . . . to cut the points — **. . . cortar as pontas**
   . . . to cut here and here — **. . . cortar aqui e aqui**
   . . . a haircut — **. . . um corte**
   . . . a hair dye — **. . . tingir o cabelo**
   . . . nail treatment — **. . . fazer as unhas**
   . . . a trim — **. . . aparar**
   . . . a wash and dry — **. . . lavar e secar**
   . . . a shave — **. . . a barba**

Cut a bit more off here.
Corte um pouco mais aqui.

Not too much.
Não muito.

How much is it?
Quanto é?

DRUGSTORE[10]

You will find drugstores almost everywhere in Brazil. All drugstores have a qualified pharmacist on duty. In drugstores you'll find products and services related to health and hygiene such as medicines, Band-aids®, minor medical implements, diapers, as well as a whole range of products for hygiene and beauty. Although most products do not require a prescription, the pharmacist is trained to help you choose the right medication and advise on dosage.

Strictly Prescription Items

The drugstore will not supply these items unless you have a Brazilian doctor prescribe them with a registration number CRM (*Conselho Regional de Medicina*). Normally prescriptions are needed for hormones, strong painkillers, and some sleeping pills.

Prescription Only Medicines (POM)

Many prescription medicines do not require a doctor's written prescription. As long as you know the name of the medicine, or the generic equivalent the pharmacist should be able to assist you.

Natural Medicines

Brazil has a wealth of herbal and natural medicines that have been used by indigenous Brazilians for centuries. They are now being industrialized and sold at pharmacies. They do not require a prescription.

---

10. See also Section's *"Medical Help"* and *"Dentists."*

Medicinal and Clinical Assistance

Similar to many other Latin American and European countries, drugstores may provide medical assistance. Injections, treatment of minor wounds and insect bites, prescription of antiseptics and antibiotics can be done through a pharmacy. They may also direct you to the nearest doctor, or call an ambulance, if needed.

analgesic	**analgésico**
antihistamine	**anti-histamínico**
anti-inflammatory	**anti-inflamatório**
antiseptic	**anti-séptico (a)**
asthma	**asma**
baby tissue	**lencinho umedecido para bebês**
bandage	**atadura**
bathroom	**banheiro**
bite	**mordida**
bug	**animal**
diabetes	**diabete**
diarrhea	**diarréia**
dizziness	**tontura**
drugstore	**drogaria, farmácia**
fever	**febre**
gloves	**luvas esterilizadas**
hangover	**ressaca**
headache	**dor de cabeça**
heart	**coração**
high blood pressure	**pressão alta**
hygienic towel (*for women*)	**absorvente**
I.D.	**identidade (R.G.)**
infection	**infecção**
influenza	**gripe**
injection	**injeção**
insect	**inseto**
itching	**coceira**
kidney	**rim**

medication	**medicação**
nagging pain	**dorzinha**
natural medicine	**remédio natural**
needle	**agulha**
noise in the ear	**zumbido**
nose tissue	**papel de assoar**
pain	**dor**
redness	**vermelhidão**
remedy	**remédio**
scissors	**tesoura**
sick	**doente**
snake	**cobra**
swelling	**inchaço**
syringe	**seringa**
syrup	**xarope**
teas	**chás**
toilet paper	**papel higiênico**
tweezers	**pinças**
vomit	**vômito**
w.c.	**banheiro**

Do you have this medication?
Você tem esse remédio?

Do I need a prescription?
Preciso de uma receita?

I don't feel well.
Não me sinto bem.

I don't understand Portuguese.
Não entendo português.

I have . . .	**Sofro de . . .**
. . . asthma	**. . . asma**
. . . allergy	**. . . alergia**
. . . diabetes	**. . . diabete**
. . . heart problems	**. . . problemas de coração**

I need to take an injection.
Preciso de uma injeção.

I want to see the pharmacist.
Quero ver o farmacêutico.

Please call an ambulance!
Por favor, chame uma ambulância!

Where is the nearest hospital?
Onde fica o hospital mais próximo?

How often do I need to take this? **Quantas vezes por dia?**

. . . once a day	**. . . uma vez por dia**
. . . twice a day	**. . . duas vezes por dia**
. . . three times a day	**. . . três vezes por dia**
. . . for one week	**. . . durante uma semana**
. . . for two weeks	**. . . durante duas semanas**
. . . for . . . days	**. . . durante . . . dias**

MEDICAL HELP

With the exception of remote areas, medical doctors and hospitals are likely to be close by. If you fall ill or have an accident leave it to others to call for medical help. They will be better qualified to call the emergency service you need. Most hotels will have a list of English speaking doctors who will come to you.

Quality and Payment

You will receive excellent medical help in any emergency. However, Brazil is struggling to standardize its healthcare system–*Sistema Único de Saúde*–to cover the whole country. You could be helped by a city (*municipal*), religious, private, or university hospital. In some hospitals they require payment immediately following treatment and in others it is free of charge. To be certain, it's a good idea to obtain travel insurance before your arrival.

First Aid (Accidents and Emergency)

Pronto Socorro posts are open 24 hours (the majority of them are free of charge). Some private hospitals and medical cooperatives also provide similar services. In an emergency you will be taken to the nearest emergency post. If you have travel insurance your doctor might redirect you to a private hospital.

Ambulance and Rescue

There is no unified system of ambulance services in Brazil. In any kind of accident someone should call *Resgate* (rescue service). These are well-trained members of the Fire Department that also serve as paramedics. (*See "Means of Communication" for emergency phone numbers*)

Notes:
1. Take a comprehensive travel insurance policy before your departure.
2. Always bring with you packages of the medicine(s) you need to take regularly. Brand names of medications vary. Be familiar with the generic name of your medication.
3. Always bring with you a certificate stating the drugs you need to take on a regular basis; this is necessary for customs inspection and to refill prescriptions in Brazil.
4. Private hospitals in Brazil have interpreters, and most doctors will understand some English.

accident	**acidente**
ache	**dor contínua**
ambulance	**ambulância**
analgesic	**analgésico**
anemic	**anêmico**
appetite	**apetite**
bandage	**atadura**
band-aid	**esparadrapo**
bite	**picada**
blackout	**desmaio**
bleeding	**sangrando**
blister	**bolha**
blood	**sangue**
bone	**osso**
breastfeed *v*	**amamentar**
breath	**respiração**
breathe *v*	**respirar**
burn	**queimadura**
capsule	**cápsula**
clinic	**clínica**
cold	**resfriado**
collapse	**desmaio**
concussion	**traumatismo**
constipation	**prisão de ventre**
contact lenses	**lentes de contato**

corn	**calo**
cough	**tosse**
cut	**corte**
diabetes	**diabete**
diarrhea	**diarréia**
discharge (*liquid*)	**corrimento**
discharge from hospital	**alta do hospital**
dizzy	**tonto**
dull pain	**dor leve**
emergencies	**emergências**
examination	**exame**
eyeglasses	**óculos**
fever	**febre**
first aid	**primeiros socorros**
first-aid center	**pronto socorro**
flu	**gripe**
fracture	**fratura**
heart attack	**enfarte**
hemorrhage	**hemorragia**
high blood pressure	**pressão arterial alta**
hunger	**fome**
ICU	**U.T.I.**
ill	**doente**
immobilize *v*	**imobilizar**
indigestion	**indigestão**
infected	**infeccionado**
infection	**infecção**
inflamed	**inflamado**
inflammation	**inflamação**
influenza	**gripe**
injection	**injeção**
insomnia	**insônia**
intoxication	**intoxicação**
irradiating pain	**dor irradiada**
itching	**coceira**
laboratory	**laboratório de exames**
medical insurance	**seguro médico, convênio médico**
medication	**remédio, medicação**
migraine	**enxaqueca**

nagging pain	**dorzinha**
nausea	**náusea, enjôo**
numb	**adormecido, sem sensação**
nurse	**enfermeiro(a)**
operation	**operação**
pacemaker	**marca-passo**
pain	**dor**
phlegm	**catarro**
pill	**comprimido**
plaster	**gesso**
pregnant	**grávida**
prescription	**receita**
private	**particular**
scald	**queimadura**
scratch	**arranhão**
sharp pain	**dor aguda**
sick	**doente**
sleep	**sono**
stabbing pain	**pontada**
sting *v*	**arder**
sting *n*	**picada**
strong pain	**dor forte**
surgery	**cirurgia**
temperature	**temperatura**
thirst	**sede**
unbearable pain	**muita dor**
vaccine	**vacina**
vomit	**vômito**
ward	**enfermaria**
wound	**ferida**
X-ray	**raio-X**

Body Parts

ankle	**tornozelo**
arm	**braço**
back	**costas**
bladder	**bexiga**

bowels	**intestino**
breasts	**seios**
chest	**peito**
ear	**ouvido**
elbow	**cotovelo**
eyes	**olhos**
finger	**dedo**
foot	**pé**
forehead	**testa**
genitals	**genitais**
gums	**gengiva**
hand	**mão**
head	**cabeça**
heart	**coração**
heel	**calcanhar**
jawbone	**maxilar**
kidney	**rim**
knee	**joelho**
leg	**pernas**
liver	**fígado**
lung	**pulmão**
mouth	**boca**
(*roof of*) mouth	**céu da boca**
nail	**unha**
nape	**nuca**
spine	**espinha, coluna vertebral**
stomach	**estômago**
throat	**garganta**
tongue	**língua**
tonsils	**amídalas**
tooth	**dente**
vein	**veias**
wrist	**pulso**

What's the problem?
Qual é o problema?

Where does it hurt?
Onde dói?

It hurts here.
Dói aqui.

How long have you felt sick?
Quanto tempo faz que ficou doente?

I can't . . .	Não posso . . .
. . . eat	. . . comer
. . . sleep	. . . dormir
. . . hold down food or water	. . . comer ou beber nada que vomito

I am sick/ I am ill.
Tenho vontade de vomitar/ Estou muito doente.

I cannot move.
Não posso mexer.

I don't feel well!
Não me sinto bem!

I don't understand Portuguese.
Não entendo português.

I feel faint.
Sinto que vou desmaiar.

I feel dizzy.
Sinto tonturas.

I had an accident.
Tive um acidente.

I have . . .	Tenho . . .
. . . attacks of . . .	. . . ataques de . . .
(*asthma, dizziness*)	(*asma, tontura*)
. . . a stomachache	. . . dor de estômago, dor de barriga
. . . blackouts	. . . desmaios
. . . convulsions/ epilepsy	. . . convulsões
. . . diabetes	. . . diabete
. . . diarrhea	. . . diarréia
. . . fits	. . . ataques
. . . a headache	. . . dor de cabeça
. . . heart problems	. . . problemas de coração
. . . hemophilia	. . . hemofilia
. . . medical insurance	. . . seguro médico
. . . a pacemaker	. . . marca-passo
. . . pain in my chest	. . . dor no peito
. . . strong pain	. . . dor forte
. . . nausea	. . . vômito

I am allergic to . . .	Sou alérgico a . . .
. . . antibiotics	. . . antibióticos
. . . insect bites	. . . mordida de insetos
. . . strawberries	. . . morangos

I have had	Tive uma . . .
. . . an operation . . .	. . . operação
. . . a bypass	. . . safena

I need a doctor.
Preciso de um médico.

I need to take an injection.
Preciso de uma injeção.

I take this medication.
Estou tomando este remédio.

I need medication for . . .
Preciso de remédio para . . .

I had an accident, please help.
Tive um acidente, favor ajudar.

Please, call an ambulance.
Por favor, chame uma ambulância.

Where is the nearest hospital?
Onde fica o hospital mais próximo?

THE DENTIST

Dentists are well trained and plentiful in Brazil. Booking for emergencies is never necessary and the waiting time is usually short.

abscess	**abcesso**
allergy	**alergia**
anesthetic gel	**gel anestésico**
anesthetic injection	**injeção anestésica**
antibiotics	**antibiótico**
back teeth	**dentes de trás**
bite	**morder**
bridge	**ponte**
broken tooth	**dente quebrado**
chew	**mastigar**
cold	**frio**
crown	**coroa**
denture	**dentadura**
drill	**broca**
extraction	**extração**
few days	**alguns dias**
filling	**obturação**
foreign body	**corpo estranho**
front teeth	**dentes de frente**
gold tooth	**dente de ouro**
gum	**gengiva**
hot	**quente**
inflammation	**inflamação**
months	**meses**
mouthwash	**bochecho**
one week	**uma semana**
painkiller	**comprimidos contra dor**
pus	**pus**
root canal	**canal**
teeth	**dentes**
temporary	**temporário, provisório**
tooth	**dente**

toothache	**dor de dente**
tooth decay	**cárie**
treatment	**tratamento**

Do I need an appointment?
Precisa marcar hora?

How long does it take?
Quanto tempo demora?

How much does it cost?
Quanto vai custar?

I am afraid of drills.
Tenho medo de brocas.

I am nervous.
Estou nervoso.

I believe that the filling fell out.
Caiu a obturação do dente.

I can feel it; it is not numb yet.
Ainda não está anestesiado; estou sentindo.

I have a toothache here.
Tenho dor neste dente aqui.

I have an inflammation.
Estou com inflamação.

I have an allergy to . . .	**Tenho alergia a . . .**
. . . anesthetics	**. . . anestésicos**
. . . antibiotics	**. . . antibióticos**

Is it necessary to have a root canal treatment?
É necessário tratar o canal?

It hurts a lot.
Está doendo muito.

It is urgent. I have a very bad toothache.
É urgente. Estou com muita dor de dente.

When do I need to come back?
Quando devo voltar?

The Dentist might say:

Open wide!
Abra a boca!

Close your mouth.
Fecha a boca!

Spit.
Pode cuspir.

Which is the aching tooth?
Qual é o dente que dói?

ENTERTAINMENT

Popular Music and Dance

Some bars and restaurants offer popular live music and dancing. Pop music shows also may take place in open spaces such as parks and beaches.

Carnival

This is an intense period of four consecutive days during the summer when the country literally "stops" for dances, parades and parties. Most businesses are closed, except for emergency-related services, hospitals and other essential services. Some drugstores, supermarkets, and restaurants may also remain open. Every year the four days of Carnival vary according to the traditional Catholic calendar. Since most Brazilians are catholic, Carnival is always the four days before Lent, which is forty days before Easter. The Carnival festival starts on a Saturday and finishes on a Tuesday (Mardi Gras). The first day of rest after Carnival is Ash Wednesday

There are several ways to enjoy this festival. You can enjoy it as a casual observer on the street; you can buy a ticket to watch the parades (some that last 12 hours or more!); or you can attend a costume ball, which are very extravagant and usually quite costly.

CARNIVAL

ball	**baile**
Carnival	**Carnaval**
costume	**fantasia**
dance	**dança**
dancing groups	**escolas de samba**

drinks	**bebidas**
hangover	**ressaca**
parade	**desfile**
table	**mesa**
ticket	**ingresso**

Sports

Soccer is the national sport of Brazil. It is certainly worth it for you to see a live match, if only to see the architecture of the stadium and to witness the enthusiasm of the supporters. Basketball and volleyball are growing sports as well. There are numerous places where a tourist can play golf, tennis, squash, or swim. Beaches for fun in the sun are a must. At certain spas thermal bathing is a healthy option.

Sports

ball	**bola**
basketball	**basquete**
club	**clube**
football	**futebol americano**, rugby
golf	**golf**
golf club	**clube de golf,** **campo de golf**
play	**jogar**
seat	**cadeira**
soccer	**futebol**
soccer field	**campo de futebol**
stadium	**estádio**
supporter	**torcedor**
swim	**nadar**
swimming pool	**piscina**
swimsuit	**maiô, calção**
tennis	**tênis**
ticket	**entrada**
volleyball	**volei**
watch	**assistir**

I want to . . .	**Eu quero . . .**
. . . play	**. . . jogar**
. . . watch	**. . . ver**
Where can I buy. . . ?	**Onde posso comprar. . . ?**
. . . a ticket	**. . . entrada**
. . . a swimsuit	**. . . maiô**

Cinemas

The most comfortable and modern cinemas are the multi-screen ones in the malls or those belonging to international networks. As a rule, recent English language films are shown with subtitles. The timetable usually indicates whether the film is dubbed or subtitled. Advance tickets are rarely necessary for cinemas or theaters. Some foreign films receive a local title, but usually the posters show (in parenthesis) the original language title.

Theaters

Even in smaller cities you can find theaters. In larger cities you are likely to see visiting performers and plays from all over the world. Contact the British Council and the *Cultura Americana Center* for information about English companies that are touring Brazil. Some theaters have magnificent architecture and decorations and are worth a visit, even if the language is unfamiliar.

THEATERS/CINEMA

act	**ato**
actor	**ator**
actress	**atriz**
audience	**platéia**
author	**autor**
ballet	**balé**
box	**camarote**

circle	**balcão**
classical	**clássico(a)**
comedy	**comédia**
concert hall	**sala**
drama	**drama**
dubbed	**dublado**
entrance	**entrada**
exit	**saída**
film	**filme**
interval	**intervalo**
language	**língua, idioma**
lounge	**sala**
movies	**filmes**
music	**música**
musical	**musical**
opera	**ópera**
original	**no original**
play title	**nome da peça**
price	**preço**
reservation	**reserva**
seat	**cadeira, poltrona**
stalls	**platéia**
subtitles	**legendado**
theater (*play*)	**peça de teatro**
ticket	**bilhete**
video, DVD	**video, dvd**

Is it in English?
É em inglês?

Is it dubbed?
É dublado?

Subtitled?
Legendado?

Are there numbered seats?
As cadeiras são numeradas?

Is this film (*play*)
    suitable. . . ?
    . . . for children
    . . . for all ages

Esse filme (*peça*)
    é própria para. . . ?
    . . . para crianças
    . . . para todas
        as idades

What is the film/play?
Qual é o filme/peça?

TOURISM IN BRAZIL

Brazil has much more to offer to the traveler than Sugarloaf of Rio. Large cities like São Paulo offer architectural jewels, good shopping, theaters, great music (classical and popular), exotic restaurants, and museums. The country itself has many types of tourism to suit all tastes. It's best to research activities and places to go before traveling.

Ecological Tourism

The Amazon Forest has a wealth of exotic plants and animals and the local cuisine is an experience in itself. Excursions include airplane flights as well as ocean and river cruises. The Amazon River and its basin are an ecological wonder to behold, as are the Pantanal, an ecological reservation, and *Sete Quedas* and *Iguaçú* two of the widest waterfalls in the world.

Colonial Architecture

Sixteenth-century buildings and architecture can also be found in Brazil. Sleeping towns such as *Ouro Preto* and many others also offer interesting Colonial architecture.

Winter Tourism

June, July and August are winter months in Brazil. Further inland, and in the mountains, there are popular festivals with bonfires, fireworks and in resorts like *Gramado* (*Rio Grande do Sul* State) and *Campos do Jordão* (*São Paulo* State), there are art festivals. Be prepared, it is cold, with frost and the occasional snowfall.

Beaches

The Brazilian coastline offers beautiful beaches with warm ocean water. Perfect for tanning, surfing, and sailing.

For visitors, the best way to enjoy Brazil is to book organized excursions. These are safer, more economical, and they offer bilingual guides. Planning your own trips can be troublesome and less complete. It can also be more expensive. *Embratur* is the name of the tourism department in Brazil.

airline	**companhia aérea**
airport	**aeroporto**
Aleijadinho, "Little Cripple"	**famous XVIII c. architect and sculptor**
animals	**animais**
apartment	**apartamento**
asphalt road	**estrada asfaltada**
baroque	**barroco**
beach	**praia**
beach chair	**cadeira de praia**
birds	**pássaros**
bus	**ônibus**
bus terminal	**rodoviária**
capital city	**capital**
cart	**charrete**
chalet	**chalés**
children's swimming pool	**piscina infantil**
churches	**igrejas**
coach/bus	**ônibus**
coach/bus station	**rodoviária**
cold	**frio**
colonial architecture	**arquitetura colonial**
comfortable	**confortável**
country	**interior**
countryside	**campo**

crocodile	crocodilo, jacaré
day charge	diária
days	dias
duration	duração
eco-tourism	turismo ecológico, ecoturismo
English-speaking	em inglês
entertainment	recreação
exhibit	mostra, exibição
expensive	caro
few days	poucos dias
field, sports court	campo, quadra de esportes
fireplace	lareira
fish	peixes
fishing	pescaria
fishing lakes	lagos de pesca
flowers	flores
forest	floresta, mata
fortress	fortaleza
game room	salão de jogos
gas station	posto de gasolina
green area	área verde
guide	guia
hammock	rede
health farm	hotel fazenda
heated swimming pool	piscina aquecida
highway	auto estrada
horseback riding	passeios a cavalo
hot	calor
hours	horas
hunting	caça
inclusive	incluído
Jacuzzi®	banheira hidromassagem
landscape	paisagem
leisure	lazer
local cuisine	comidas regionais, pratos típicos

luxurious	**luxuoso**
modest	**simples**
mountain	**montanha**, **serra**
museum	**museu**
nature	**natureza**
playground	**parque infantil**
price	**preço**
programs	**programação**
rain	**chuva**
restaurant	**restaurante**
return ticket	**passagem de ida-e-volta**
river	**rio**
room	**quarto**
room with bath	**suíte**
roundtrip	**ida-e-volta**
rustic style	**estilo rústico**
sand	**areia**
secondary road	**estrada local**
ship	**navio**
swimming pool	**piscina**
timetable	**horários**
tour	**turnê**, **tour**
tracking	**trilha para caminhadas**
travel agency	**agência de viagens**
tree	**árvore**
umbrella	**guarda-sol**
vacation	**férias**
waterfalls	**cachoeiras**, **cascatas**
week	**semana**
wind	**vento**

Preparing a Trip

Does anyone here speak English?
Alguém fala inglês aqui?

I want an excursion with an English-speaking guide.
Queria excursão com guia em inglês.

Is there an English-speaking guide?
Há um guia que fale inglês?

Where is the nearest travel agency?
Onde fica a agência de viagens?

I want a good sightseeing tour.
Queria uma boa excursão de ônibus.

Are the roads good? May I go by car?
As estradas são boas? Posso ir de carro?

What is worth seeing?
O que é bom ver?

Which is the best?
Qual seria o melhor?

Is it near or far?
É perto ou longe?

I would like to go . . .	**Eu gostaria de ir . . .**
. . . camping	**. . . acampar, num acampamento**
. . . on an excursion	**. . . numa excursão**
. . . on a boat trip	**. . . numa viagem de**
. . . into the forest	**. . . nas florestas**
. . . fishing	**. . . pescar**
. . . hiking	**. . . caminhar**
. . . rafting	**. . . nos barcos de águas rápidas**
. . . tracking	**. . . tracking nas trilhas**

I want to see/visit . . .	**Quero ver . . .**
. . . the museum	**. . . o museu**
. . . the cathedral, the churches	**. . . a catedral, as igrejas**
. . . Colonial architecture	**. . . a arquitetura colonial**
. . . the waterfalls	**. . . as cataratas**

How do we get there? **Como se vai até lá?**
   ... by airplane   **... de avião**
   ... by bus   **... de ônibus**
   ... by boat/ship   **... de barco/navio**

How is. . . ? **Como é. . . ?**
   ... the hotel   **... o hotel**
   ... the ship   **... o barco**
   ... the tour bus   **... a excursão de ônibus**
   ... this tour company   **... essa companhia de turismo**

What is the transportation?
Quais são os meios de transportes?

Could I have a map?
Pode me dar um mapa?

What are the dangers?
Quais são os perigos?

Is there a danger of disease?
Há perigo de doenças?

Do I need any vaccinations?
Preciso de vacinas?

Are there any doctors?
Há médicos lá?

What are we going to see?
O que vamos ver?

What clothes should I wear?
Que roupas levar?

How many days?
Quantos dias?

A few days.
Alguns dias.

One week.
Uma semana.

How many hours does it take?
Quantas horas leva?

How much is it per day?
Quanto é a diária?

Is it in dollars or reais?
É em dólares ou reais?

What is included? | **O que está incluído?**
... meals | **... refeições**
... accommodation | **... acomodação**
... travel | **... viagem**

How much is the whole package?
Quanto custa o pacote?

Is there a discount for seniors/students?
Há desconto para idosos/estudantes?

ON A TRIP

What is that?
O que é aquilo?

How old is that?
Qual a idade daquilo?

Is there an entrance fee?
Cobram entrada?

Is it a round trip?
Ida e volta?

What is the price of admission?
Qual é o preço da entrada?

Can we swim here?
Pode-se nadar aqui?

Is it safe to get out?
É seguro sair por aí?

Are there dangerous/poisonous animals here?
Há animais perigosos/venenosos aqui?

I have a complaint.
Tenho uma queixa.

SAFETY

In Cities

Follow the advice of hotel personnel, guides, and cab drivers. Do not go to certain areas after dark, especially if advised not to do so. Always carry on you R$50 in cash for eventualities. Never resist muggers. Dress modestly when walking around. Should you be mugged, always report the event to the police. You will need to obtain a police note called *Boletim de Ocorrência* (*B.O.*) "Report of Happening." This *B.O.* might be necessary later for your insurance company, customs services, etc.

documents	**documentos**
gun	**arma, revolver**
help me please	**me ajuda por favor**
kidnapping	**seqüestro**
knife	**faca**
money	**dinheiro**
police	**polícia**
robbery	**roubo**
safe *adj*	**seguro(a)**
safe *n*	**cofre**
take it	**toma** (*give your money, watch, etc.*)
thief	**ladrão**
wallet	**carteira**

My . . . was/ were stolen.	**Roubaram meu . . .**
. . . car	**. . . carro**
. . . wallet with money	**. . . minha carteira de dinheiro**
. . . watch	**. . . relógio**
. . . jewels	**. . . minhas jóias**

In Remote Areas

When venturing into the outdoors dress appropriately. High boots are advisable for protection against venomous animals and insects. Brazil is one of the largest exporters of anti-venom in the world. If you are bitten by something there is a good chance someone nearby will have a universal antidote. However, it is best if you can describe the animal/insect that bit you for more specific treatment. Some rivers might have crocodiles or piranhas, so ask locals before taking a dip. The locals know their environment very well and will advise you to the dangers accordingly.

bite	**mordida**
insect	**inseto**
piranha	**piranha**
scorpion	**escorpião**
shark	**tubarão**
snake	**cobra**
spider	**aranha**

Where is the nearest hospital?
Onde fica o hospital mais próximo?

Call . . .	Chame . . .
. . . a helicopter	**. . . um helicóptero**
. . . the rescue department	**. . . o resgate**
. . . an ambulance	**. . . uma ambulância**
. . . a doctor	**. . . um médico**
. . . a pharmacist	**. . . um farmacêutico**
. . . the police	**. . . a polícia**
. . . the fire department	**. . . os bombeiros**

I have been bitten/stung...	**Fui mordido por ...**
... by a snake	**... uma cobra**
... by a spider	**... uma aranha**
... by a scorpion	**... um escorpião**
... by an insect/ animal	**... um inseto/ animal**

I have not seen the animal.
Não vi o bicho.

I am dizzy.
Estou tonto.

I feel faint.
Sinto que vou desmaiar.

I am wounded.
Estou ferido.

I cannot move ...
Não consigo mexer ...

I cannot see.
Não enxergo nada.

I had an accident.
Tive um acidente.

It is painful.
Está doendo muito.

Can you help me?
Pode me ajudar?

QUICK REFERENCE

This section lists vital words regarding communications: colors, numbers, fractions, calendar, seasons, days of the week, hours, time orientation, and directions.

<u>Colors</u>	<u>Cores</u>
beige	**bege**
black	**negro**, **preto**
blue	**azul**
brown	**marrom**
gray	**cinza**
green	**verde**
mauve	**roxo escuro**
navy blue	**azul marinho**
orange	**laranja**, **alaranjado**
pink	**cor-de-rosa**, **rosado**
purple	**roxo claro**, **lilás**
red	**vermelho**
white	**branco**
yellow	**amarelo**
dark	**escuro**
medium	**médio**
pale	**claro**

<u>Numbers</u>	<u>Números</u>
1	**um**[11] *m*, **uma** *f* (only the numbers 1 and 2 have genders masculine and feminine)

---

11. In bank checks and other important documents the word **um** is written sometimes with a **h** (**hum**) to avoid tampering and falsification.

2	dois *m*, duas *f*
3	três
4	quatro
5	cinco
6	seis
7	sete
8	oito
9	nove
10	dez
11	onze
12	doze
13	treze
14	catorze, quatorze
15	quinze
16	dezesseis
17	dezessete
18	dezoito
19	dezenove
20	vinte
21	vinte e um
22	vinte e dois . . .
30	trinta
40	quarenta
50	cinqüenta
60	sessenta
70	setenta
80	oitenta
90	noventa
100	cem
200	duzentos
300	trezentos
400	quatrocentos
500	quinhentos
600	seiscentos
700	setecentos
800	oitocentos
900	novecentos

1.000[12]	**mil** [in money matters it is customary to write **hum mil** to avoid tampering]
2.000	**dois mil**
3.000	**três mil**, and so on.
1.000.000	**um milhão**
2.000.000	**dois milhões**
1.000.000.000	**um bilhão**

EXAMPLES:

a) 1.800.765.432, 21 = um bilhão, oitocentos milhões, setecentos e sessenta cinco mil, quatrocentos trinta e dois, *vírgula*, vinte um.

b) R$1.545,34 = um mil, quinhentos e quarenta e cinco reais e trinta e quatro centavos.

<u>ORDINAL NUMBERS</u>[13]	<u>NÚMEROS ORDINAIS</u>
1º, 1ª	**primeiro(a)** *m(f)* *1ˢᵗ*
2º, 2ª	**segundo(a)** *m(f)* *2ⁿᵈ*
3º, 3ª	**terceiro(a)** *m(f)* *3ʳᵈ*
4º, 4ª	**quarto(a)** *m(f)* *4ᵗʰ*
5º, 5ª	**quinto(a)** *m(f)* *5ᵗʰ*
6º, 6ª	**sexto(a)** *m(f)* *6ᵗʰ*
7º, 7ª	**sétimo(a)** *m(f)* *7ᵗʰ*
8º, 8ª	**oitavo(a)** *m(f)* *8ᵗʰ*
9º, 9ª	**nono(a)** *m(f)* *9ᵗʰ*
10º, 10ª	**décimo(a)** *m(f)* *10ᵗʰ*
11º, 12º, etc.	**décimo primeiro, décimo segundo, etc.** *11ᵗʰ, 12ᵗʰ, etc.*
20º	**vigésimo, 21º vigésimo primeiro etc.** *20ᵗʰ*
30º	**trigésimo** *30ᵗʰ*

---

12. In Portuguese, contrary to English, the **decimal point** is used to indicate thousands and millions, and the **comma** indicates decimals (fractions).

13. In Portuguese, all ordinal numbers (indicating order in a sequence) carry the gender of the noun it describes.

Notes:

- Ordinal numbers higher than this are rarely used. Instead, the words *lugar, posição* (place, position) are used followed by the ordinal number. Examples: *25º lugar na fila* = 25th place in line; *o tenista está no ranque 178º* = the tennis player ranks 178th.
- In writing, the ordinal numbers are usually indicated by a superscript º, ª or more commonly by a simple **o, a** after the number (as in the examples above).
- In the days of the month, only the **first day** of the month is indicated by an ordinal number, e.g. *1º maio, 1º outubro*, but *2 de maio, 3 de outubro*.

FRACTIONS	FRAÇÕES
a half	**um meio ½**
a third	**um terço**
two thirds	**dois terços**
a quarter	**um quarto**
a fifth	**um quinto**
0,5 (*zero*) *point five*	**zero vírgula cinco**
3,4 *three point four*	**três vírgula quatro**
10% *ten percent*	**dez por cento**
100% *one hundred percent*	**cem por cento**

Months, Seasons, and Days of the Week[14]

MONTHS	MESES
January	**janeiro**
February	**fevereiro**
Mars	**março**
April	**abril**
May	**maio**
June	**junho**
July	**julho**
August	**agosto**
September	**setembro**
October	**outubro**
November	**novembro**
December	**dezembro**

SEASONS	ESTAÇÕES DO ANO
Spring	**primavera**
Summer	**verão**
Autumn	**outono**
Winter	**inverno**

DAYS OF THE WEEK	DIAS DA SEMANA
Monday	**segunda-feira**
Tuesday	**terça-feira**
Wednesday	**quarta-feira**
Thursday	**quinta-feira**
Friday	**sexta-feira**
Saturday	**sábado**
Sunday	**domingo**

---

14. In Portugese, the names of the months and days of the week are usually lowercase. Only dates of major significance, which became proper names (such as historical dates, road names, etc.) are written with capital letters.

Note:

- In colloquial Portuguese the word *feira* is usually omitted.
- *Feira* means open market; *sábado* comes from the Jewish "Sabbath," *domingo* comes from the Christian religion (*Day of the Lord*).

<u>Hours</u>   <u>Horas</u>

Officially one should use a 24 hours cycle (military time) when telling time. In practice, however, this is only done in newspapers and television. In everyday speech Brazilians divide the day into four sections: *manhã, tarde, noite, e madrugada.*

6 A.M. to 12 noon	**manhã**
Noon to 6 P.M.	**tarde**
6 P.M. to 12 midnight	**noite**
12 midnight to 6 A.M.	**madrugada**

In everyday speech, one says, for example,

9 A.M.	**9 da manhã**	(*in the morning*)
3 P.M.	**3 da tarde**	(*in the afternoon*)
8 P.M.	**8 da noite**	(*in the evening*)
3 A.M.	**3 da madrugada**	(*in the early morning*)

What is the time?
Que horas säo?

EXAMPLES:
9 A.M.   **nove da manhã, 9 horas**
9:30 P.M.   **nove e meia da noite, 21:30**

In Brazil, some people do not say "15 minutes," or "30 minutes," but "one quarter" and "half." So, 9:15 can be said *nove e quarto* (nine and a quarter), and 9:30 can be said *nove e meia* (nine and half), and 9:45 will be *quarto para as dez*.

9:15	**nove e quinze**, or **nove e quarto**
11:45 A.M.	**quinze** (*minutes missing*) **para o meio dia**, or **um quarto para meio-dia**
11:40 P.M.	**vinte** (*minutes missing*) **para a meia noite, 23:40**
12:00 noon	**meio dia** (*mid-day*)
12:00 (midnight)	**meia noite, 24:00** (*midnight*)

Note:
Avoid saying 12:00 A.M. and 12:00 P.M.—this may be confusing to Brazilians. Always say 12 noon and 12 midnight.

<u>TIME ORIENTATION</u>	<u>ORIENTAÇÃO DE TEMPO</u>
last month	**mês passado**
last week	**semana passada**
last year	**ano passado**
next day	**dia seguinte**
next month,	**mês seguinte,**
coming month	**mês que vem**
next week,	**semana seguinte,**
coming week	**semana que vem**
next year,	**ano seguinte,**
coming year	**ano que vem**
previous day	**dia anterior**
previous month	**mês anterior**
previous week	**semana anterior**
previous year	**ano anterior**
today	**hoje**
tomorrow	**amanhã**
tonight	**hoje à noite**
when?	**quando?**
yesterday	**ontem**

<u>DIRECTIONS</u>	<u>DIREÇÕES</u>
Where?	**Onde?**
Where to?	**Para onde?**
North	**norte**
South	**sul**
East	**leste**
West	**oeste**
back	**atrás**
behind	**atrás**
deep	**fundo**
down	**baixo**
far	**longe**
fast	**depressa** (*time word*)
here	**aqui**
in front of	**na frente de**
later	**depois** (*time word*)
left	**esquerda**
middle	**meio**
near	**perto**
now	**agora**, **já** (*time word*)
opposite	**do lado oposto**
over there	**ali**
quick	**rápido** (*time word*)
right	**direita**
shallow	**raso**
straight on	**em frente**
there	**lá**
up, top	**cima**